*L*earning to Teach Inductively

Bruce Joyce

Emily Calhoun

Foreword by

David W. Johnson
Roger T. Johnson
University of Minnesota

Allyn and Bacon
BOSTON ■ LONDON ■ TORONTO ■ SYDNEY ■ TOKYO ■ SINGAPORE

ces Helland
ger: Kathy Hunter
t: Kris Lamarre
tion Service: Omegatype Typography, Inc.
nd Prepress Buyer: Linda Cox
g Buyer: Suzanne Lareau
istrator: Linda Knowles
er: Omegatype Typography, Inc.

ght © 1998 by Allyn & Bacon
om Company
ould Street
dham Heights, MA 02194

ernet: www.abacon.com
merica Online: keyword: College Online

Library of Congress Cataloging-in-Publication Data

Joyce, Bruce R.
    Learning to teach inductively / Bruce Joyce, Emily Calhoun.
        p.   cm.
    Includes bibliographical references (p.).
    ISBN 0-205-26778-5
    1. Elementary school teaching.   2. Induction (Logic)—Study and teaching (Elementary)   I. Calhoun, Emily.   II. Title.
LB1555.J65   1988
372.1102—dc21   97-30860
                                                                          CIP

Printed in the United States of America

10 9 8 7 6 5 4 3 2 1   02 01 00 99 98 97

Dedicated to teachers everywhere:
to those who taught us,
to those whom we have taught,
and to those many who work passionately to teach all children

$\mathscr{C}$ ontents

The Picture-Word Inductive Model: Literacy As the Fundamental Objective of Education 53

chapter *4*

Teaching Beginning Readers and Writers of All Ages 53

Few things are more important to successful progress in our school and our culture than the development of literacy, and no aspect of teaching is more important than inducing our students to read and write effectively. The **Picture-Word Inductive Model (PWIM)** *takes advantage of children's natural inductive capacity and their natural language development, using both to support productive inquiry into language. Reading and writing are taught together from the beginning. In a scenario taken from a real set of teaching episodes, we watch a teacher using the model with a group of kindergarten students in the initial stages of learning to read and write. The students develop sight vocabulary, connect that vocabulary to books, classify the words, learn phonetic and structural generalizations, and begin to write words and create sentences for classroom publication and study.*

chapter *5*

Literacy across the Curriculum 96

Once students can read and write to some extent, the task is to expand their ability to inquire into increasingly complex materials and forms of expression. The inductive process becomes routine: They learn to collect and synthesize information and to consolidate their knowledge and to convert that knowledge into skills. In this scenario, we watch a sixth grade teacher use *the **Picture Word Inductive Model** to take a group of students into the study of ancient and modern Egypt. The students use pictures, videotapes, data bases, and books to collect and classify information, understand their prior conceptions, and develop hypotheses to test as they gather further information. Reading and writing to learn social studies are at work.*

---

chapter *6*   Building the Learning Community   **121**

How do we begin the school year, developing a warm and rigorous learning community where students can learn alone and together in a space both safe and challenging? In this chapter, we build on the scenarios in Chapter 3 and discuss how those teachers developed communities of learners. The study of student learning and the accommodation to individual differences are addressed as integral components of creating a healthy learning community in the classroom.

chapter *7* **Curriculum Topics for Inquiry** **139**

We invite you to identify domains in each curriculum area that are amenable to inductive inquiry.

chapter *8* **Inquiring into Inductive Inquiry: The Formal Research** **149**

We explore the formal research on inductive inquiry, from the early development of language to the pursuit of literacy in the academic subjects. We invite you to conduct your own inquiries.

chapter *9*   **The Teacher Scholar—The Professional Learning Agenda**   185

How do we acquire teaching strategies, polish them, and develop executive control over them? What is in the storehouse of ways of teaching that we can explore? How do we build a learning environment for ourselves—one that sustains our inquiry and feeds us as we try to nurture our children? This chapter seeks to engage readers in life-long inquiry into teaching and learning, a form of continual professional development.

appendix *A*   **Peer Teaching Guide: Inductive Model of Teaching**   198

appendix *B*   **"Just Read" Forms**   206

*F*oreword

> *I* always found myself unable to think as a single person.
>
> —*Kurt Lewin*

For thousands of years teachers learned how to teach by observing their elders and following their example. When problems arose, teachers shared their wisdom and experiences. In *Learning to Teach Inductively*, Bruce Joyce and Emily Calhoun provide aspiring, new, and experienced teachers with a book that furnishes a clear model of how to teach and that shares their considerable teaching and educational knowledge and experience. They include the two essential aspects of improving teaching—a conceptual model and clear examples of how to apply it in elementary, middle, and high school settings. They provide a refreshing look at how to nourish students' natural curiosity, problem-solving abilities, and sense of community.

Many instructors are given misinformation about how to teach. They believe that *teaching is telling* and *told is taught*. Joyce and Calhoun go beyond this old paradigm of teaching and focus attention on inquiry and inductive learning. *Induction*, (in + ducere = to lead) means "leading into" a conclusion. Inductive learning may have first been formalized in 1620 when Sir Francis Bacon described inductive reasoning in his famous *Novum Organum, sive indicia vera de interpretatione naturae* (The New Instrument, or true evidence concerning the interpretation of nature). He proposed that reasoning should proceed by collecting and analyzing evidence and then coming to a tentative conclusion that is stated as a probability, not a certainty. (Unfortunately, Bacon died prematurely from a cold caught while stuffing a chicken's carcass with snow for an inductive test of refrigeration.) Students should be willing to be led to whatever conclusion the facts direct them, while remembering that all decisions are temporary, tentative, and always open to modification on the basis of new evidence. The inductive leap to a conclusion is always risky because *all* the evidence cannot be known. No amount of evidence can logically prove an assertion because "one and some can never equal all." Students must, therefore, keep an open mind to new facts that might disprove what we currently conclude.

Inductive learning takes place within the inquiry process. As Jerome Bruner pointed out, students should not become little living libraries on a subject, but rather they should learn how to engage in inquiry to *acquire* knowledge. Richard Suchman described inquiry teaching as providing a focus (to catch the curiosity of the learners), freedom (to allow the learners to guide their own journey), and a responsive environment (which includes materials, teacher, peers, and time). Students formulate a problem, select data sources, gather data, analyze data, and make inferences and conclusions. As Joyce and Calhoun so aptly point out, teaching is far more than presenting information. It involves creating a learning situation in which students learn how to work with data to go beyond the information given and make inferences based on discovering new insights and generalizations (i.e., learn the procedures of inquiry). Learning is a process, not a product.

Two keys to successful induction and inquiry are building a cooperative context and encouraging intellectual conflict. Neither intellectual isolation nor competition (with its resulting obstruction of classmates' learning and high anxiety levels) promote insight and learning. Inductive learning (and teaching) and inquiry best take place within a cooperative context in which there is support, encouragement, and assistance for discovering insights and achieving mastery.

The easiest way to build a cooperative context is through the use of cooperative learning. The keys to cooperation are positive interdependence, individual accountability, promotive (face-to-face) interaction, appropriate use of interpersonal and small group skills, and group processing. Students must understand that when engaging in induction and inquiry, they are part of a learning community in which they are responsible not only for their own learning and insights, but they are also responsible for helping their classmates learn and discover insights. In this learning community there are no "free rides" and each student must do his or her fair share of the work. Students work together—helping, sharing, and challenging each other's reasoning and conclusions. In working together, students need to provide leadership, communicate effectively, facilitate problem solving and decision making, and resolve conflicts in constructive ways. Finally, learning groups should regularly discuss how effectively members are working together and how they can improve and be even more effective in the future.

Once cooperative learning is firmly established, the next step in promoting induction and inquiry is to encourage intellectual conflict. Dewey described problem solving as starting with "a felt difficulty" and Piaget described the learning process as triggered by disequilibrium. Constructing one's own knowledge begins with realizing there is a discrepancy between one's initial conclusions and the conclusions of others. When faced with such an intellectual challenge, students develop a rationale for their conclusion, argue its validity, challenge and refute opposing positions while defending their own, seek to view the issue from all perspectives, and strive for a synthesis of the best information and reasoning from all sides. It is intellectually "disputed passages" that create uncertainty about the validity of one's conclusions and spark the induction and inquiry process.

In *Learning to Teach Inductively,* Joyce and Calhoun challenge the traditional view of teaching as *telling* and explain how teachers may structure learning situations in which students induce their own understanding of the material being studied. Students do so by engaging in inquiry within a cooperative context that allows for constructive intellectual challenge and conflict. As Joyce and Calhoun note in the final chapter, you (the reader) teach yourself how to use inductive instruction by doing it over and over again. Taking advantage of the opportunity this excellent book presents by putting into practice the procedures clearly presented is one of the smartest decisions a teacher can make.

David W. Johnson
Roger T. Johnson
University of Minnesota

*F*or teachers, learning never ends. For your authors, the desire to share the results of this learning has been ever strong. We are, at heart, teacher–learners. After 70 years of combined experience in education, it's difficult for either of us to be in any educational setting and not teach—or at least feel compelled to share more than most folks want to know—or to ask a barrage of questions and begin to classify them as we help a group gnaw an issue. With natures like ours, we see this book as one more teaching opportunity, another chance to have a large class of future and current colleagues "go to school" with us.

We've tried to make *Learning To Teach Inductively* serve two purposes: The first is sharing what we wish we'd known when we started teaching, and the second is sharing what seems to have been most beneficial to our colleagues and their students as we worked with them. First, we've looked back at our early years in teaching and asked ourselves what we've learned that we wish we had known at the beginning. Answering that question generated quite a large list (one of us has taught for 25 years and the other for 45), so we winnowed the inventory down to a critical few, including how to teach and learn inductively. Second, we looked at the relationships we have with experienced teachers (between us, we've worked in school-renewal projects with over 2,000 teachers during the past five years) and asked: "What is the most important outcome of our work and our interaction with these colleagues?" We decided that it is, for them and for us, an increased ability to teach and learn inductively.

That's how this book came to be organized around inductive thinking as a way of learning for children and adults. There are many other models of teaching we might have dealt with, and many other aspects of teaching we might have dealt with. But we decided that we'd leave it to others to survey the field, and we'd concentrate on one thing that has enabled us to continue to grow and that will serve our colleagues and their students across ages and subjects. We believe that the inductive model of teaching is one of the major powerhouse instructional strategies, and that inductive thinking is a tool for life: learning to gather and organize information for use, to invent concepts and create possibilities, to apply one's knowledge and skill—used altogether or by themselves, the cognitive processes that shape the full model work to help us make sense of our world and to bring order and utility to massive amounts of information.

Another decision we made was to concentrate primarily on the teaching of reading and writing. While we have included examples of the inductive teaching of science, social studies, and mathematics concepts, we also focused on literacy within those curriculum areas. From listening to teacher candidates and experienced teachers alike, we concluded that the most-asked questions have to do with literacy and communication. Primary teachers want to know how to introduce children to reading and writing, and all other teachers want to know how to increase reading/writing capability and how to generate literacy in all subjects. In addition, teachers in the upper elementary grades and secondary school want to know how to help those of their students who do not read or write very well.

Our colleagues and students have told us repeatedly that examples of teaching are vital to them. Thus, examples of inductive teaching and learning at work in kindergarten through eighth grade classrooms comprise much of this book. We have attempted to make these examples serve two roles: first, to provide mental images of the inductive teaching model at work, thus adding to your definition of the model and of the concept of inductive reasoning; and second, to provide mental demonstrations to support your practice with the model as you develop or expand your teaching repertoire.

Probably, knowing us, we've tried to do too much. We have been accused of high expectations before! We've tried to write for people just beginning their careers as professional teachers and for experienced colleagues who want to learn more about or expand their use of the inductive process. We think the book is suitable for both, although sometimes we speak to novices and sometimes to persons with considerable experience with induction. Our thanks go to those who spent considerable time reviewing the manuscript: Ava Belitzky, University of Toronto; Barrie Bennett, University of Toronto; and Gary Hillman, University of Colorado at Denver. Also, special thanks to David and Roger Johnson for taking the time to read the book and write such a thoughtful and scholarly foreword.

With you and your future or current students in mind, let's go to school on teaching and learning inductively!

B. J. and E. C.

$\mathcal{A}$ ha! Scenes

Aha! One

Ten-year-old Charlie is engrossed in examining two sentences. He and his classmates are studying various kinds of devices that authors use to generate images. Charlie has been stuck for a couple of days as he has tried to classify a number of sentences in a data set that George Henry, his teacher, presented to the class. Charlie has put together a couple of sentences that really intrigue him. He feels he's getting close to something, but he doesn't know what it is. He reads the two sentences again:

> Every clear morning when the sun rose in the sky over the hills, Alison felt that the day would be wonderful.

> Every clear morning the sun reached over the hills and touched Alison's house, telling her the day would be wonderful.

Charlie is talking to himself silently. "They both begin with 'every morning.' Then 'the sun rose in the sky' and 'the sun reached over the hills.' The sun rises, or that's what it looks like to us. It doesn't reach. It can't reach unless it's alive. And it sure doesn't talk. *That's* it! The author is pretending the sun is alive, like a person. It reaches, it touches, it talks!"

"Now, **why** did the author do that? I don't think she's trying to fool us into thinking the sun is alive. . . . Maybe she's trying to tell us how Alison feels. That's it! Alison sees the sun as a kind of friend, a real, personal friend, who wakes her. It's like, it's like the 'sun friend,' who arrives and makes her feel like it's going to be a good day, is giving her a message."

"I think I've got it!"

Charlie starts to examine another pair of sentences:

> As we bolted past, shivering in the wind and rain, the willow tree shook its hair and wept.

> The willow tree was dripping wet and swaying in the wind as we ran home.

Aha! Two

Aletha's parents drop her at school a half hour early because they have an appointment. Humming to herself, Aletha makes her way to the door of her second grade classroom to deposit her backpack. To her surprise, the door is open, although she doesn't see her teacher, Pam Eastman, inside.

Going to her desk and putting the backpack on top of it, she heads for one of the two plants she has been tending for the last four months and feels the soil to see if it is dry. She inspects one plant critically, especially a tiny bud that has appeared on one of the branches. She opens the notebook next to the plant and makes a note that the bud seems to be starting to open. Her class has been tending 30 plants since the first week of January, and now is in the process of classifying them according to their characteristics, their growth, and their response to fertilizer, light, and water. Yesterday, everyone was trying to make hypotheses about why four plants had developed brownish leaves. Because they had been well-tended and were quite different types of plants, making hypotheses was difficult. However, those plants had been next to each other most of the spring. A hypothesis about bugs had apparently been disconfirmed with a careful examination of the leaves of the plants, although something infecting the roots was still not ruled out.

A sound makes her turn, and she sees Alex, the custodian, enter, banging his cart of mops and cleaning supplies through the door.

"Hi, Aletha," he says, unconcerned that she is in the room.

"Hi, Mr. Callahan," she replies.

Alex bustles around, and Aletha decides to go outside for a while. At the door, she turns and stands stock still as she realizes that Alex has two of the brownish plants in his hands and is moving them along the ledge where the plants have been living. She watches as he goes back for the two others. "Mr. Callahan?"

"Yes, Aletha."

"I don't mean to be rude, but why are you moving those plants?"

"Oh, you couldn't be rude if you tried, Aletha. The reason I'm moving those plants is that for some reason Robert (the other custodian) moves them at night when he cleans. I'm not sure why, but he does it every night. I like things to be tidy so I move them back when I come in."

Aletha has been moving closer and points at the grill on top of the heating unit. "Does he always put them there?"

"Almost always, why?"

"Is the heater turned on at night?"

"Just on low, to keep away the mildew. Now what's up, honey?"

"Oh, Mr. Callahan, you've just solved a mystery. The *mystery of the brown-leaved plants!*"

Aha! Three

Nancy and Enrique are in Bruce Hall's eighth grade class, studying the nations of the world. In the early stages of the inquiry, the whole class has been using several data bases and classifying the countries. They have data on population, economics, education, religions, political systems, and a host of other topics. They have been learning to look at the relationship between variables, such as finding whether physical size is related to population, whether per capita income is related to levels of education, and so forth. As the inquiry has developed, some of the work groups have questions they want to explore. Nancy and Enrique have become interested in life expectancy.

They have sorted out the ten countries with the lowest and highest life expectancies for females. They have found that Chad, Western Sahara, Guinea, Afghanistan, Angola, Mali, Sierra Leone, Guinea-Bissau, Central African Republic, Bhutan, and Mozambique have female life expectancies between 40 and 49 years. Hong Kong, Switzerland, Spain, Japan, Italy, France, Sweden, Norway, Netherlands, and Austria have female life expectancies between 81 and 84.

They are developing questions that they hope will lead them to explanations of why people in some countries live so much longer than do people in others. They have three questions so far. Nancy has suggested that they find out whether the difference is due to wealth, so they are asking, "Do the countries where people live longer have higher per capita incomes?" Enrique has suggested they ask whether medical care is responsible, so they are asking "Are the number of physicians and hospital beds per capita associated with longevity?" They also are searching for information about the effects of education on longevity.

Their problem is how to arrange the information so that they can answer their questions. They think that they've got something, but how to put the information in a better form stumps them. They don't ask Bruce because part of the task is to use what they have learned in math and social studies about tables, frequencies, graphs, and displaying data and information. And they are determined to develop a display that clarifies any relationships they find and that will be easy to "read."

They agree to meet at Enrique's house that afternoon and think it over. When Nancy arrives, she finds Enrique reading an issue of *Sports Illustrated*.

"More macho stuff!" she snorts.

"Not so," he growls back. "Look, there's an article on women's volleyball right here."

She picks up the magazine and leafs through it while he gets them some iced tea. She comes across some tables of information about the National Basketball Association teams and stops for a minute to look at it. Nancy stares at the table and then asks Enrique what are "assists" and "steals." He defines them offhandedly, balancing the iced tea and a plate of cookies. "Assists are when a player makes a pass that sets up another player to score. They are only counted when the player *does* score. Steals are when a player takes the ball away from the other team, usually by knocking it away or intercepting a pass. Don't tell me you're getting interested in basketball!"

"I don't understand it, but look at these tables. In one table, the players are listed in order of the average points they have scored in the games they have played this year. In other tables, it's the average rebounds, steals, and assists. Look at this one on rebounds. What do *off* and *def* mean?"

Nancy shows Enrique the table. This is a small part of it.

Rebounds

Player	Off	Def	Total	Avg.
Rodman	282	495	777	15.9
Motumbo	212	518	730	11.8
Mason	148	541	689	11.3

"Offensive and defensive. An offensive rebound is when one of the players on your team has tried a shot and you get the rebound, so your team gets the ball. A defensive rebound is when the other team shoots and you get the ball."

Nancy opens her notebook and starts scribbling. "I wonder if we can use the same kind of table with our data?" She shows him these headings and fills in the data for two countries.

Country	Life Expectancy	Per Capita Income	Physicians Per Capita
Guinea	45	352 USD	1/11,000
Sweden	81	22,000 USD	1/337

"If we make a series of tables where we list data on each variable for the countries, then we can tell whether any two of the variables go together. I sure didn't think that sports statistics would help us with problems like this one."

Enrique has forgotten the basketball data entirely. "Umnh! look at those differences. Let's make two tables, one for the high longevity countries and another for the low longevity countries. I can't believe the differences between those countries. No one thing can explain that."

chapter 1

Constructing Knowledge about Teaching

In a perfect world, we would come to adulthood knowing we have full-blown knowledge about how to raise children and how to teach. At least we'd know we have those knowledges and attendant skills latent, lying just below the surface and ready to come to life when we have babies or accept jobs as teachers. In our imperfect world, we are not so lucky; most of us have to learn how to parent and how to teach. But we are not without equipment, because what we need *does* lie within us, if we will allow it to find its way into our consciousness.

What We Bring to Life: Natural and Unlimited Learning Capability

From birth, we reached out to living and nonliving things. Think how we loved our pillow, and our blanket, or some stuffed toy. We not only loved them, we imbued them with a love that they returned to us. In the most desolate circumstances, a baby will treasure a stick or a stone, if that's all there is at hand. Now, knowing how to love and care for others beyond ourselves is a great tool to begin with. We *know* that everybody needs affection and attention, and we know something about how to provide these developmental staples.

We're also natural scientists. We experiment continually at birth, trying things and seeing what happens. We just can't help it, for we want to know how our world works. We make hypotheses and test them. We are a handful at that point, and those who care for us have to scoop us up at times just before we connect ourselves to the electrical system or the oven. But we continue experimenting with our world, crawling around and poking things into other things to find out what happens.

Along with our experimental capability, we're inborn scholars—constructors of concepts and generalizations. We're born with an innate ability to discriminate things from each other and build categories. As infants, we sorted things as hard or soft, comfortable or uncomfortable, rough or smooth, noisy or quiet, learned to tell Mom from Dad, the cat from either, the cat from furry toys, and words. *There's* a big one—as we listened to the world around us, we sorted *words,* one from one another, rapidly gaining control and making choices as we shouted, *Da* to access Dad, *Baa* for our bottle, and *Ju* for our juice.

Early language acquisition is easy because we're natural linguists. As our minds seek to make sense of our world, we figure out which words are used for what. Wherever we find ourselves, we listen and learn to speak. In Greece, we learn Greek; in Thailand, we learn Thai; in Argentina we learn Spanish. In Switzerland, we may learn French, German, and Italian, all at once. By the time we're four or so, we know the structure of our language and can understand and speak several thousand words—a basic storehouse that we will hear and process all our lives.

In the same fashion, we're born anthropologists. We learn the norms of our culture rapidly, watching the people around us and imitating them. We'll eat literally anything, if our people do. And we'll stay away from any food our social environment shuns. Most of us mimic, then follow, the customs of our immediate world. If the people around us shake hands on greeting, we shake hands; if they hug, we hug; if they bow, we bow. In China, we'll learn Chinese customs. In England, we'll soon look like miniature English people.

What can we—the teacher candidate, the formal educator, the experienced schoolteacher—do to strengthen, nurture, and channel this wondrous human capability. What is our role? our work? *Learning to work with nature and to avoid working against it.* If we learn to build classroom and school environments that capitalize on the way we are—the way *people* are—the natural learning ability of children will make us great teachers and parents. One of the inherent premises of inductive teaching, and therefore of this book, is that we do not have to feed all our knowledge of language, science, social studies, and mathematics to our students. Rather, if we present our subject matter so that students engage with it conceptually and organize it for use, they will learn. And, they will be learning more than our specified curriculum objectives: they will *learn how to learn* ever more powerfully, because they are practicing their thinking, because they have more information, because they are using this information, and because learning and having more control and understanding are satisfying.

What We Bring to Teaching: Our Wondrous Learning Capability and Its Continual Application

Learning to teach well fits our nature. Learning to remember our own wondrous learning capability, using it in our work, and nurturing and extending it in our students is the foundation of great teaching and self-sustaining professionalism.

Our children come to school filled with words that exist in their memories of listening and speaking, and experience the transformation of the words and all they mean into reading and writing. The words will never be the same again, for they take on a new dimension. Where they could be heard before, they now are seen as well. Where they could be produced before as sounds, they now can be written down. The fundamental reality of the words continues, but something very important has happened to them, and that happening is the property of each unique mind.

We, the teachers, help bring those changes to the children by arranging the learning environment and providing tasks that generate those new realities. As teachers, we would like to peer inside to find out what learning has taken place and what readiness there is for new learning. But teachers cannot crawl inside and look around—we have to infer what is inside from what we can see and hear. Our educated guesses are the substance of our craft as we try, continually, to construct in *our* minds the pictures of the minds of our students. The never-ending cycles of arranging learning environments, selecting content, providing tasks, and building pictures of the minds of the students makes the character of teaching—the continuous inquiry into mind and environment—evolutionary.

At its core, the teaching process is exactly the same in the secondary phase of education and in the university and graduate school as it is with young children. The algebra teacher and professor of physics arrange learning environments, select content, provide tasks, and try to learn what is going on in the unique minds of their students, in parallel cadence with the teacher who first introduces reading and writing to students.

To teach well is to embrace this adventure of learning about minds and how ideas and emotions interact with environments and become transformed. To teach well means to be caught up in an inquiry that has no end: we are never finished with this adventure, never satisfied with the arts and sciences of making those inferences, never done with the construction of models of learning and teaching that are built on the guesses we make about what is going on in all those minds.

How We See Ourselves and Our Students: Perceptions, Expectations, and Behaviors

What does the rhetoric of the previous sections have to do with planning lessons and units, with daily instruction, with making it 'til the end of the quarter?

How we perceive our role as teachers—as facilitator of learning, or as owner of the knowledge of most worth, or as *(fill in your own image)* —has a large impact on our daily behavior, on our willingness to continue to develop teaching competence, and on our students' abilities to educate themselves.

Do you see yourself as a charismatic teacher, with your students enthralled by the force of your personality? Do you see yourself as a persuasive presenter, with your students bound by the elegance of your rhetoric? Do you see yourself as the sole authority, with your students listening to you and following your guidance because you have "the knowledge"? Do you see yourself as the one in charge, officially sanctioned by society and the local school board, with your students compliant and learning efficiently because it is thus?

No . . . most of us would say we see ourselves as working with children, as helping them learn, or as teachers of mathematics or science or social studies. But what is our actual, operational stance as we interact with students and design instruction for and with them? And how do they respond to our stance?

Thankfully, successful teachers are not simply charismatic and persuasive presenters. Rather, they engage their students in robust cognitive and social tasks and teach the students how to learn more efficiently. Effective learners draw information, ideas, and wisdom from their teachers and use learning resources effectively. For example, although learning to lecture clearly and knowledgeably is highly desirable for a teacher, it is the learner who does the learning. Successful lecturers teach students how to mine the information in the talk and make it their own; when this does not happen, the teacher who organized and presented the information remains the primary learner in the instructional environment, not the students. Thus, a major role in teaching is to create powerful learners who forage for knowledge, not dependent learners who wait passively for the next morsel to be brought to them.

Inquiring teachers learn quickly that they do not have to feed knowledge to their students. They learn to organize their lessons and curriculum so that students learn how to use their learning abilities; thus enabling their students, whether they are five years old or fifteen or fifty, to memorize information, to attain concepts, to invent concepts, to build hypotheses and theories, and to use the tools of science to test them. Their students learn how to extract information and ideas from lectures and presentations, how to make their writing and problem solving more lucid and creative, and how to work with others to initiate and carry out cooperative programs of inquiry. Their students become both more challenging and more exhilarating to teach because their expanded learning styles enable them to engage actively in attaining the many goals of education. For successful teachers are brave teachers: they have learned to let go of the desire to recreate their students as images of themselves, and they celebrate individual differences because they do not see these differences as deficits.

In our profession and our society at this time, it is all too easy to lose touch with our wondrous learning capability. Maybe this loss is encouraged by the comfort of civilization; by the familiar routines in schools and classrooms which have changed little across the past 100 years; by our pleasure in being entertained in courses, at workshops, and at conferences instead of being engaged and challenged; by our personal desire to remain conceptually comfortable. If we cannot remember our own natural learning and how it worked, if we do not look back at those teachers who helped us expand our own capability, we can become resistant to learning, shrinking our developmental capability and possibly inhibiting the potential of our students.

For education—inside the schoolhouse and beyond—continuously builds ideas and emotions. The flux of human consciousness gives the process of education its distinctive character and makes teaching a wondrous ever-changing process, as ideas and feelings are built and rebuilt. To enter teaching fully one must desire to experience this flux.

Entering the profession, many of us have an image of who we will teach and what we will teach. We have images of our students and our work with them. Some of us see ourselves in the primary school with young children, helping them to explore their world and learn to read and write. Others of us see ourselves in the upper elementary grades and middle school with preadolescents and adolescents, helping them to reach further into their world and use their reading and writing tools to extend their knowledge. And, of course, some of us see ourselves in the high school with young adults, helping them prepare for citizenship and college through courses introducing them to academic study.

These images often lead us to conceive of teaching in quite different terms. We know many teachers of the primary grades who feel that teaching young children is completely different from teaching in the high school, and we know high school teachers who believe that their work is almost a different profession from the work done by elementary teachers.

Despite the obvious differences between young children and young adults, the dimensions of effective teaching and learning bear remarkable similarities.

Whatever age we teach, we learn to teach through inquiry: trying strategies and activities, studying how they work with our students and our curriculum goals, and modifying them based on our analysis of their effectiveness.

Whatever age we teach, the learners do the learning. Teachers whose students learn the most, teach by expanding and refining the learning capability of the students.

Whatever age or subject we teach, our goal is that what we teach be used. The purpose of learning is not to pass tests given in school, but to develop knowledge and skills that are continuously applied in life out of school. Thus, we teach children to read so that they can begin consuming the library of the world, the storehouse of books that has been assembled by our society. While literature provides understanding and pleasure, it also provides for many people an avenue to good writing. Our young readers need to read and read and read, educating themselves and enjoying themselves simultaneously. How do we make this happen?

We teach children to think scientifically so that they can use scientific knowledge and methods to understand their natural and human world and to solve problems. We teach children about society and social life so that they can understand their social world, learn more about it after they have left us, solve problems in their immediate social setting, and participate in shaping the world in which they will live. How do we organize instruction so this learning lasts beyond the classroom door or the final exam?

The mathematics we teach at all levels needs to be part of the students' permanently available intellectual storehouse. Too often, the content of courses like algebra and chemistry is "learned to be forgotten," which is a terrible shame and a waste of life and quality time. Similarly, foreign languages need to be learned as permanent tools for communication. From our perspective as teachers, how sad it is to think that one's course, one's subject, is simply a credential for graduation to be discarded, never used; for our students, what an opportunity lost. How do we prevent such a loss?

Whatever age we teach, in order to develop useable knowledge and skills, the learner has to strive for mastery—for the conceptual control that will lead to productive use of those knowledges and skills. Without this conceptual control, much of the curriculum covered by us as teachers and experienced by our students will slide rapidly through the sieve of short-term memory, despite the constant reviews and repetitions built into the spiral curriculum in many textbook series and district documents. The learner has to become a determined inquirer. How do we foster this unquenchable spirit?

In every primary child, we need to see a lifelong learner in the making. In today's world, higher education (whether it be formal or informal) has become almost essential for a quality economic and social life. We need to nurture the self-esteem and vision that will help students create an ever-better world for themselves as individuals and for society as a whole. How do we foster a better vision, a better world view than our own?

In every high school student, we need to see the insecure child that still lives in every adolescent (and probably in most of us), so we can nurture them to self-confidence and the determination to live a life of high quality. At all levels, building collaborative, inquiring processes is crucial, for from our classrooms come our citizens.

As Socrates reminded us over two millenniums ago, "We cannot live better than in seeking to be still better than we are." From the perspective of professional teachers, we translate this into: "The more powerful we become as teacher learners, the broader the opportunities for our students."

chapter 2

The Flow of the Inductive Model of Teaching

*T*he students do the learning, however we teach. We design the environment to make it likely that the students will learn. We organize the kids, assemble learning resources, and provide tasks. We teach the students to work in that organization, use those resources (including ourselves), and respond to those tasks. We draw on various models of teaching to help us design those environments, to help us decide how to organize the students, how to arrange materials, and what kinds of tasks to provide and in what order. Always we have objectives in mind: the kinds of learning that we hope will happen.

Objectives of the Inductive Model

The inductive model is designed to accomplish some very broad purposes, but can be focused specifically as well. Some of the broader objectives occur over fairly long periods of time through many experiences with inductive processes; others can be accomplished quite quickly and efficiently.

■ **Thinking inductively.** Every inductive experience should help students learn to work inductively—collecting and organizing information, forming categories and hypotheses, developing skills, and using the knowledge and skills appropriately. Through these experiences, they learn how to construct and use information while consciously improving their skills in doing so. Thus, the model gives students a powerful tool for learning, one they can use from the time they enter school and which will serve them throughout their lives. As we teach, we want them to get better and better at learning by thinking. Essentially, we want to help them increase their intelligence.

▪ **Inquiring collaboratively.**   Most inductive activity is the product of an individual mind. We think about data and form categories within our own heads. However, our minds do not exist in a social vacuum. The learning environment needs to operate so that the students learn to build and test ideas with others, helping one another and testing their minds against the ideas of others. Thus, we want to build a learning community in the classroom where individuals learn to share the products of their inquiries and where groups and the whole class plan studies together.

▪ **Using the ideas in learning resources.**   Books and electronic media connect the learner to all manner of sources for information and ideas. Students need to learn to mine those sources for information and to use their contents to test ideas and to find ideas to test.

▪ **Building conceptual control over areas of study.**   The inductive process asks students to form concepts by organizing, grouping, and regrouping information so that areas of study become clear and hypotheses and skills can be developed and tested.

▪ **Acquiring and retaining information and skills.**   Induction is built on collecting and organizing information and building conceptual structures that provide for long-term retention of information. The process of organizing data, building hypotheses, and converting information into skills is designed to increase the likelihood that what is learned "stays learned."

The Flow of the Model

The concept we refer to as *syntax* depicts the **structure of a model of teaching: its major elements or phases and how they are put together** (Figure 2.1). Some models, such as concept attainment, have relatively fixed structures within which some of the elements or phases need to follow each other for maximum effectiveness. Other models have a rolling or wavelike structure where phases are recycled. The inductive model has a rolling structure that

FIGURE 2.1   **Syntax of the Inductive Model of Teaching**

Phase One: Identify the Domain

Establish the focus and boundaries of the initial inquiry.

Clarify the long-term objectives.

Phase Two: Collect, Present, and Enumerate Data

Assemble and present the initial data set.

Enumerate and label the items of data.

Phase Three: Examine Data

Thoroughly study the items in the data set and identify their attributes.

Phase Four: Form Concepts by Classifying

Classify the items in the data set and share the results.

Add data to the set.

Reclassification occurs, possibly many times.

Phase Five: Generate and Test Hypotheses

Examine the implications of differences between categories.

Classify categories, as appropriate.

Reclassify in two-way matrices, as well as by correlations, as appropriate.

Phase Six: Consolidate and Transfer

Search for additional items of data in resource material.

Synthesize by writing about the domain, using the categories.

Convert categories into skills.

Test and consolidate skills through practice and application.

evolves over time; inductive inquiries are rarely brief. The flow of the inductive process is made up of several types of inquiry that overlap considerably:

- identifying an area of study—a domain that contains conceptual or actual territory to be explored;

- collecting and sifting information relevant to that area or domain of inquiry;

- constructing ideas, particularly categories, that provide conceptual control over territories of information;

- generating hypotheses to be explored in an effort to understand relationships within that domain or to provide solutions to problems;

- testing hypotheses, including the conversion of knowledge into skills that have practical application; and

- applying concepts and skills, practicing them and developing "executive control" over them so that they are available for use.

In this flow of cognitive operations, we find the definition of *induction,* for in these types of inquiry, **the student constructs knowledge and then tests that knowledge through experience and against the knowledge of experts.** *Induction,* rooted in the analysis of information, is often contrasted with *deduction,* where one builds knowledge by starting with ideas and proceeding to infer further ideas by logical reasoning.

Although it is convenient to imagine a prototype inquiry that begins with data collection and organization and proceeds to the development of categories, the generation and testing of hypotheses and perhaps then to the development of skills, the inductive process may begin at any of these stages or phases. Now, consider how the inductive process emerges.

Phase One: Identify the Domain

What information will be gathered for analysis, from which discipline(s) and in what form(s)? What material will students burrow into in their inquiry? Will it be a set of words? of poems? of picture story books? of opening paragraphs of books or magazine articles? of cartoons? of arithmetic problems? of paintings? of maps? of information about different species of animals?

To begin a given inquiry, we **lead the students toward information that is conceptually related.** Thus we create for them, or help them create, territories or productive arenas for concentrated study. We call these territories or arenas selected for academic study *domains for inquiry.* Domains form arbitrary boundaries for study and are quite various: they can be defined geographically ("Let's study everything in the town center"); they can be selected from domains within the academic disciplines (the economic systems of all nations, the political systems of Asian nations, poems written last year by Chinese women); they can be derived from student work (organizational patterns in expository prose, as in "We need to learn about organizing ideas more explicitly in our informative pieces"). They can be very broad, such as the mammals living in North America today, or quite narrow, such as specific literary devices like personification and foreshadowing. Domains can be quite pragmatic and immediately applicable, as when primary children study the structure of written words, or very abstract, as when those same children, grown older, study the tenets of the world's religions.

When we think about selecting content and organizing for instruction, we try to select domains that, if studied in-depth, will provide students with greater conceptual control over the world or with skills that are needed to navigate the world. For example, respectively, understanding how changes in communication technology are affecting the kinds of work we do and the people we relate to or developing the ability to write well-organized prose. Essentially, we try to lead students to domains that are significant by some academic standard or that will have practical utility for them.

At this point, the teacher's knowledge of curriculum and of what is worthy of sustained study by individuals and the class as a learning community comes strongly into play. Not that curriculum knowledge and resource knowledge are unimportant in other phases of the inductive model; however, if the major domains selected for concentrated study are substantive and if worthy substance and materials are selected for analysis, then (as your authors have experienced many times over the years) the teacher can learn along with the students, discovering many heretofore elusive relationships within language arts, science, mathematics, social studies, music, art, and so on. For when it is conducted well, the inductive model of teaching can lead to the clarification of concepts and relationships that have dangled disconnected for years within our minds or the minds of our students.

The academic domains or territories that have developed over the years as part of the curriculum within disciplines (for example, phonetic analysis; the properties of numbers; the study of quality in writing; the relationships among geography, climate, and natural resources; the Romance poets; optics; algebraic equations—just part of an enormous list) provide a rich source for in-depth academic explorations by students across the grades.

Selecting domains for inquiry requires us to think from a curricular point of view. As we organize the year's study in the curriculum areas, we identify the areas or domains that we want to be sure the students study. Other domains will emerge as the year progresses, with smaller domains and lines of inquiry emerging within the major ones, but the long-term planning of the year is the context within which the domains as units of study emerge.

Setting Objectives for an Inquiry.   As we stated earlier, the inductive model has many overlapping processes. As your mind plays across the curriculum and the time you will have with students, and you tentatively identify domains and units of study, you are also thinking about specific learning objectives. If you select as a domain "the study of quality in writing expository prose," you want students to develop skill in announcing their topics, developing logical organizational plans to help the reader, and providing accurate and ample support for their major points. Other objectives will surface as the students engage with the substance of the domain. If the Romance poets become a domain for exploration, you want students to understand the characteristics of their poetry, how it related to earlier literary works and affected later works, and the context of this movement in society at that time in literary and world history. Again, other objectives will surface for individual or collective pursuit; some identified by you, and others by the students.

Summary: Domain Identification Phase. When planning an inductive inquiry, we select a domain or unit of study or work with the students to identify one, and we think simultaneously about the ultimate objectives of that unit. We need to see these objectives in our mind's eye as knowledge and skills our students will develop through their explorations. As we engage in these processes, we know that other domains and other objectives will evolve as students engage intellectually with the information and materials that comprise the initial domain.

Phase Two: Collecting, Presenting, and Enumerating Data

Moving the inquiry on, we lead the students toward information that forms a domain or is within a given domain or territory. We may begin by presenting information to them or by helping them to gather or produce data, because inductive operations involve organizing data and pulling it apart and reorganizing it in the search for ideas. Thus, collecting data occurs early, and new data may be added or discarded as an inquiry proceeds.

Within the inductive model of teaching, we call the information presented or gathered *data sets*. These data sets are **assemblies of information.** This information comes in myriad forms: objects; literature and prose in its many forms—poems, stories, paragraphs, sentences, words; the results of experiments; perceptions; and combinations of various forms—all can be assembled into data sets. Almost any set of related information can become a data set: the table of numbers 1–100, modes of transportation, major cities and their locations, power plants and their locations, accident rates and locations, particular jobs and ethnic prejudice, stars and their locations. In this phase of the model, we bring the learners and the data together.

As learners and data interact, expected and unexpected results transpire. We are born with both the drive and capacity to sort the things we perceive, and we find connections among all kinds of things. The creation of the items we call constellations came from the linking of points of light to creatures and legends, which seems an improbable connection from some perspectives but which represents a natural function of the human need for understanding. Your students will make many improbable connections; they will often see things in the data that you did not see or make connections that have little utility. For example, in a set of poems students may notice that a number of poems have the word *yellow* in them, that a number of poems mention foreign countries, that a number of them all begin with the word *When*. At other times, students will notice information that you missed, or make useful connections that were not "visible" to you.

While we do not want to inhibit our students' spontaneous ability to seek unlikely connections, when we organize them for inquiry we develop boundaries for the search for information. Thus we create for them, or help them create, sets of data within the domains selected for academic study. For example, if we decide to help upper grade or middle grade students learn to use metaphoric devices in their writing, then they will have to understand categories of metaphors and be able to produce them as they write and to assess the effects of doing so as they decide whether to use those devices in a given piece. The data sets, thus, need to include examples of metaphors and examples of other devices so that students can distinguish them from metaphors. To build the set, we draw on samples of writing, possibly sentences, where authors have used metaphors and other devices such as personification or hyperbole.

Similarly, if we wish students to be able to generate prepositional phrases, we know that they will need to comprehend the nature of such phrases and practice producing them, our higher-order objective. The data sets will need to include many prepositional phrases and other structures, such as clauses, that need to be distinguished from them.

Let's look at how the two phases we have discussed thus far—the domain identification phase and the data collection/presentation phases—might work out in the primary grades, the upper grades, and the middle school.

Primary Grades.   In grade one, we may lead students to the domain of phonetic structures and provide them with a set that contains the subdomain of the sounds represented by the letter *c*. The objective is that they comprehend the rules governing the sounds of *c* and be able to use those rules in reading and spelling. The data set might look like this:

cat	crib	cake
catch	crayon	cotton
ice cream	October	nice
Carl	church	cable
Christine	choo-choo	cement
race	accident	act
face	duck	cold
mice	bookcase	luck
chicken	coat	actor

Or, we might have the students look through picture-story books and find words that contain the letter *c*. Or, working from devices such as the Picture Word Inductive Model (see Chapter 4), we might have them select the words containing *c* from a large set that includes words of many spellings.

Similarly, we can lead students to the study of plurals by presenting a set of nouns, some of which are plural and some of which are singular. The objective is that they develop categories containing singular and plural words and develop the skill to use those categories when reading and writing. That set might look like this:

1. book—books	11. word—words	21. library—libraries
2. city—cities	12. sentence—sentences	22. window—windows
3. girl—girls	13. boy—boys	23. crayon—crayons
4. woman—women	14. church—churches	24. lady—ladies
5. story—stories	15. farmer—farmers	25. slipper—slippers
6. cat—cats	16. teacher—teachers	26. table—tables
7. child—children	17. principal—principals	27. kitten—kittens
8. face—faces	18. man—men	28. bookcase—bookcases
9. desk—desks	19. chair—chairs	29 blouse—blouses
10. pan—pans	20. party—parties	30. cake—cakes

Again, we might send the students on a hunt for such words or have them sort them from a larger set that includes many types of words. (As an aside, we might do exactly the same thing with older students who have needs in the area of phonetic and structural analysis.)

Upper Elementary Grades.   To lead students into the domain of Native American Peoples, where we want them to comprehend the types of tribes, their differences, and the consequences to the different types as a result of European settlement, we might present a data set containing information about a number of tribes. The data set would include where the tribes lived before European settlement began, their numbers then and now, their type of life (hunting and gathering or agricultural, nomadic or settled, leadership structure), and any pictures and artifacts available. A few items from such a set might look like this:

1. The Southwest is spectacular country. Nature has carved the land forms into magnificent sculptures. Steep, multicolored mesas give way to deep canyons, and vast areas of dry land with a sparse growth of stubby grasses reach out toward the high snowcapped mountains in the distance. It is

beautiful country, but it seems a harsh and forbidding place for people to live. Wide stretches of desert are separated by rocky cliffs. The climate offers droughts, sandstorms, flash floods, and blizzards. But the Pueblo Indians and their ancestors have lived there for so long that it is as if they have always been there.

About thirty pueblos are still inhabited today by Pueblo Indians. The Hopi village of Old Oraibi . . .

The Pueblo, "The People and the Land," p. 1, by Charlotte and David Yue

2. In the summer of 1540, in what is now New Mexico, the Zunis looked down from their mesa-top pueblo named Hawikuh and saw a strange sight. Approaching from the desert to the south was a caravan of more than a thousand people. Most of them were Indians, but there were also several hundred men carrying long lances, wearing metal helmets and breastplates that glistened in the sun, and riding monstrous animals no western Indian had ever seen before—horses.

The caravan was led by Francisco Vasquez de Coronado, who had traveled north from Mexico on behalf of the king of Spain, pursuing rumors of tremendous treasure said to exist in the fabled Seven Cities of Gold. . . .

The Zuni warriors went down to find out what the strangers wanted. Through an interpreter, Coronado told them that he was on a sacred mission. If they did not peacefully submit to the Spanish soldiers and priests, he warned, "we shall . . . do to you all the harm and damage that we can." The Zunis answered by hurling stones and shooting arrows. Coronado himself was knocked twice from his horse, but in the end, the Zunis were overpowered by the Spanish horses, lances, and guns, whose thunderous sound they had never heard before.

Coronado's men took over Hawikuh, seized the Indians' food for themselves, and set up a wooden cross, demanding that the Zunis pray before it. But they found no gold or silver.

The West: An Illustrated History for Children,
"The People," pp. 4–5, by Dayton Duncan

3. The Indians had suffered plenty before the U.S. started moving into the West in the early 1800s. By then, the Spanish had been in the Southwest for more than two centuries. Under their rule, pestilence and slavery, along with raids by other Indians, had reduced the population of New Mexico's once stable and prosperous Pueblo communities from at least 60,000 Indians to about 9,000. The death toll in California was equally dire. By 1800, a string of Spanish missionaries had converted some Indians, enslaved others, and by means accidental and intended managed to kill off a lot more, perhaps up to 90 percent of the indigenous population.

Horses, which Spaniards had introduced to America, also profoundly altered Indian existence. Hunting buffalo from horseback and trading the skins to whites for weapons and other goods proved so profitable that a few previously agricultural nations, such as the Cheyenne and the Crow, gave up their permanent settlements for the nomadic life. Meanwhile, Indians who were pushed onto the Plains by westward-moving white Americans also embraced the horse and nomadism—the Sioux from Minnesota, for instance, and the Blackfeet, who were known as the Algonquian back East.

The Wild West, "The Way West," pp. 29–30
by the Editors of Time-Life Books

Or, we could present the students with the names of the tribes, the books listed above, plus any good sources they find, and have them locate the information and create the data set.

In the study of reading and writing, we might have students study contextual definitions with the use of a data set containing items such as these:

1. To the Plains Indians, the buffalo, or American bison, was the most important animal on earth.

   Buffalo Hunt, p. 8, by Russell Freedman

2. Even the buffalo's droppings were valuable. On the treeless plains, firewood was scarce. But there was an endless supply of sun-dried buffalo dung left behind by the grazing herds. These prized "buffalo chips" burned slowly, produced a hot fire, and were ideal for cooking.

   Buffalo Hunt, p. 42, by Russell Freedman

3. Humans ranged across the Old World for thousands of years, leaving behind sufficient skeletal remains to reveal their general, although incomplete, evolution from ancient forms. However, because only the remains of modern humans have been found in the Americas, a majority of archaeologists (scientists who study the remains of past human societies) have concluded that modern humans must have evolved elsewhere and then migrated to the New World at a relatively later date.

   The American Indians, p. 13, by R. W. and M. T. Force

4. Many New World cultures depended on hunting and gathering, although agriculture came to be the economic base of more advanced civilizations. The focus in the new world was on corn (maize), beans, squash, and tubers as the staple crops, as contrasted to the Old World reliance on such cereal grains as wheat, barley, and rice.

   The New Encyclopaedia Britannica, "Native American Peoples," V. 13, p. 349

5. The largest and tallest living things on earth, the giant sequoias of California are named for the exalted Indian leader Sequoyah, who invented the Cherokee syllabary, which not only made a whole people literate practically overnight but formed the basis for many Indian languages. . . . [When a hunting accident left him lame], Sequoyah turned his attention to the "talking leaves," or written pages, of the white man and set out to discover this secret for his own people. Over a period of twelve years, ridiculed by family and friends, he listened to the speech of those around him, finally

completing a table of characters representing all eighty-six sounds of the Cherokee spoken language. His system, which he devised by taking letters of the alphabet from an English spelling book and making them into a series of symbols, was adopted by the Cherokee Council in 1821. . . . The redwood tree (Sequoia sempervirens) was named for him not long after his death.

The Henry Holt Encyclopedia of Word and Phrase Origins, p. 474

Our objective in this case is that students will learn categories of contextual devices and develop the skill to use those categories to determine the meaning of words and phrases *and* be able to use those types of contextual devices in their own writing.

Middle School.   We could lead an eighth grade class to the study of the nations of the world with a data set containing statistical data like the following pairs on per capita income and urbanization.

Country	Percent Urban	Per Capita Income
Nepal	7.0	179 USD
Cambodia	11.0	84 USD
Kenya	22.0	376 USD
Japan	77.0	25,000 USD
Spain	91.0	9,578 USD
Sweden	83.0	22,000 USD

Asking the students to ruminate on the data and a possible relationship between these two variables, we then organize them to search for those same data on many nations and to begin generating hypotheses that explain the results of their findings.

Here, our objective is to lead the students to develop categories of nations based on demographic information so that they can better comprehend the variety in the nations of the world, understand which variables are and are not correlated, and be able to develop and test causal hypotheses—hypotheses leading to theses that explain variation among nations—for instance, why some are richer than others.

Let's move from our classroom examples back into our discussion of the technical aspects of the inductive model of teaching.

Enumerating and Tagging Data.   The data in the set need to be labeled or numbered so that we can keep track of them. In each of the sets just above (except the first grade set that was on word cards), the items are numbered so that they can be conveniently referred to. Pictures and objects can be numbered, tagged by color, or provided with meaningful names. For example, if primary students visit a number of local businesses and take notes about them, the data about each business can be labeled with the names of the businesses: bakery, delicatessen, shoe store, and so on. Rocks from the seashore can be tagged with blue, rocks from the mountain with yellow labels, rocks from the grasslands with green labels, and so forth. Lines from poems by various poets can be labeled with numbers, plus the poet's names and the titles of the poems.

Enumeration or labelling is extremely important. In a set of any size, we simply cannot manage to communicate with terms like "the one in the middle but slightly left." As we categorize, placing items together in groups, communication is facilitated because we can say, "Items four, seven, and twelve go together; they have '*xxx*' in common." The listener can refer to those numbers, track down those items, and follow our line of reasoning.

Summary of Phase Two.   In summary, in the data collection, presentation, and enumeration phase, the teacher collects the data that the students will delve into, enumerates the items in the data set, presents it to the students, and their inquiry begins. *Or,* the students and the teacher collect and enumerate the data, and their inquiry begins.

When teaching students to work inductively, we may present sets of organized data to them that we believe will help develop specific knowledge and skills, such as the different ways that *s* works in our language, or inflected endings, or text structures for expository prose, or information about major rivers, cities, or transportation. At other times, we may present data to them that represent a very broad domain—for example a large set of words, posters, math problems—and observe how the students interact with the information, then select the substance for their initial inquiry. We also teach students how to collect data and create data sets, because many inductive inquiries begin with a collection phase. Eventually, students leave our primary, elementary, and middle school classrooms. When they do, we want them to be able to use the inductive process as a problem-solving strategy and to support their learning about any topic: be it school reports on the influence of the union on the American economy or a report on the different types of land formation, or a project being tackled professionally, such as investigating the rapid reductions of the water table in their state or the stability of pension funds in their corporation.

Phase Three: Examine Data

Once a data set is assembled and enumerated, we are ready to have the kids examine the items in the set very carefully, richly teasing out the attributes. The examination of the set needs to be thorough; otherwise the inquiry will be superficial.

Returning to the earlier examples: for the primary grade's data set on the letter *c,* the students need to look carefully at each word, noting the spelling, where the *c*'s are placed, and how the letter, alone and in combination with others, sounds. For the upper grade's data set on Native American tribes, the students need to note each bit of data on each tribe. For the middle school data set on nations, the students need to be sure they are clear about the variables and what they mean (see pp. 49–51 for an example where the teacher works with the students to clarify the terms) and to familiarize themselves with the information about each country (how large it is, what is its population, the educational levels reached, and so on).

We have found that many teachers tend to rush through the examination of data, which is almost always a mistake. Sufficient time must be allowed so that the students have begun to discriminate the items from each other, seeing how their attributes are similar and different.

Phase Four: Form Concepts by Classifying

As we have said before and will reiterate often throughout the book, classification is a natural activity, almost as if it were built-in to our brains. The inductive model of teaching sets up a learning environment that facilitates and disciplines this natural tendency, making the process formal and conscious.

At this point in the inquiry, data have been collected and organized for examination, the attributes of the items in the set have been studied, and the students are familiar with the material. Their minds have already begun to play over the items, noting similarities and differences. Now, we ask them to reorganize the items into groups according to common characteristics. Using the language of the inductive model, these groups, or *categories,* help students form *concepts* as they put items together that share common characteristics, or *attributes.*

In Phase Four, we say things like this to students who are just becoming familiar with the inductive process:

To those primary school children: "Let's study these words and make groups of them. Put into a group, words that have something in common in how they are spelled and how the *c* sounds."

To those upper elementary students: "We know something about each tribe. Now, let's put them in groups that have some attributes in common, and see what we can come up with."

To those eighth grade students: "Using what you know about these countries so far, make groups based on common characteristics."

As students become more familiar with the formal inductive process, they will move through the phases with little prompting. They will know what to do before we suggest it, and individuals and groups of students (as well as the class) can carry out the phases while we, as teachers, serve as a guide and resource. The students will become more powerful and efficient as they become conscious of the process and gain metacognitive control over it. For now, let's continue as if the students have little experience with the process.

Initial Classification.   For the classification phase to be most productive, we generally classify data several times. The first passes are important, but we have a tendency to classify on gross characteristics and just use one or two attributes, confining ourselves to one-way classification. For example, when classifying poems, we rely on the more obvious differences in subject matter, mood, and device. Although it is limited, this first pass gets us going at building and sharing categories.

Our primary students might make their first pass by grouping together the words by position of *c,* as to whether *c* or *cl* or *cr* are at the beginning, regardless of the differences in sound. Thus, *cook, certain, clank,* and *crack* end up in the same category and *back, race,* and *reclaim* are in another. That is fine for a beginning.

Our intermediate students may make their first pass purely on location, grouping the Eastern, Western, and Plains Indians together. That is also fine for a beginning.

Our middle school kids may put countries together according to similarities and differences in single variables, such as size or wealth, and do nothing with combinations of attributes. Again, that's fine for a first pass.

Sharing Categories.   Generally, we ask individuals and small groups to share their categories at this point. We ask them to point out the attributes they used and explain why they grouped items together.

Adding Data.   Information processing is the essence of inductive inquiry, and without adequate information an inquiry stalls. Fresh information can be needed at any point in the process. For example, when building categories from a set of data, one may find that one has to collect more information because the data set is too thin. Sometimes after the first exercise in classification, we find we need to add more data to our set. Sometime, we begin to see things we didn't notice when we were collecting and examining the data. In those cases, we cycle back and collect or examine again, or both.

Further Classification.   Digging into the data again, our students reclassify, refine or collapse categories, split them or make subcategories, experiment with two- and three-way classification schemes. Categories emerge and are shared. Students gradually gain control of the information.

We ask them to examine the data again and see if they can discover more bases for grouping items. We might even give them some explicit suggestions:

- We might ask our primary students to pay close attention to sounds as they re-examine the data.
- We might ask our upper grade students to use variables other than location to expand their classifications.
- We might ask our middle school students to develop two-way classifications, prompting them to learn whether size is associated with any other characteristics (see pp. 35–36 for an example).

New or Refined Categories Emerge. Our primary students may discover that *cl* generally refers to the same sound regardless of position in a word. They may discover that *c* and *ck* and *k* can all represent the same sound. They need to learn that *c* followed by *o* or *a* will have the "hard" sound, as in *cone* /kon/ and *cake* /kak/. Gaining full control of how *c* works in the English language provides students an opportunity to learn and apply a number of phonetic generalizations.

Our upper elementary students may discover relations between methods of gathering food and the region where the tribes lived, or that population was reduced by war or disease among tribes having particular characteristics. They will surely come to have a picture of the overall pattern of change that occurred as a consequence of European settlement.

Our middle school students will discover whether per capita income is associated with educational level, fertility, or other variables. They will discover the enormous differences in life expectancy among nations and regions.

Reclassification can occur several times, depending on the complexity of the set and the students' experience with the inductive model. Greater experience leads students to develop more refined categories. They will develop a better sense of when to "categorize categories," or collapse them, and when to pull them apart to make more subcategories.

Phase Five: Generate and Test Hypotheses

In this phase of the model, students build hypotheses from the data and form generalizations for application and skill use. They continue to analyze information, but the focus is on studying the function and utility of different concepts and how they can be applied.

Of course, just having categories is educative, giving us greater conceptual control over portions of our world. When we classify character sketches drawn from novels and short stories, we discover ways that authors introduce characters; knowing those ways enables us to read with a more refined eye. However, if we keep pushing at the categories, we can form hypotheses about them and convert some of these hypotheses into useful skills. Suppose we discovered that female writers used analogies more frequently than male writers when introducing characters: we might hypothesize that women would use analogies more in all phases of their writing. We can develop a new inquiry to test that hypothesis. If we pursue the subject, test our hypothesis, and find it to be true, we can try to find out why.

To build skills from categories requires students to learn how to produce something that fits the category; to support increasing knowledge and appropriate use, they need to be able to explain their product. Suppose we discover metaphors as a device used by poets. If we want to produce metaphors, we need to practice creating them, and compare our products with the metaphors generated by expert writers.

Generally speaking, we need at least a half-dozen examples to generalize, another half-dozen to consolidate a category, and another half-dozen to convert a category into a skill. Thus, if an initial data set contained a half-dozen metaphors, the students need to find ten or fifteen more items with metaphors as they try to practice making them. Essentially, they need to synthesize their information into operational categories that they can transfer into action, using metaphors powerfully in their own written and oral communication. Thus, they proceed from identifying the characteristics of metaphors, into the development of a formula (list of attributes and the relationship among the attributes) that tells how to make them.

For example, our primary students need to convert categories into skills for use in reading and writing. We can present more words and ask the students to decode them, using what they have learned (words beginning with *co,* words ending with *ck,* and so forth). We can ask them to look through their books for more examples and place those examples into their categories. We can ask them to spell words that are in their listening/speaking vocabularies, but not in their sight vocabulary, and place them in the correct category. Our goal is for students to be able to use productive categories: can they recognize items that belong and can they create new items that match the attributes, or formula, they developed to describe each category.

Our upper elementary students need to consult authoritative sources that will help them interpret what they have learned. They need to express what they have learned in writing, discussing the similarities and differences among the tribes, formulating hypotheses related to those similarities and differences, and explaining how events evolved into the conditions that exist today.

Our middle grade students need to generate hypotheses that will explain the relationships they found, such as common attributes in terms of location (as in where the richer and poorer countries are located). They need to consult authoritative sources to see if they can find corroboration of their ideas. They, too, need to write extensively as their inquiry proceeds, using their categories to help structure their writing, explaining their hypotheses and what they have learned to support or disconfirm them.

In this phase, students continue to analyze data, focusing on the similarities and differences among the categories, seeking to understand the reasons and implications of these similarities and differences, and producing items that belong to different categories or relating the hypotheses they have formed to other settings, events, or situations.

Phase Six: Consolidate and Transfer

The concepts and skills produced by the inductive process are to be available in the students' minds for *use*. They need to be consolidated and applied. For this to happen, thinking has to be precise and clear. You can't identify metaphors or use them at an optimum level of expressiveness if your understanding of the definition is vague. Our students, thinking about metaphors, need to call several examples to mind, "see" their attributes, and use them to analyze things they read, identifying metaphors and distinguishing them from other types of imagery. In addition, when writing, the students need to bring those images to bear as they construct metaphors. They need practice in appropriate use, exploring when a metaphor seems to enhance the message and when it doesn't. They need practice, practice, practice.

Let's look at our primary, intermediate, and middle school students as they make the transfer from "lessons and assignments" to knowledge and skills they own for life.

- Our primary students need to decode and to write many words using their letter *c* in all its combinations.

- Our intermediate students need to use the concepts they have built about Native American tribes when they think about other groupings of people and when they encounter contemporary discussions about Native Americans.

- Our middle school students need to bring what they have learned about nations to bear when they think about the emerging international world.

Here, our responsibility as teachers and the students' responsibility as learners is to ensure practice, practice, practice in using what has been learned.

Studying Student Learning: Production, Diagnosis, and Next Steps

In the context of the inquiry, we study student learning of information, concepts, hypotheses, and skills. During the exploration of each domain, we study how well students are progressing with their mastery of the inductive process itself. We study the students by observing them, by examining their products at each stage of the process, and by giving them problems to solve that require applications of what they have learned. We will explicate this process in great detail in Chapters 3, 4, and 5. For now, let's see how the study of student learning might look in our primary, upper grade, and middle school classrooms.

Primary Students

As our primary students classify their words, we note the distinctions they make and the attributes they concentrate on. We find out whether they can "see" both sound and letter. Do they lump the hard and soft *c* sounds together or discriminate between them? We note whether they understand relationships between the sound of the consonant and the vowels that follow it. We note whether they generalize with respect to the position of the *c* in the word. We discover how they handle *ch, cl, cr,* and *ck*. We learn whether they can find, through reading, new words that belong in their categories and whether they can decode them phonetically. We present spoken words to them and learn whether they can spell them. Altogether, we are trying to learn whether they have mastered the little domain of *c*.

With respect to the inductive process and transfer of learning, we now provide them with another set and another domain—for example, words defined by the presence of the letter *t*—and we observe whether they are more proficient in the phases of that inquiry than they were with their first. Where they have trouble, we model the process. We might, in fact, choose another domain and demonstrate all the phases to them: gathering the words, enumerating the items, examining them for attributes, classifying, reclassifying, making and testing hypotheses, and sharing examples of how we use the different categories in our own reading (decoding) and writing (encoding).

Upper Elementary Students

We behave similarly with our upper elementary students. We note which attributes they pay attention to as they classify the tribes, and, depending on what we observe, we organize further passes through the items in the data set. We may have to teach them how to classify on more than one variable at a time, and if we need to do so, we will demonstrate. ("Here's a category I made to find out if nomadic or settled tribes lived in particular sections of the country. And here's how I built those categories.") We observe the types of hypotheses they make and what they are curious about: learning, for example, whether they explore how the hunters and gatherers fared when they were confined to reservations. We will provide them with some hypotheses to test and observe the skill with which they explore them.

As we prepare our upper graders for their next inquiry, we will use what we have learned to prepare sessions that will add to their knowledge base *and* to their inductive thinking skills. As we present them with a new domain to study, say, the forty largest population centers in the United States, we will observe whether they are more skillful and, based on these observations, decide what needs to be done next to add to their abilities.

Middle School Students

You can probably predict, now, what we will look for in our middle school students. As they categorize the nations, we will note the variables they concentrate on and how well they can handle categories based on multiple variables. We will study the hypotheses they develop and the questions they ask (Why is life expectancy so short in Afghanistan, Ethiopia, and Angola?). And we will give them problems to solve, such as learning how the small, wealthy countries in the world became that way. Depending on what we find, we will demonstrate techniques for handling data and ask them to make new passes through the data using those techniques. And, of course, their next domain of inquiry will be another opportunity for us to observe their developing skills. Figure 2.2 summarizes the inductive thinking model that will be explored as we proceed.

Summary

The inductive model reaches out to students and invites them to construct knowledge and skill through disciplined inquiry. Long-term retention and the ability to use the knowledge and skills developed during the process are our curriculum goals. The learning that results is not to end with the immediate classroom experience or the "end of unit" assessments, but is to be applied in further schoolwork, in out-of-school work, and to life in general. Another goal is the learning of the inductive process itself, so that students have conscious control of a powerful tool for learning.

The best inductive inquiry rolls along naturally, not rigidly, much as does good problem solving in the "real" out-of-school world. Thus, it is designed to facilitate, discipline, and extend what the mind does naturally: examine information, develop concepts, generate hypotheses, and take actions whose consequences are assessed.

Therefore, we intentionally design the learning environment—through the classroom organization, the content selected (initially and evolving from individual and collective inquiry), and the tasks we give as instructional moves—so that inductive reasoning occurs and students learn facts, learn concepts, and learn how to learn.

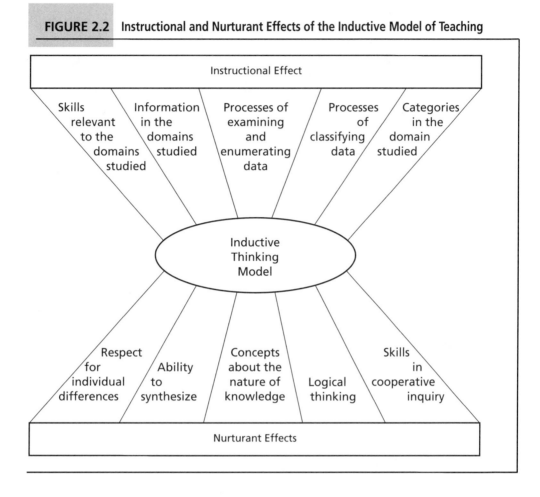

FIGURE 2.2 Instructional and Nurturant Effects of the Inductive Model of Teaching

In planning inductive inquiries, it is important to select worthy domains for in-depth study. You may want to identify territories that contain concepts essential to understanding a discipline and controlling its knowledge and processes for current and future learning development. For students, the cumulative effect of moving through the phases of the inductive model needs to include a degree of mastery that transfers to their future studies and their work.

The pace of learning needs to be commensurate with the importance of thorough study. Of great importance is not to let students rush through a shallow exploration, for this will not help them consolidate knowledge nor lead to transfer and use. In-depth study, allowing time for thorough study of content and for learning how to think, runs counter to normative practice in many classrooms where rapid but superficial coverage is common. Some teachers allocate as much time to similar topics/content units as those suitable for inductive inquiry, but the content is "covered," not explored and exploited for knowledge and beyond-classroom use. Inductive inquiry is an antidote to superficial study.

The inductive model works for efficient learning across disciplines and across ages. It can be used to design a large portion of the learning experiences in the major curriculum areas. It reaches out to all ages and to a wide range of individual differences.

In terms of professional development, teachers who have led many in-depth inductive inquiries cite two major effects. The first is a greater knowledge of the underlying structures of the disciplines they teach—just ferreting out the important topics and most productive concepts has an effect in itself; then leading the inquiry broadens and sharpens their knowledge. The second is a greater understanding of how children learn, gained by studying their ability to examine information, build lasting concepts and skills, generate and test ideas, and use what they have learned.

As students repeatedly use the model, they become more skillful information users and more powerful thinkers. The cumulative impact of practice in disciplined inquiry and the study of how to make it better is significant—our students look smarter, work smarter, and *are* smarter.

3

The Cooperative Inductive Classroom: Scenarios from Primary, Upper Elementary, and Middle School

*W*e don't advocate that you use *only* inductive strategies. You can use quite a few powerful models of learning to accomplish your objectives as teachers. However, we want you to know that you can accomplish a wide range of objectives by teaching your students to construct knowledge as they work alone and collaboratively. To help you form a picture of how teachers use the inductive model to shape the instructional day, we have provided three scenarios of cooperative inductive classrooms at work: a fifth grade class, a second grade class, and an eighth grade class.

The first scenario follows an elementary school class through a day when they pursue inductive inquiries in all the major curriculum areas. As you read the scenario, please note the ways that the class has been organized into a learning community and taught how to work, as individuals and together, to master the curriculum.

A Cooperative Inductive Classroom: Fifth Grade

8:30 A.M.—A Day in Early October 1996

Evelyn Burnham's fifth grade class assembles, pulling books and notebooks out of their backpacks. Figure 3.1 shows a diagram of her classroom.

They spend the next twenty minutes organizing themselves for the day. The computer crew for the week turn on the eight old 286 computers that Evelyn has scrounged from local businesses (and added memory and CD-ROM drives to them) and the Pentium, with its modem and classroom-size monitor, that is provided by the school district.

The students bring their Just Read files up to date and several add items to the "I Recommend This Book" list.

Working on the Pentium, one of Evelyn's "assistants for the month," using slips of words handed to her by the other students, enters words on the "Words We Need To Know" list that will be used at 9:00 A.M. The list comes from the students' scan of encyclopedia articles on several of the United States. For homework last night, all students had read articles and identified

FIGURE 3.1   **Layout of Evelyn Burnham's Classroom**

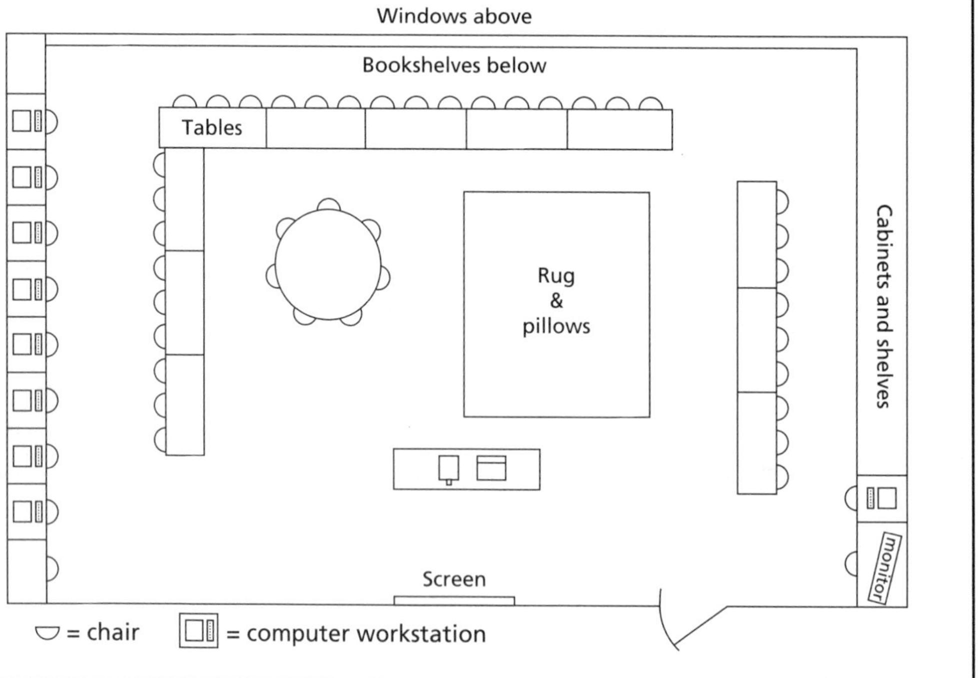

any words that were new to them and whose meanings were not apparent from context.

The science crew for the week sets up paper and instructions for making a variety of experimental paper airplanes that will be used to open a new stage of a science unit.

Another student assistant prints out one of Evelyn's files that contains sentences using adverbial words, phrases, and clauses, a data set that will be used in their study of writing.

While the students work at their organizational tasks, Evelyn has conferences with two of them on books they are reading, concentrating on comprehension of plot and character and assessing their needs in the comprehension area.

8:50 A.M.

The "Words We Need To Know" list pops up on the screen. The class is engaged in a long-term study of the human geography of the United States that has followed a study of its physical geography. The kids have made maps of the river and mountain systems, studied their geological histories, and mapped the plains. Now they are going to study the states. They are getting ready to classify them, using demographic information from a data base (see pp. 35 for a description of that phase of the inquiry). They are developing a list of items of further information they want and are using encyclopedias, the *Grolier Electronic Encyclopedia* and the *Britannica,* as a first source of information. Yesterday, each student took home an article on a particular state and a set of demographic data from *PC USA*. Their assignment was to scan the material and identify words and phrases they could not decipher from context so that the class could study those words to facilitate their inquiry. They have the *American Heritage Dictionary* on CD-ROM to help them.

The student who tapped in the list had noted the frequency with which the words were mentioned by her cohorts. The highest-frequency words and phrases were:

per capita income	crime rate (various crimes/1000 people)
unemployment rate	agricultural products
total land area	urban population density
ethnic composition	industries
immigration	public school expenditure per pupil
annual rainfall	mean annual temperature
persons per sq. mile	tourism
early settlements	capital city
annual gross product	admitted to the union

The class agrees that these words need to be the first priority, with other words to be studied after these are thoroughly mastered. For this unit, the class is organized in ten work groups of three students. Each group takes responsibility for two words, assigned randomly. Their task is to use the dictionary to ferret out the meanings of the words and to generate sentences that provide information about the words in context. The product is then passed to another group which reads it and makes suggestions for editing. Here is an example of the product.

The annual (yearly) rainfall (amount of rain) in the Olympic Mountains in the state of Washington is about 80 inches (between seven and eight feet). Usually annual rainfall is reported as the average amount over several years. In the Olympic mountains the low in the 1980's was 70 inches and the high was 120 inches, about one-third of an inch on an average day.

If a group has serious problems developing a product, Evelyn has them display their draft on the Pentium and helps them edit it while the class watches. The first few times her students wrote their definitional pieces, some had difficulty providing accurate and adequate information; some students added much nonessential information. But they are doing much better now. The "public" editing and discussion allows Evelyn to "think aloud" to her students about organizing their paragraphs and about different strategies for providing contextual information to their readers.

As each contextual definition is shared, Evelyn questions the students closely to ensure that they understand the meaning of the terms. The pieces that emerge will be used by the students as the class builds a data set on the states. For example, each student will use the above definition while building the part of the set containing rainfall information for various locations in the United States.

Each group enters their products on the "Words We Need To Know" disk and a set is printed out for all the students to study.

The next step, for homework, is for each student to classify the definitions. Evelyn gives the instructions:

> We're going to have more data to organize under these headings and others. I want you to become more familiar with these definitions and find out whether there are larger categories that can hold some of them, because they tell us similar things about the states. Remember how we studied poems last month? We found five ways the authors used images to convey their messages. Those five ways were grouped under "types of images our poets used." I want you to see whether we have the same thing here: definitions that share characteristics of the states. Grouping the definitions will help you clarify their meanings and help us organize our data as we collect it.

10:00 A.M.

The class begins their study of flight, which will begin with gliders and proceed to powered craft. The science crew distributes paper and the designs for the paper airplanes. Altogether, there are six types of gliders, and five students will make each of them. Having five of each model permits replication accounting for variation in manufacture.

Today, the class will begin to study the characteristics of the airplanes (size, shape, and length of wings, fuselages, etc.). In this stage of the inquiry, the airplanes are constructed and then placed around the room. The students examine them and make notes about their characteristics. As a class they discuss what they have learned, and the emerging descriptions are entered into a data set. Then they plan to fly the planes. They will be flown several times and the characteristics of flight and the airplanes studied. The students decide to begin by flying them inside, where there will be few air currents. Someone suggests that the flight might be affected by how hard they are flown. Another suggests that angle might affect flight. Several suggest that how high they are released might be a factor. They decide to arrange to use the gymnasium and to fly each plane several times, varying height and angle of release and the strength of the toss.

Evelyn has told them that they will make about fifteen models altogether and, by experimenting with them, develop concepts about the characteristics of the airplanes and their flight. The class will then compare what they have learned with information from a variety of sources including encyclopedias, books on the subject, and several films Evelyn has obtained from the Smithsonian.

Today's session ends with each student writing predictions about how each of the first three models will behave in flight. They will keep these, along with the descriptions of the three models, as part of their running accounts of the inquiry. Tomorrow when the flights begin, each flight will be preceded by the students' sharing of their predictions; these predictions will be tested when the students observe the flights.

Evelyn has been taking notes about the discussion, paying particular attention to the part where the students identified variables that might affect how the paper airplanes will behave. She wants to lead the inquiry so that students develop sets of principles about the relationships between the structural characteristics of the airplanes and how they behave in flight. She wants them to learn why they fly and how they can be controlled. Eventually, all the students will design their own paper airplanes, deciding how they want them to behave and making them according to the principles they have learned. They will also take a field trip to the airport, where pilots will discuss particular airplanes with them, showing how these principles work in the design and manufacture of aircraft.

11:30 A.M.

The students read independently until lunch, and Evelyn has conferences with three more students.

12:00 Noon Until 1:00 P.M.

Lunch and play. Evelyn confers with another student just before the period ends.

1:00 P.M.

The data set containing adverbial words, phrases, and clauses, all underlined in the context of sentences, is passed out by the Language Arts Crew. Here are some examples of the thirty sentences:

> Mary walked slowly across the field.
>
> With a leisurely pace, Mary walked across the field.
>
> Although she was walking slowly, Mary made her way across the field in twenty minutes.

Evelyn opens this domain of inquiry by explaining that they are beginning a unit on the ways verbs are elaborated. She asks the students to examine the set for three structures that are used to relate words to verbs. (The class had been studying verbs and their many functions and forms during the two previous weeks.) She adds that she wants the students to look both for the structures and the kind of information that is added to the verbs.

For about thirty minutes, the students read the set silently, making notes on the characteristics of the sentences. If students need help with a word, they use the electronic dictionary to check pronunciation and meaning. Evelyn moves around the room, studying what the students are doing and conducting miniature dialogues with them about what they are finding. She also confers with one of the faster readers about a book he has been reading, concentrating on his independent vocabulary development; he has chosen a fairly complex book on a topic he is unfamiliar with, the Pueblo Indians, and is being exposed to a number of new terms whose meaning he is having difficulty inferring from context.

Evelyn calls "Time," and the members of the work groups compare notes, explaining what they see and getting ideas from one another.

The last activity is a general discussion and sharing time, concentrated on the first half-dozen items in the set. Evelyn calls on students to share the characteristics they see in particular sentences, asks other students to add ideas, and clarifies ideas.

Their homework assignment is to continue to study the set. Tomorrow's session will be built around classification of the items.

2:00 P.M.

Outdoor play for twenty-five minutes. Evelyn has another reading conference with two students who are reading the same poet and are discovering some ways of conveying feeling that are new to them.

2:25 to 3:00 P.M.

Evelyn demonstrates several ways to build tables and graphs representing statistical data on the states. Using information from the New England states, she uses physical size and population as examples and shows students how to set up tables comparing size and population, and demonstrates one way of converting the data on the states to a graph. Using the Pentium display, she builds the following table.

NEW ENGLAND STATES

NAME OF STATE	SIZE IN SQUARE MILES	TOTAL POPULATION
Maine	33,265	1,235,396
Vermont	9,614	569,789
New Hampshire	9,279	1,110,801
Massachusetts	8,284	5,998,375
Connecticut	5,018	3,280,959
Rhode Island	1,212	1,005,091

Evelyn then reorganizes the table, ordering the states by population. The students can see immediately that size and population are not correlated. "Maine is bigger than all the rest put together and hardly has more people than Rhode Island, although it's thirty times bigger!" says one. They discuss the tables and peer at their maps.

Now, Evelyn plots the data, making the graph shown in Figure 3.2.

Over the next few days, Evelyn will demonstrate how to handle multiple variables. She will lead the students to the concept of population density and how to compute it. Students will use these techniques as they collect data on the states and classify them in various ways.

Shortly before the school day ends, the Just Read crew reports on the class's reading. They also share the number of books they have to read before

FIGURE 3.2 New England States Ranked by Size

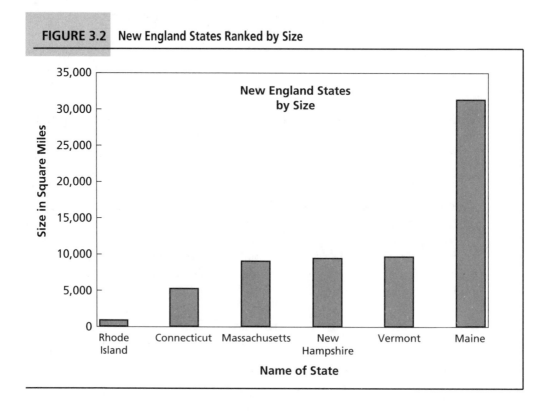

qualifying for the next class celebration. Two of the crew members take a few minutes to "advertise" several books that have been added to the class library. They leave the following table on the screen:

Just Read Totals, Week Ending October 5 (Week 5 of School Year)

There are 30 of us	
Books reported last week	52
By boys (n=15)	25
By girls (n=15)	27
Students reporting no books read	0
Fiction books read	36
Non-fiction books read	16
Total books to date	195
Books to first celebration	305

3:00 to 3:15 P.M.

As the room is cleaned and made orderly by the various crews, Evelyn holds her ninth reading conference of the day.

Commentary

In this sketch of a relatively typical day, we can see that Evelyn has used the inductive model to design the units in all her curriculum areas. In the social studies, she and the students are building a very large and complex data set on the states. To build the set, the students have to understand the conceptual meaning of a number of terms that are unfamiliar to them. Evelyn teaches them how to use the context provided by the author to determine the meanings of those terms, and when that does not work, how to use sources beyond the text as easy reference tools. Then, in order to increase their understanding and conceptual control of the terms, she has students classify them. In science, she has built an experiential inductive unit around the domain of flight. In the language arts, the unit on adverbs is opened with a data set she has constructed. Eventually, the students will add a great many adverbs, adverbial phrases, and adverbial clauses to the initial data set. The data sets and Evelyn, working together, will help students strengthen their prose, making it more active and providing better transitions to move the reader toward their message or though their narrative. In mathematics, she is teaching skills for developing tables and figures to represent data. Those tables and figures will facilitate inductive activity within the social studies inquiry.

The curriculum for these fifth graders is naturally integrated in a number of ways. The consistent use of cooperative inductive methods integrates the students socially and requires them to process information at different levels of understanding. Students are expected to think like social scientists—the tasks of creating knowledge and testing it with authoritative sources pervade the classroom. Each curriculum area feeds the others. Reading and writing are pervasive as tools for learning and are taught in the context of all the curriculum areas. Evelyn has a dual focus of building students' competence in reading and writing, and of using wide reading and informative writing as tools for learning and consolidating knowledge within each discipline. On the day we have observed, the mathematics and social studies lesson provide skills and content for one another. The study of flight, taught first from the point of view of science, will evolve into an examination of the impact of the airplane on the society.

Evelyn assesses student performance constantly and uses the information diagnostically to determine the next instructional moves, both for individuals and for the class as a whole. Within each domain of inquiry she tracks the students' learning closely, noting categories formed, hypotheses made, and vocabulary being developed. She confers with each student over reading at least once a week and concentrates on comprehension skills. In this week's round of conferences, she is gathering information to guide the content of the next unit of work in the language arts, which will focus on the skills for comprehending books as a whole.

The Management of the Classroom Community

Evelyn teaches the students to work cooperatively and to inquire together. All students learn to share the products of their studies and to work together, building and sharing hypotheses to test and generating questions to answer. And she teaches them that what they are learning—both the content and process of learning—has long-term implications: they are to remember and apply what they learn, rather than treating the products as schoolwork only.

Each month, Evelyn organizes the class into work groups of two or three persons. These work groups carry out many learning tasks together. The inductive process defines the types of tasks the students need to learn, whether they are working as individuals, in small work groups, or as a class. When necessary, Evelyn teaches the students the skills they need to carry out those tasks.

She also forms crews. The "crews" are different from the work groups described above. The crews are groups of students who work with Evelyn to prepare and organize instructional materials, equipment, and records. The class has six crews, with five students in each crew:

1. Assistants to Evelyn

2. Computers

3. Plants and Aquarium

4. Science

5. Just Read

6. Library

Evelyn organizes the students as work groups and crews to create a real workplace, with everyone having responsibilities for themselves and for the group as a whole. She relates to the students easily and respectfully, treating them as responsible people, and most of them respond. Within the flowing, evolving process of the model, she provides the structures that ensure that everyone knows what to do and why.

She has scrounged computers from various sources. These computers serve multiple purposes: they are used as tools for writing, as sources of information, for the production of materials, and for displays of information for the whole class. All students are expected to use the computers to make themselves proficient in the major applications, such as word processing, databases, spreadsheets, graphics, and communications, including the electronic searching of databases and networks such as the World Wide Web. Individuals also keep "Words I Need To Learn" lists parallel to the class lists and are expected to acquire new vocabulary from every book they read. Every week, each student has at least one and a half hours working on computer-related skills. Evelyn would like another dozen computers, preferably more, so that each student can have a work station. You can predict she will find them before long.

During the day we have just described, Evelyn worked alone, without paid or volunteer aides or a co-teacher. However, she recruits parents who assist with particular units (we will see an example of this on pages 41 to 43) and, of course, she has enlisted all the parents to help with the Just Read program. She has encouraged parents to form their own miniature PTO (Parents and Teachers Organization) program. This gives her an opportunity to explain the curriculum to them and ensures that they know what kinds of homework the students will be doing and how to help them with it. Her bi-weekly newsletter also tells the parents what is going on and enlists their help.

Next, we observe a primary school teacher at work.

A Cooperative Inductive Classroom: Second Grade

Now let's look in on Bonnie Brigman's second grade classroom. Her school is in a neighborhood where about half of the heads of household are recent, Spanish-speaking, Filipino immigrants to the United States. The other residents are relatively young English-speaking couples and women raising children alone who, like the immigrant families, have moved into the neighborhood seeking affordable housing. For a close-to-the-border California city, the neighborhood is old; the houses were built right after World War II. Nearly every household has one employed adult, and many have two, working mostly at semi-skilled jobs.

As in Evelyn's case, we're going to depict Bonnie as working mostly alone with thirty students. Although people like Evelyn and Bonnie are proactive, you can bet that by October they would have several regular volunteers—parents, senior citizens, and personnel from local businesses—even if the school district was unable to provide a paid paraprofessional. However, Bonnie will have two parents working with her for the first hour of the day.

As with Evelyn, we're going to show how Bonnie organizes her second grade into a learning community and designs the major curriculum areas with the inductive model, teaching the students to work independently and in groups and providing them with the tools of the inductive model.

8:30 A.M.—A Monday in Early May 1997

The class assembles, pulling books and notebooks out of their backpacks. Students use the first twenty minutes organizing themselves for the day at various tasks around the room (Figure 3.3). The computer crew for the month turn on the fifteen old Macintosh computers that Bonnie has corralled as the computer labs in the district have been updated. She has two relatively new Macintoshes—one with a classroom-size monitor, both with CD-ROM drives and modems—that were purchased last year by the school district. Bonnie has also loaded English–Spanish dictionaries and translation programs into all the computers, and sound in the case of the two newer computers.

FIGURE 3.3 Layout of Bonnie Brigman's Classroom

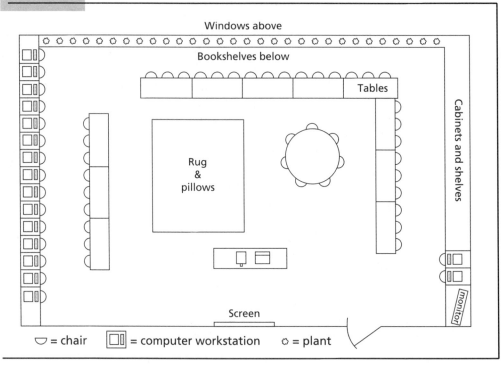

The library crew check books in and out of the classroom library. Each child takes a minute to water one of the thirty plants that are arranged across the window side of the room. Each plant is labeled, and there is a small notepad in front of it. The children inspect their assigned plant and some make notes. A few measure the height of their plants. The students also bring their Just Read files up to date.

While the students work at their organizational tasks, Bonnie has conferences with two of them on books they are reading, concentrating on their vocabulary and their ability to decode new words and infer the meanings from context. The two parent volunteers are printing out, in a large font, a list of words for each child and cutting the lists apart so that each student will have what amounts to a set of vocabulary cards. The words are taken from what looks like a diagram on one wall of the classroom. On close inspection, the diagram turns out to be a large photograph of the courtyard of a California mission, with lines extending from objects and actions in the picture. The photograph was taken during a reenactment of mission life, performed at a festival celebrating the founding of the mission. At the end of each line on the wall chart is a word or phrase representing the object or action the word is connected to. Bonnie and her students are using a strategy called "The Picture Word Inductive Model" to build reading/writing vocabulary and to study the early settlements of California. (Chapter 4 presents a detailed explanation of the Picture Word Model.)

8:50 A.M.

Bonnie reads a couple of announcements and goes over the plan for the day, inviting the students to comment and add specific items. She reviews the work of the last two days, during which students identified items in the picture of the mission courtyard and created the picture word chart. She then holds up cards containing each word and asks the students to read the word silently, then aloud, and asks its meaning. If students have difficulty reading a word (meaning Bonnie *hears* something other than that exact word when the students respond orally as a group), she asks one of the children to locate the word and identify what it is connected to on the picture word chart. When she is satisfied that the students can read the words and know what they refer to, she passes out the vocabulary cards and asks the children to create a subgroup of words that connect to some feature or aspect of life in the mission. Because of their extensive work on the structure of words earlier in the year, students tend to group the words by common phonetic or structural elements. This time Bonnie is focusing them on classifying their words by content relationships or meaning.

She illustrates by saying, "If someone were to group the things in this classroom the same way—by how they are used, what they do, how they were made, where they are located, and so on—they might put the computers, telephone, and overhead projector together because they are all tools run by electricity that we use for communication." Seeing some puzzlement on some students' faces, she elicits a few more categories from them. One suggests things used for writing: pencils, papers, chalk, markers, whiteboard, computers, and the overhead projector and transparencies. Someone suggests the plants because they are all growing things, all green, and all there to be studied. Everyone appears to understand so she asks them to proceed by making one category. Here is a partial list of words and phrases they have to work with.

horses	two carts	baskets filled with flowers
sword	soldiers	baskets filled with vegetables
bucket	rope	women grinding something
oven	cross	men wearing crosses around their necks
singer	guitar	women wearing brightly colored dresses
hoe	sombreros	men wearing only short skirts
wall	iron gate	men carrying wood
trees	children	children playing
bell	weaving	flowering bushes

The students, working as individuals, peer at the words and begin to sort them. Bonnie and the parents move around the classroom, watching and listening as the children share the categories they are building. Whenever a child asks them what a word is, they indicate the picture word chart and send the child to find the word and what it represents. If a child can think of a Spanish word but not the English one, he or she goes over to one of the computers and uses the translator program. After a while, Bonnie calls for order and asks some of the children to share their groups. One says, "I put a bunch of things together because they have to do with clothes: brightly colored dresses, armor, short skirts, sombreros, and crosses." Another child has some items to add to the same category: flower necklace, trousers, shawls. Three or four other categories are shared, then the children go back to their task, this time to make as many categories as they'd like.

At the end of the period, they share more categories, with one of the parents typing them into the computer. Bonnie asks the children to keep thinking about ways of grouping the words and phrases, actually the objects and actions they represent, and announces that tomorrow they will watch a film on mission life and see if anything is mentioned that needs to be added to the word chart.

As the study proceeds on subsequent days, the children will read a couple of short books on mission life and continue to add to their lists of things and actions. Bonnie has assembled a number of short books, some fiction and some nonfiction, that the children will explore as individuals. Eventually, they will compose descriptions of mission life and write stories set in the missions. They will also visit one of the missions and match what they have learned from secondary sources with what they see and what they are told by the mission guide. By the time they visit the mission, they will have many questions to try to answer.

Throughout the year, inquiries such as these have been building the sight reading/writing vocabularies of the students. Building the sight vocabulary through the picture word chart, the film, and the electronic encyclopedias brings more books within the reach of the students, while the categories they are developing provide structures around which they can write as the inquiry proceeds. Bonnie estimates that the social studies–related units have enabled her average student to add about five hundred sight words to his or her reading vocabulary and almost as many to their available writing vocabulary.

10:00 A.M.

Outside play. The parents stay until the recess is over. They will be needed again tomorrow.

10:20 A.M.

The class has been reading Dr. Seuss books. Ten of the books have been passed around until all the students have read them. Bonnie also has read a number of them aloud to the students and begins today's session by reading *The Circus McGurkus*. Then she says, "To get ready for some important writing—describing characters—we're going to study the Seuss characters and how Dr. Seuss made them come to life. Let's start by describing some of the characters in *Circus McGurkus*. We'll do these first ones as a group. Then, let's make a list of some of the characters in the other books and make descriptions of them and how Dr. Seuss tells us about them."

The members of the class volunteer information about Sneelock, an important character in the book. They talk about what he looks like, what he does, and the kind of person he is in the little boy's imagination. With each bit of information, they describe how that information is conveyed. ("We see his clothes in the picture." "He *does* very brave things, like. . . .") The children's ideas are collected on a flip chart page which will be pinned up on what will become the "Seuss Characters" wall in the room.

After the charts contain the descriptions of the two main characters and the ways they are revealed, Bonnie asks the students to use the information and write short descriptions of the characters. They work in groups of two around the computers, tapping in their descriptions. Before the day is over, these descriptions will be collected in a file on one disk, to be printed out for use the next day.

Over the next couple of days, pairs of students will take characters and make the same kind of description that emerged from the class activity. Soon the wall will be covered with descriptions of about fifteen Seuss characters. The students will classify these descriptions, then take the categories they developed and invent their own characters, writing with some of the same devices that Seuss used.

This activity, too, builds sight reading/writing vocabulary and helps students use what they have read to expand their writing skills.

11:30 A.M.

The students read independently until lunch, and Bonnie has conferences with three more students.

12:00 Noon Until 1:00 P.M.

Lunch and play. Bonnie confers with another student just before the period ends.

1:00 P.M.

This week's arithmetic is built around the Just Read data for the year. Every Friday afternoon, the students have entered on the computer the names of the books they have read—mostly at home. The numbers of books read have been totaled and plotted on the Just Read chart posted on the classroom door. The students are familiar with their own weekly and cumulative data. Bonnie is about to lead them through a series of analyses of the data that will introduce them to a number of ways of partitioning and aggregating numerical information. They have mastered the addition and subtraction facts and have practice adding and subtracting up to three-column numbers and adding lists of four or five numbers.

Each student prints out her or his reading record for April. The record includes the number of books read, the titles of the books, and the total number of books read by the student thus far. Each individual record also includes the total number read by all students for the year to date.

Bonnie begins, "I'm going to give you a series of tasks as we begin to look at our Just Read data in some new ways. I want to see if you can think of some questions we might ask, and we'll see what we can do with them. First, I want you to look over the names of the books you have read and count the number of fiction and nonfiction books you read."

The students take a few minutes counting the books, while Bonnie turns on the computer and sets up a format that has two columns. She asks one of the children to enter the numbers as the students report. Without saying anything, she calls on the girls first, then the boys. The class watches as the two columns of thirty numbers are entered and displayed on the screen. Then, Bonnie asks, "How can we find out if we read more fiction titles or more non-fiction titles?" There is some discussion, and the students agree that the two columns could be added and the totals compared. Each student does so, but their totals for fiction, when compared, range from 216 to 246.

Bonnie asks Tracy to come up to the monitor and add the numbers aloud. Tracy adds the first column while she is carefully checked by the others and comes up with 160. Then she adds the second column and comes up with 80. She adds the two totals for a grand total of 240. Another student says his total was 240, also, but he did it differently. He divided the long list into three lists of ten numbers, totaled each list, and then added the sums. The students discuss whether doing it that way will work. Robert comes to the monitor and demonstrates what he did. Sure enough, he gets 240.

The process is repeated for the nonfiction books. Then Bonnie leads them to figure out how to compute the number of fiction and nonfiction books read by males and females.

The session ends as the students begin to develop other questions: finding out how many of the books they read were about people, animals, combinations, and so forth; how many were mysteries; how many were fantasies; how many were realistic; and so on.

The subsequent sessions will deal with these questions and others, such as in which months the children read the most books. At the end of the week, they will make decisions about what kinds of books should stock their classroom library as they return one hundred books to the central school library and check out one hundred for the next month.

2:00 P.M.

Outdoor play for twenty-five minutes. Bonnie has another reading conference with two students who have finished reading books by the same author. The students have noticed that the books have virtually the same plot, only different characters and settings.

2:25 to 3:00 P.M.

Since January, the students have been tending and observing the plants. (There have been some casualties. Bonnie's assistants have been tending extra plants which are used as replacements. There were six of these the first week of January and two are left. She will use these for demonstrations.)

Now the time has come for the classification of the plants. The first task is for students to consolidate their information. Bonnie asks each student to write about her or his plant, describing its structure, what amounts of water and food it seems to respond to best, how much it has grown, whether it has produced flowers or fruit, and so on. Their descriptions will be duplicated and passed around.

Over the next few days, each student will give a brief oral report, showing the plant and discussing its characteristics. When all are thoroughly familiar with the plants (when they have been studied and examined by all the students), the classification process will begin. Each work group will develop categories and, in presenting their category, will actually move the plants around. Some days this phase of the activity will take an hour or an hour and a half. Eventually, the class will write a collective informative book about their plants and present the book to their parents.

Bonnie already has the meeting scheduled with the parents. She will use it as an opportunity for students to celebrate what they have learned. At the meeting, students will show off their plants and discuss what they have learned. After the meeting, each student will take a plant home to keep.

3:00 to 3:15 P.M.

The crews clean up and organize their areas, and everybody tidies her or his work space. Bonnie holds her ninth reading conference of the day.

3:15 P.M.

Right after school, Bonnie does her preparation in the classroom, using the computer extensively. During those hours, she keeps the classroom open, letting children and parents use the computers or read from the classroom library, with the understanding that they bother her only when they are stuck.

Commentary

In this sketch of a relatively typical day, we can see that Bonnie, like Evelyn, has used the inductive model to design the units in all curriculum areas. In the social studies, she and the children are building a very large and complex data set on the mission. To build the set, the students have to understand the conceptual meaning of a number of terms that are unfamiliar to them. Bonnie teaches them to dig out the meanings of those terms and to classify them in order to increase their understanding and conceptual control of the words. In the language arts, the unit on writing about characters is centered around the set of Dr. Seuss books. The mathematics lessons are built around the Just Read data. And in science, she has built an experiential inductive unit around the plants.

As can be seen throughout the day's lessons, the curriculum is naturally integrated in a number of ways. The consistent use of cooperative, inductive methods is central. Creating knowledge and testing it with authoritative sources pervades the classroom. Each curriculum area feeds the others. Reading, writing, and the inductive models of learning are pervasive and are taught in the context of all the curriculum areas. In the day we have observed, the language arts curriculum, through Just Read, provides skills and content for mathematics. In the Dr. Seuss unit, the students work on their reading comprehension skills as well as their writing skills. And Bonnie uses the extensive study of the mission in social studies to build sight vocabulary, to build skills using context to determine word meaning, and to develop competence in writing expository prose.

The Management of the Classroom and the Students

Bonnie teaches the students how to work cooperatively and how to inquire together. Each month, they are organized into work groups of two or three persons. Those work groups carry out many learning tasks together. When necessary, Bonnie teaches them the skills they need to carry out those tasks. The entire class shares the products of their studies and works together to build and share hypotheses to test and generate questions to answer. The inductive process defines the types of tasks the students need to learn whether they are working as individuals, in small work groups, or as a class.

The "crews" are groups of students who work with Bonnie to prepare and organize instructional materials, equipment, and records. There are six crews with five students in each crew:

1. Assistants to Bonnie

2. Computers

3. Just Read

4. Library

5. Sports Equipment and Games

6. Wall Displays

Bonnie organizes the students to create a real workplace, with everyone having responsibilities for themselves and for the group as a whole. She relates to her students easily and respectfully. Within the flowing, evolving process of the model, she provides the structures that ensure that everyone knows what to do and why. She teaches them that what they are learning, both the content and process of learning, has long-term implications: they are to remember and apply what they learn, rather than treating the products as schoolwork only.

The computers are used as tools for writing, as sources of information, for the production of materials, and for displays of information for the whole class. All students are expected to use the computers to make themselves proficient in word processing. Individual students keep "Words I need to learn" lists parallel to the class lists and are expected to gain new vocabulary words from every book they read.

Like Evelyn, Bonnie has enlisted all the parents to help with the Just Read program. Her students' parents have their own miniature PTO program. She explains the curriculum to them and ensures that they know what kinds of homework the students will be doing and how to help. Her bi-weekly newsletter tells the parents what is going on and enlists their help with everything from materials to time in school.

She tracks the students' learning closely, noting categories formed, hypotheses made, and vocabulary being developed. She confers with each student over reading at least once a week and concentrates on word attack and comprehension skills. In this week's round of conferences, she is gathering information to guide the content of this year's last language arts unit, which will focus on gathering information from nonfiction books.

And last, we visit a middle school teacher at work.

A Cooperative Inductive Course: Eighth Grade

We'll now look in on Bruce Hall's eighth grade social studies course. Bruce's middle school receives the students from Bonnie's school. The school is run traditionally, with separate-subject courses in the basic subjects. The eighth grade "team" of teachers is actually four individuals who teach their own courses. Bruce would like to see a schedule where social studies and language arts or science, or all three, are taught together, but he is a lone voice in the school and has had to design his social studies course within the confines of five 45-minute periods each week.

The curriculum guide for the school district assigns "multicultural education" to the eighth grade, but provides few guidelines other than the title. So Bruce has designed his course from a "global literacy" perspective, which includes a lot of basic information about the nations of the world and in-depth study of three nations representing three cultural groups. He teaches four sections of the course, with an average class size of thirty-two.

Much of Bruce's work with parents and his interactions with the business community has stemmed from his individual initiative. He has tried without success to persuade the faculty and principal to develop a schoolwide Just Read program, so he runs his own, and, like Evelyn and Bonnie, has developed his own miniature PTO program. He also has developed strong miniature "business partnerships" with several local businesses that are engaged in international trade and uses them extensively, as we will see.

Bruce is a skilled computer user and wants to foster similar skills in his students. With the school's limited budget, he has had some difficult choices to make, the most difficult being the choice between purchasing a large number of computers of low power or a small number of high-powered ones. He ended up with four high-powered Pentiums and is looking for resources to obtain a set of Alpha Smarts so his classes can use word processing at will.

Last year he applied for a grant from the state department of education for $5,000, and the reviews were favorable. However, the grant stipulated that the local board of education had to chip in $1,000 in matching funds, and the board declined on the grounds "that it wouldn't be fair to the other classrooms." Bruce was furious because the middle school athletic program costs $150,000 each year and provides "only the best" football, baseball, and basketball equipment for the players. Undismayed, however, he approached his business partners and they are discussing whether they can raise the money to make his a demonstration classroom. They probably will, but for now we will visit him and see what he has designed with the equipment he has.

The four Pentium computers have modems and CD-ROM drives. Bruce has assembled data-based programs, encyclopedias, and a host of other references. Like Bonnie, he also does his after-school preparation in the computer lab, keeping it open so that the kids can have access for an hour in the afternoon.

Bruce has assembled a classroom library of books about the regions and nations of the world, world religions and cultures, a large number of World Bank and United Nations publications, and sets of documents including constitutions, treaties, and speeches by politicians. The Saturday/Sunday edition of the *International Herald Tribune* arrives weekly in classroom quantities.

Some of his colleagues grumble that Bruce teaches graduate courses in a run-down middle school. Other colleagues are put off by the offhand remarks he makes, like, "If you aren't computer literate, then look down and you'll find the world has driven off without you." Bruce appears not to notice and is more than willing to help any of the teachers in computer use. He provides regular technical assistance to the teacher who operates the school computer laboratory. While frustrated with the district's progress in technology and its attitude toward funding, he has continued to serve on the district technology committee.

Let's look at the physical organization of Bruce's classroom (Figure 3.4), then we'll visit his first-period class for a while.

8:30 A.M. on a Monday, the Second Week of School in September

The students enter to find on their desks folders containing several maps of the world, of its regions, and of the middle eastern countries. Some of the maps are blank except for political boundaries; some are topographical; and some are political. Each student also has a copy of *The New State of the World Atlas* that Bruce ordered for $2.95 each from Edward R. Hamilton, Booksellers. The students look at each other, not sure about what's going on, and then give Bruce their attention.

"Last week we spent most of the time getting to know each other. I asked you to write about the United States Constitution and the United Nations, and we held discussions about current events. I used your papers and our discussions to explore what you know about the other nations on our planet.

FIGURE 3.4 **Layout of Bruce Hall's Classroom**

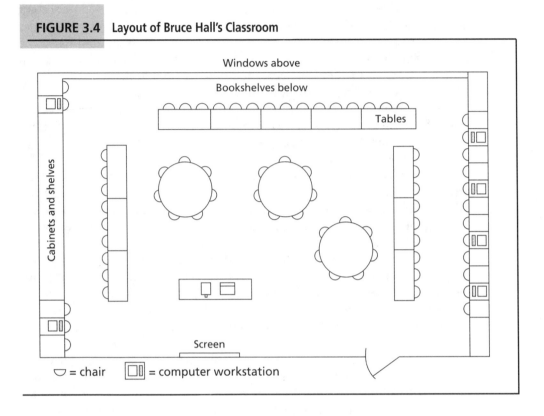

"This week, we begin our study of the world's nations and its cultures. By the end of the year, I want you to know enough about the people on this planet that it will be as if you have a little globe in your brains. You'll be able to scan that globe and see countries grouped into regions; you'll know which cultures dominate those regions and something about those cultures. You'll have a good idea about how the wealth of the planet is currently divided, how a sample of those countries are governed, what education is available and what portion of the population participates, what size families they have, and what's happening to them medically and financially. We'll use many sources of information: books, maps, computerized data bases and encyclopedias, the Worldwide Web, and other sources we think of as we search for information and ideas. Each week, two of you will be assigned to each of the four computers. I'll teach you how to use them. We'll read the *International Herald Tribune* each week. We'll study one article together, and then you can choose one to study for special interest. What questions do you have?"

There is a brief discussion as some of the students ask questions for clarification. Then Bruce continues. "We'll work inductively, for the most part, and take the world a region at a time. You will look up information, and then we'll use that information to classify countries until we get mental control of their differences and similarities. As the year progresses, you'll have many opportunities to ask questions, pursue them, build hypotheses and test them. You told me last week that inductive work would be new to most of you, so we'll begin today with a little inductive exercise."

Bruce opens the exercise by having students look at the maps of the Middle East. He has them read the names of the countries and helps them with pronunciation. Then, he asks them to take out a table shell labeled "Middle East." The names of the countries are in the left column, but the remainder of the columns are not headed, and the cells are blank. Bruce taps a key on each of the computers and the monitors come to life, each with a table containing the names of the Middle Eastern countries and information about geographic size, total population, gross national product, and percent of budget spent on military personnel and supplies. He asks the students to fill in the data on their tables. "You'll find definitions of the variables, including gross national product, in your folders. See if you can figure them out. Tonight, I want you to study your table. Please think about whether geographic size and population size go together—are correlated—and so forth. We'll discuss what you find tomorrow, and I'll help you further define the variables. Oh, and take a look at the *State of the World Atlas*. Find out what's in it."

The kids begin to work, and Bruce moves around the room, responding to queries and providing assistance. By the time the bell rings, the tables are completed. The kids leave, a little dizzy, but they know they are in a *real* course.

Commentary

Notice how carefully Bruce explains the long-term, higher-level objectives of the course, dealing with both content and process. Also, the first tasks he provides the students place much responsibility on them—the students will have to dig for knowledge with his guidance. The application of reading comprehension and writing skills pervades the course. He will help students develop the concepts and the vocabulary to attack the domains that are before them, modeling and demonstrating the behavior of a highly literate person. If a student reads poorly, Bruce will help that student develop a larger sight vocabulary and better word-attack skills. If students need skills for organizing expository pieces, he will provide direct help; he will not leave the teaching of reading and writing to the teachers of English, working alone.

In social studies, Bruce expects "to open up the globe" to them. More accurately, he will teach the students how to open it up for themselves. And, he expects the knowledge of the geography of the world to be available to them for the rest of their lives.

Bruce is working to help his students retain the information they are gathering: he wants major concepts to become embedded in their long-term memories and he wants the inductive/inquiry process to become part of their permanent learning repertoire.

Summary and Reflections

On first looking into cooperative inductive classrooms, many people are struck by how similarly the teachers organize students of various ages. As the students mature, more learning resources become available to them and they have stronger tools for collecting, organizing, and reflecting on data; however, young students are organized for instruction and are taught much as are older students. We have found that many, many people underestimate the learning ability of students of all ages. Young children can think quite well, and given a chance, can learn at fine rates and deal with considerable complexity. In many schools, the upper grade and middle school students are similarly underestimated. Many courses for these young adolescents are paced too slowly and cover too much too lightly.

In these three scenarios, we have provided examples in which teachers are teaching the students to work cooperatively and inductively. Imagine what those teachers could do if their students, from their earliest days in school, had been taught to inquire!

We'd like to end Part I and leave our three cooperative inductive classrooms by sharing some reflections on the American Tradition. In the formative years of the American government, Thomas Jefferson became the spokesperson for a universal school system that would prepare people for the social and cognitive demands of building a democracy and would ensure that literacy did not become a barrier to quality of life for any citizen. During the twentieth century, the great American philosopher John Dewey became the spokesperson for those same themes, and also spoke eloquently to the issue of how teaching influences the kinds of citizens we will become and the quality of life-long learners we will be. In his view, the classroom needs to mirror the social and intellectual demands of a complex democratic society through the development of inquiring learning communities. Recently, Carl Glickman has reaffirmed the Jeffersonian and Deweyan stance, making for a span of more than 200 years in which our heritage undergirds the practice of the teachers we have been visiting.

chapter **4**

Teaching Beginning Readers and Writers of All Ages

*I*n Part II, you will explore an inductive model that uses pictures as a stimulus for language with beginning readers and writers, and as a stimulus for inquiry into social studies domains with older students.

In this chapter, we introduce you to the picture word inductive model (PWIM) with beginning readers first, providing a rationale for its use, followed by an eight-day scenario with a kindergarten class, and concluding with a section that explains the moves of the model and how to get it started in your classroom.

Rationale for Using PWIM to Teach Beginning Readers of All Ages

The picture word inductive model draws its rationale from several lines of inquiry into how children learn and how to enhance their learning: children's development of language, the process of learning to read and write, and the reading/writing connection. Because the original concept of using pictures as a stimulus for language experience activities in the classroom was developed for application in the language arts, specifically for teaching young beginning readers to read and write (see, for example, Adams and Johnson, 1980), we will approach the rationale first from the point of the early literacy curriculum.

Children's Development of Language

The first part of this rationale is based on children's natural acquisition of language. By the time most children in the United States (and most other cultures) are five years old, they are able to listen to and speak between four and six thousand words with understanding and have developed the basic syntactical structure of the language (Chall, 1983; Clarke and Clarke, 1977). They can listen with understanding to complex sentences and longer communications. They produce sentences that include prepositions and conjunctions and make causal connections like "If we go to the store now, we could watch *Thomas* on TV when we get back." They gobble up words, play with them, and have conversations with stuffed animals and dolls—composing ideas and manipulating words very much as they will later when they write.

This acquisition of language is one of the most exciting inductions into their culture and brings with it a great sense of personal power and satisfaction as these young learners receive communications and learn to put ideas into words.

In the structure of the picture word inductive model, young children are presented with pictures of relatively familiar scenes (see Figure 4.1). They "shake out" the words from the picture by identifying objects, actions, and qualities they recognize. A line is drawn from the object out to the chart paper, where the word or phrase is written. Thus, the items they identify are connected to words already in their naturally-developed listening/speaking vocabularies.

The structure of the model respects the language development of the children and enables them to begin reading by using that language to operate over the pictures. ➤

The connections between the items and actions in the picture and the children's language enables them to transition naturally from spoken (listened to and spoken) language to written (read and written) language. **They see the transformations.** They watch the words being spelled and spell them with the teacher. They connect something in the picture with a word and then watch that word appear in print. They can now read that word. Shortly, they learn that we always spell that word the same way. They identify a dog in the picture, see *dog* written, hear it spelled, spell it themselves, and on the way home from school they see a "Lost dog" sign on the street corner and read "dog."

Thus, a major principle of the model is to build on children's growing storehouse of words and syntactic forms and facilitate the transition to print. ➤

FIGURE 4.1 Example of a Picture Word Chart

Most children want to "make sense" of the language around them and they will engage with us eagerly in unlocking its mysteries. A corollary principle is that the approach respects the children's language development. Their words are used and their ability to make connections is central.

The Process of Learning to Read and Write

Much remains to be learned about the almost magical process whereby children make connections between their naturally developing language and the world of print, surely a cognitive marvel. Our understanding at this time is that several types of learning need to be accomplished as reading and writing develop.

To learn to read and write, children need to:

■ **Build a substantial "sight" vocabulary, that is, a storehouse of words they can recognize instantly by their spellings.** About 400 to 500 words are necessary to bring children to the stage where picture-story books are available to them, although, as we will see, even 100 to 150 words bring very simple books like *Go, Dog, Go* within reach.

The picture word inductive model approaches this development of sight vocabulary directly. First, the students read and spell the words as they are "shaken out" of the picture. Then, these words are placed on large vocabulary cards that they can look at and the teacher can use for group instruction. Students also get their own set of smaller vocabulary cards. They sort these words and consult the picture dictionary to check their understanding and refresh the meaning of the words. The students keep their word cards in "word banks" or word boxes, consulting them as they wish and eventually arranging them to compose sentences.

■ **Build concepts about the conventions used in language to connect sounds and structures to print forms.** With respect to sound/print forms (phonetic, often called sound/symbol or letter/sound relationships), children need to learn that nearly all the words that begin with a particular sound begin with particular letters representing those sounds. Periodically, a teacher using PWIM will ask students to pull out all the words they have in their word bank that contain the letter *b* and they will concentrate on that letter for a while. Another time, all the words with *at* will get attention. After the students have learned to read most of the words on the picture chart, the teacher may ask them to pull out all the words in which they can hear an *s* sound.

With respect to the structure of words, students need to build an understanding of inflection, the change in form that words undergo to indicate number, gender, person, tense, case, mood, and voice. While it may seem impossible to believe, these structural conventions that have developed over time do eventually result in more rapid and accurate communication of their ideas. In the scenario that follows, you will find the teacher directing her kindergarten students to notice the similarities and differences between singular and plural words (as in how *dog* and *dogs* are alike and different; or *lunch* and *lunches*).

The picture word inductive model induces students to classify their new words, building the concepts that will enable them to unlock words they have not seen before. The English language has about fifty sounds that are represented altogether in about one hundred forms, because some have multiple representations (shut, nation). As students work with their words, they will develop many categories: these words all begin like *boy*, these all have two *d*'s in the middle like *ladder*. They will develop word families (*bat, cat, hat*) that they will use to read and spell words they have not memorized previously (*mat*). And, they will learn that the generalizations they make will enable them to unlock about seventy percent of the new words they encounter.

Students will be amused at some of the ways we spell words (*ate, eight*), and, like the rest of us before them, they will sigh occasionally at our insistence that they learn the peculiarities our language has developed. They will be perplexed by *see* and *sea* and want to know why we "made them sound alike"; at times, all we can say is what some of our teachers said to us: "You'll just have to memorize them."

In summary, the picture word inductive model capitalizes on children's ability to think inductively. It enables them to build generalizations that form the basis of structural and phonetic analysis. And, **it respects their ability to think.**

Thus, a major principle of the model is that students have the capability to make those generalizations that reveal to them the conventions of language. ➤

The Reading/Writing Connection

As the students mine a picture for words, those words are spelled correctly by the teacher and written on the picture dictionary, which launches the students into the early stages of formal writing. Later, the students will be asked to make up sentences about the picture, and with the help of the teacher, they will begin to write longer pieces. Through much repetition, the words in the sentences are added to their storehouse of knowledge, and maybe even physically to their word banks.

Gradually, as they read more and more trade books, the students learn to analyze how other authors write and use the devices of these authors to enhance their ability to express themselves. Essentially, they come to use our great literature and prose base (the library of the world) as models for learning even more about writing to share and communicate one's ideas. As they read more picture-story books and short informative books, they will discuss them, in a sense, "making up sentences" about the book they are reading or have just read. Many will come to feel that the reading of a book is not complete until they have said something about it in their own words, completing the communication loop between the writer (author) and the reader in constructing meaning.

From kindergarten on, the students and teacher work together building words and sentences and paragraphs and books. As they build paragraphs, they will select and discuss titles. The teacher will lead metacognitive discussions on why this title or that title: talking to the students about which title is most comprehensive, which title might be most interesting to one audience or another, which sentences would go with one title, which with another. When writing a paragraph or creating a title, she will help students focus on the essence of communication: what do we want to say to our readers, to ourselves. Her students will use the reading/writing connection as she has them think about what they want to share, what they most want the reader to know, how they will "help" the reader "get" this information, and, finally, did we (our class group), as writers, share what we wished. She will continue to work on this link until it becomes explicit and accessible for their use as independent learners.

Thus, another major principle at work in the picture word inductive model is that reading and writing are naturally connected and can be learned simultaneously, and later can be used together to rapidly and powerfully advance one's growth in language use. ➤

Questions Often Asked about PWIM

Before you take a closer look at the model in action, here are the answers to some common questions.

Would we use the model as described here to introduce older children or adults to reading and writing, say a ten- or twenty-year-old who could not read? The answer is "Yes." The primary difference is that older students can often progress faster.

Would we use the model to teach English as a second language? The answer is "Yes." A major difference is that the students are learning to listen and speak the words simultaneously with reading and writing them. Could we shake words out in two languages at a time? "Yes."

Now, let's visit Iva and her kindergarten students for a few weeks.

Scenario: PWIM in the Kindergarten—Learning to Read and Write

Iva Carter's five-year-olds at Perry Elementary School are learning to read through their teacher's expert use of the picture word inductive model. In this two-week classroom scenario, you will see these kindergarten students at work building their reading and writing vocabularies. They are also beginning their study of phonics by analyzing the structures (spelling) of words that are in their listening and speaking vocabularies.

Day One—A Week in Mid-October

The children are seated on the floor, facing a poster that features a teddy bear in the countryside. The poster is mounted in the middle of a large, blank sheet of paper. Iva says, "We're going to get some of the words for this week's reading by shaking words out of this picture. I want you to study the picture carefully and then, when I call on you, come up and point to something in the picture and say what it is. Then I'll draw a line from the thing in the picture and write the word. We'll start learning to read the words as we go along."

The children study the picture. After a few minutes, Iva asks them if they have found something they'd like to share. All the hands go up, and Iva calls on Jessica.

Points to note...

1) *Iva selected a picture with many common items: trees, leaves, apples, sky, items of clothing, fences, ladders, and so on; therefore, most of her students recognize many items and can contribute to the class vocabulary list. They have a feeling of successful participation in their learning and the learning of the group, and they are correct.*
2) *The social setting is conducive to learning from each other and from Iva. They learn about their personal space and working together in a limited amount of space and about how to share ideas with each other, not just with the teacher during individual instructional interchanges.*
3) *The physical setting means they are near the poster, can see the letters and words and their formation as they are printed, making it possible to provide much informal instruction in spelling, penmanship, and the separation of letters within words and words one from another.* ➤

Jessica comes up, points, and says, "That's a ladder." Iva draws a line from the ladder and writes the word *ladder* in large print, announcing each letter as she writes it: "l . . . a . . . d . . . d . . . e . . . r . . . spells *ladder.*" She then spells *ladder* again, pointing to each letter as she says it, while the children watch and listen.

"Now, I'll spell it again, and you say each letter after me." She does, and then asks another child for a word.

The large number of repetitions—pronouncing the words, spelling the words, and having students practice reading the words—help move the words rapidly into the students' sight vocabulary and spelling/writing vocabulary. ➤

"Basket," says Helena. Iva draws a line from the basket and writes the word *basket* in large print, announcing each letter as she writes it: "b . . . a . . . s . . . k . . . e . . . t . . . spells *basket.*" She spells *basket* again, pointing to each letter as she says it, then asks the students to spell it with her.

"Sit," says Brian, and points to the teddy bear. "The bear's sitting."

Iva draws a line from the bear's seat and writes, *The bear's sitting.* She spells each word aloud as she writes the phrase and then takes the children through each word in turn: saying the word, spelling the word, and then asking the children to spell the word with her.

Iva says, "Let's practice reading these words." She then points to the word *ladder,* runs her hand down the line to the ladder in the picture, and asks, "What is this word?"

"*Ladder,*" they chorus.

"And this word?" she asks, pointing to *basket.*

"*Basket,*" the students respond.

"And if you saw a word and couldn't remember it or weren't quite sure, what could you do?"

"Go down the line to the ladder in the picture," they say.

"Right," Iva responds. "Find the word or the group of words, trace the line, and check your reading."

Points to note...

1) *Students "practice" their reading and Iva models the use of the chart as an illustrated dictionary to help students "read" the words correctly.*
2) *The connection between the item in the picture and its symbolic representation in the word is reinforced.*
3) *Some of her students are still learning the moves of the model. Iva provides much modeling of how to use the chart, more than she will in later picture word inquiries.* ➤

Iva continues, "And what's this?" running her hand under the phrase *The bear's sitting.*

"*The bear's sitting,*" the students respond.

"Now, this is a bit tricky." Iva places her hand under the word *The.* "Let's read these words together slowly. Look carefully at each word." She takes the students through each word in the phrase, in order, then calls on individual students to read the words.

"Hannah, what's this word?" pointing to the word *bear's.*

"*Bear's,*" says Hannah.

She repeats the process with *The* and *sitting* and then asks for the whole phrase, but calls on Bruce.

"*The bear's sitting,*" shouts Bruce.

"Who thinks he's right?" asks Iva. The children's hands go up.

Some children have not learned the concept of words as separate units. Here Iva is helping students notice the difference between the sentence and the words that comprise the sentence. ➤

Iva continues to elicit words from the children, picking up the pace a bit. By the end of the session, the following list has been accumulated, and the children can say each word as the teacher points to it and runs her hand down the line for them to check their reading. Iva finishes this segment of the picture word inductive model by asking them to see if they notice any of the words from their picture word chart in the books they are taking home for the evening to share with their parents.

Points to note...

1) *Iva wants additional reading practice beyond the lesson time.*
2) *She also wants to help students begin to put these words in their long-term memory for mastery as sight words.* ➤

As the session ends, an older child who has been recording the words on a computer saves the file and hands Iva the disk. On the file are these words the students have generated from studying the picture.

ladder	sitting	bear's	apples
teddy bear	apple tree	basket	grass
tree	tree	basket	apple core
gate	ladder	apple with a leaf	little trees
tree trunk	The bear's sitting.	apple	leaves
half-eaten apple	bear	trunk	teddy
core	leaf	half-eaten	trees
apple	little		

Points to note...

1) *Iva wants the words on a computer file for ease of manipulation and for later activities.*
2) *Also, students are watching their words go up in D'Nealian manuscript; later, the words on their word cards will be in a large, typed font. Thus, they have an opportunity to learn to recognize multiple representations of their letters and words, and the typed font helps students see the spacing among and between words more clearly and differentiate among lengths and shapes of words.* ➤

Day Two

The following day, as the children enter the classroom, some of them go up to the picture and look at the words, saying them to each other and following words they don't remember down the lines to the objects connected to those words.

Again, the children sit near the poster. Iva leads them in reading and spelling the words, using the picture to help them locate the referents for the words.

> *In this brief time, Iva engages the students in reading practice, spelling practice, choral reading, more repetitions to aid the building of sight vocabulary, the recognition of letters of the alphabet, and the combination of letters that make or spell a particular word.* ➤

Iva has taken the file of words that were shaken out of the picture, put them into a large font, printed them out, and cut them apart, making a set of word cards for each student. Where the students had identified two ladders, several trees, two baskets from studying the picture, she included duplicates of those words. She gives each child a complete set. Now she asks the children to read their set and, if they can't remember a word, to go to the word chart, find the word, and trace it down to the part of the picture it represents.

ᗡoints to note . . .

1) *For most students, this initial reading or matching time is a joyous language learning activity.*
2) *Students have an opportunity to move around, to search for their words, to learn from and help each other.*
3) *Iva can diagnose who can match words correctly, who has their words upside down, who can read several words, who is confusing **apple** and **apples**—so she can reinforce the idea that having multiple lines from the picture indicates more than one apple, more than one tree, and so on.*
4) *If several words are repeated on the chart, they go into the data set of words. For some students, it is excellent learning if they recognize that **tree, tree,** and **tree** are all the same word or include all the same letters in the same order.* ➤

Much activity ensues. The children find their personal space, spread out their words, peer at them, take one or two and head for the picture word chart, search for the word, find it and say it (usually aloud) to themselves. Occasionally, they ask Iva if they are right ("Is this word *apple*?"), and she sends them to the picture to find out for themselves. Soon, most students are getting up and down, holding a word card and locating the word on the chart.

Students read/match the words with varying ability and speed. Within fifteen minutes, Pauline and Juan have read all the words and are clamoring to have Iva listen to them. She takes a couple of minutes to listen to them read their words while she keeps an eye on the traffic at the chart. Juan reads every word correctly; Pauline has difficulty with some of the phrases that have been separated into two or three words: she reads *teddy* as *teddy bear*, *trunk* as *tree trunk*, and *leaf* as *apple with a leaf*. Iva asks Juan to help Pauline study how these three pairs are alike and different.

As she moves through the students and word cards sprawled on the floor, she notes which students are reading their words correctly and which students need to visit or re-visit the chart.

As she hears Ricardo shouting quietly to himself, *"ladder, leaf, little,"* she says, "Good reading, Ricardo." As she moves on, Ricardo tugs at her pants leg and shouts, "Ms. Carter! Ms. Carter! *ladder, leaf,* and *little* all have one's at the beginning!" Iva smiles at Ricardo, and says "What a good detective you are, Ricardo. *Ladder, leaf,* and *little* all begin with the same letter, the letter *l,* and it does look a lot like the numeral *1."*

Nina, on her way back to her workspace, excitedly says, "This word is *ladder*!" "Good reading, Nina," says Iva.

Points to note . . .

1) *For Ricardo, Iva is acknowledging his performance in inquiring into how letters and words work **and** extending his concept of the letter **l**.*
2) *For Nina, Iva's acknowledgement focuses on the joy of reading.* ➤

Iva notices that Luis has brought all his words to the chart and is dominating the center space. She gently moves Luis to the side and asks him to take his bundle of word cards back to his personal space and see how many he can read. Then bring just one or two to the chart. She promises to come over in a few minutes and listen to him read.

Iva notices that Brad has his word card with *ladder* upside down as he is searching the chart. She takes his card and turns it right-side-up, saying "Try it this way, Bruce. Some of these letters are tricky and you have to study them very carefully." She notices that Kirk is getting a bit frustrated as he searches for *basket* and gives him a clue by saying, "Kirk, take a look on the other side of the chart."

She observes and listens to the six or seven students currently at the chart, looks around at the students at work on the floor and tables, then walks over to listen to Cynthia and Andrea, who have managed to wiggle closer and closer together and mingle their words.

She asks Cynthia to go to the chart and check out *gate* which she is "reading" as *grass*. She says, "Cynthia, this word begins with the letter *g* just like *gate,* but it isn't *gate*. Go to the chart and see if you can find this word. Then study it so you will know it next time you see it."

Iva asks Andrea to go and check out *apple* and *apples,* which she is reading as *apple.* Iva points to *apple* and says to Andrea, "Yes, Andrea, this word is *apple.*" She points to *apples* and says, "And this word has the word *apple* in it. Do you notice anything different about these two words?" Andrea points to the *s.* "Yes," responds Iva, "this word has an *s* at the end. Go to the chart and see if you can figure out what this word is."

Iva informally diagnoses what is happening, provides students with assistance and extensions, directs their attention to looking for other attributes of their categories, encourages them to look for other words that might belong in their group/category, reinforces correct generalizations, and facilitates discrimination between letters and words. ➤

After thirty minutes, most of the students are still actively engaged with studying and reading their words, although Hannah has started to wander over to the book center and Luis is crawling under the table. Iva decides this is enough for one day. "All right, guys, let's put our word cards back in their envelopes."

Day Three

As is usual in the sequence of the picture word inductive model, the first day of reading/matching their words provides students with a lively and chaotic lesson in language learning. The following day's lesson is often very similar, with students using approximately one-half of the lesson time individually reading/matching/studying their words.

Iva opens the lesson by having students as a group read the words on the chart. Next, she takes out seven word cards that she has selected for special attention by the group. (These words are written in large print on sentence strips.) In yesterday's lesson, these seven words were the ones she observed students checking most frequently at the picture word chart: *teddy bear, ladder, ladder, leaves, grass, apple, basket.* She has students as a group (remaining in their loose semicircle on the floor in front of the chart) practice locating each word visually on the chart, calls on an individual to come up and take her large word card and match it to the word, asks the students to raise their hands if this is a correct match, then has everyone read, then spell, the word aloud. She does this for each word, then places these seven word cards in the pocket chart.

She says to the students, "Look carefully at the words in our pocket chart. Think silently. What do you notice about them?" Iva waits a minute until several hands are up, then calls on several students.

[Tommy] "I can read all of them."

[Iva] "That's great, Tommy."

[Jordan] "They all have letters."

[Iva] "You're right, Jordan, they all have letters."

[Helena] "We have two *ladder*s."

[Iva] "Raise your hand if you agree with Helena, 'we have two *ladder*s.' " Most hands go up. Iva says to Helena, "Will you come up and put the two *ladder*s on the other side of the pocket chart." Then she calls on Miranda.

[Miranda] "*Teddy bear, ladder,* and *ladder* all have two letters just alike, right by each other."

[Luis blurts out] "They all have two *d*'s!"

[Iva] "Yes, Luis, those are *d*'s." Then says, "Miranda, would you come up and place *teddy bear* under our two *ladder*s and point to the two letters, the two *d*'s, that are alike in each word." Miranda does so and returns to her seat. Iva finishes this segment of the lesson by saying, "I am going to leave our word cards in the pocket today. Study them, practice reading them, and see if you notice anything else about them."

Iva is focusing on the first six sight words to be mastered by everyone. This day's activities have provided additional reading and spelling of these six words and focused students' attention on their similarities and differences. Recognizing these similarities and differences will help students learn to read these words and will help as they begin classifying words according to their structural and phonetic properties. ➤

Then students take their envelopes, find their personal space, and resume their independent reading of the words on the chart. They spend about twenty minutes reading their words.

Day Four

The following morning, Iva again reviews the chart with the children, reading the words and spelling them together. She has selected *apples, tree, tree,* and *trees* for special attention. She leads students in a brief silent and oral reading practice on these words, similar to what they did with the words in yesterday's lesson. Several students eagerly share that *apples, tree, tree,* and *trees* all have two letters just alike, side by side. Part of the visual study and practice in this segment of the lesson emphasizes how to discriminate *apple* from *apples* and *tree* from *trees,* with some discussion of how *s* by itself at the end of a word often indicates more than one object.

Points to note . . .

1) *Iva noticed the day before that some students were reading **apple** as **apples** and **tree** as **trees** and vice versa.*
2) *She is moving students toward recognizing the concept of singular and plural and how the letter -s works in forming many plural nouns.* ➤

Then she prepares her students for classifying their words. She reviews briefly what they have been working on in math: putting their red cubes together, their green triangles, and making patterns. She holds a set of pattern blocks of various colors and shapes in a small tray and asks the students to look at them. Then she says, "Watch carefully, see if you can be a very good detective. I am going to select three of these that go together. Your job as a detective is to think of as many reasons as you can why they go together." Iva selects three green triangular shapes and asks the students to think about how these three are alike. She gives students a minute to study. Here are some of their responses as she calls on individual students:

"They're all green."

"They all have three sides."

"They are pattern blocks!"

"On Saturday, we went to the store to look for some."

"Three points."

"Green triangles!"

Iva says warmly, "What good detectives you are. Now, look carefully and think silently. Would this pattern block fit in my group?" (Iva holds up a green square.) She calls on Ricardo.

[Ricardo] "It's not a triangle."

[Iva] "You're right, Ricardo. Now, can you tell us why it's not a triangle?"

[Ricardo] "It's not the same."

[Iva] "How is it not the same?" Iva waits for a few moments as Ricardo thinks, then calls on Jake.

[Jake] "The one in your hand has four sides."

[Anne blurts out] "It can't belong because it's a square! Triangles have to have three sides."

[Jessica] "Like the roof of a house."

[Iva] "You're right. This pattern block does not belong in my set because it has more than three sides. It is not a triangle. Now look carefully. (Iva holds up a red triangle.) Would **this** pattern block fit my group?"

"No," chorus the students.

[Iva] "Why, Angela?"

[Angela] "It's a **red** triangle. Yours has only green triangles."

Iva wraps up: "What good detectives you are. You noticed that the pattern blocks in my set were all green, had three sides, had three points, and are called triangles. You have been using a very important thinking skill called 'classifying.' Let's do one more practice classifying together before you do it by yourselves. Watch carefully."

Iva then picks up the large name cards the class has been using each morning as the students learn to read each others' names (and she takes attendance). She calls Jessica to the front and hands her name card to her; then Jordan; then Jeanette; then Jake. She asks the class to study each name card carefully and figure out how they are alike. She gives them a minute to think silently, then calls on individual students. Here are some of the responses:

"They're all kids."

"They're in kindergarten."

"Two boys and two girls."

"They all have *j*'s!

"They're all alike at the start."

[Iva] "Bruce, could you come up and point to where they are 'all alike.'" Bruce comes up and points to the *J* at the beginning of each name.

[Iva] "Raise your hand if you agree with Bruce." (Iva writes the letter *J* on the chart nearby.) "*Jessica, Jordan, Jeanette,* and *Jake* all begin with the same letter."

[Jessica can't stand it any longer and blurts out] "It's a *j*!"

Iva calls on Luis who has been waving his hand energetically but patiently for several minutes. "Thanks for waiting quietly, Luis." Luis gets up and walks up to the cards. He points to the *J* and *a* in each word and says, "They all have *j*'s and *a*'s." Iva says, "Everyone watch carefully. Luis, would you point to those letters again." Luis does so and returns to his seat. Iva collects the name cards from the students and places them one under the other in the pocket chart, "Thank you, Jeanette, Jordan, Jessica, Jake."

Iva, holding up Anne's name card asks, "Would this name fit in our group?" She calls on several students who give varying but correct responses about why it could not belong. When she holds up Jan's name card, students easily identify it as a member of the group. Iva places it in the pocket chart and helps her students think about writing and spelling by saying, as she points to the *J* in each name, "Yes, if we want to write Jeanette's, Jordan's, Jessica's, Jake's, or Jan's name, we have to begin it with an uppercase or capital *J*."

She brings the group practice to a close and reinforces and extends the students' comments/thinking by saying, "You were good detectives. I did put these names together because they all begin with the letter *J*. I did not think about the letter *a* being in every name, but Luis spotted it. Now, it's your turn to be a 'classification detective.' "

Points to note...

1) *Iva brings her students into formal classification of their words: connecting the classification work they have done in forming groups/sets and working on shapes in mathematics. She begins with objects that are tangible and concrete (the pattern blocks); then moves them to relatively familiar words (their names) and to looking at the letters in these words. After these demonstrations of classification with objects and words, she has students begin their first individual classification of the words from the chart.*
2) *Each student has his or her own set of cards, so everyone can be fully engaged in studying the words.* ➤

She asks her students to take out their word cards and find some words that go together because they are alike in some way. Students find their personal space and spread out their cards. There is a regular stream of traffic as students go to the picture chart to check their reading of a word. Iva walks around observing and asking students about their groups. Here are some of the categories she sees and the students' reasons for putting them together:

/apples, trees, bears, little trees/	"They have *s*'s and *e*'s."
/tree, trees/	"They have two *e*'s."
/tree, tree, little trees/	"They all have the same letters (pointing to the *t, r, e, e* in each word)."
/ladder, teddy bear, tree, apple, apples/	"They all have two letters alike."
	[Iva] "Can you find any other words that go in your set?"
/apple tree, little trees, teddy bear, apple core, tree trunk, half-eaten/	"They all have two words."
/teddy bear, apple, grass, tree, little trees, ladder, ladder/	"These are all words I can read."

/ladder, ladder/	"They are both *ladder*."
/bear's, apples, grass, trees/	"They all have *s*'s at the end."
/tree, gate, core, apple core, apple, apple tree/	Jeanette has lined up her word cards one under the other so that the *e* at the end of each is obvious. She says nothing when Iva asks her how they are alike, but points to the *e* at the end of each.

Iva says, "What a good detective you are, Jeanette!" Iva points to each word and reads it aloud, "*tree, gate, core, apple core, apple,* and *apple tree* all end with the same letter, the letter *e*. Now let's read them together." Iva says each word, and Jeanette echoes after her until they get to *apple,* which Jeanette rushes to say first for *apple core, apple,* and *apple tree.*

Iva allows the students about fifteen minutes to work individually on reading and classifying their words. Some students read their words to her when they describe their group; others do not. Some students identify the likenesses by pointing and saying "They have the same two letters in them." Iva extends their learning by pointing to these letters and saying, "You're right, *apple, apples, apple tree, apple core* all have two *p*'s in them. Can you find any more words with two *p*'s in them?" A few students are still practicing their reading; Iva praises them for their good reading and asks them to see if they can find at least two words that go together for some reason.

Note that students are expected to share the attributes of their groups—their conceptual basis for putting these items in one group—encouraging students from the beginning to be thoughtful about their groups and to articulate what they are noticing about how our language works. ➤

By this time, the students have been at work (from reading the chart as a group until now) for almost fifty minutes. Iva decides to stop while she's ahead. Lessons in the picture word/inductive model often last twenty-five to thirty minutes in grades kindergarten through two; however, some lessons may last fifteen minutes, others an hour. Iva generally stops when students have explored or extended the major concepts in language learning planned for that day, or when the students get squirmy. She wants their interest and attention to be focused; some days, fifteen minutes is all she and they can manage. But, she has been constantly amazed at how long these five-year-olds stay on-task as they explore how language works, and at how "smart" and thoughtful their responses are.

Day Five

Iva ended the previous day's work by having the students read the words on the chart as a group just before school was dismissed. She begins the Day Five lesson: "Today we will continue to read, study, and classify our words. As you are working with your word cards, pay close attention to which letters go together to make up a particular word. The more carefully you study a word—and how the letters fit together—the more likely you are to recognize it next time you see it. Let's look at a few together."

Iva places *ladder* and *ladder* under each other in the pocket chart. She says, "Study these two words. Read them silently. When you have something to share about them, raise your hand." She waits until most hands are up and calls on Tommy.

[Tommy] "They are both *ladder*."

[Iva] "How do you know, Tommy?"

Tommy gets up, goes to the pocket chart, takes both word cards over to the picture word chart, puts one and then the other under the word *ladder* and says, "Because they **are** *ladder*!"

[Iva] "Good reading, Tommy." [She calls on Helena.]

[Helena] "*Ladder* starts with an *l* and has two *d*'s and they both have all the same letters."

Iva adds *leaf* to the pocket chart under *ladder* and *ladder*. She says, "Study these three words. Read them silently. When you have something to share about them, raise your hand." She waits until most hands are up and calls on Miranda.

[Miranda] "They all have *l* first." Iva asks Miranda to come up and show everyone the *l* at the beginning of each word. Then she calls on Luis who is about to burst.

[Luis] "They all have *l*'s and *a*'s and *e*'s."

[Iva] "Good detective work, Luis."

Pointing to the word and the designated letter in each word, she says, "*Leaf, ladder,* and *ladder* all have *l*'s as the first letter." Then she points out the *a*'s and *e*'s in a similar fashion. She talks briefly about the tricky silent *a* in *leaf,* "*Leaf* and *leaves* (pulling out the word card for *leaves* and adding it to the pocket chart) are tricky words to spell . . . because we cannot hear in *leaf* or *leaves* any of the sounds that *a* stands for. We just have to study and study until we remember that *leaf* and *leaves* are spelled *l e a*. . . ."

Points to note . . .

Iva leads students in activities that help them notice and attend to:
1) *the characteristics of words and the order of letters;*
2) *the fact that specific letters form one word; if only one letter is added, it is a different word;*
3) *the concept that letters make similar sounds (as in* l*); and*
4) *the concept of "silent" letters.* ➤

Now Iva has them continue classifying their words just as they did in yesterday's lesson: "All right, let's get busy with classifying our words. See if you can find some words that go together because they are alike in some way, and be ready to tell me why. See if you can come up with some new groups, different from yesterday's." Students find their personal space and spread out their cards. As yesterday, there is a regular stream of traffic as students go over to the picture chart to check their reading of a word. Iva walks around observing and asking students about their groups.

Points to note . . .

Reasons for classifying **again***:*
1) *students can discover much about how our language works from classifying again and again the same list of words; and*
2) *students learn there is more than "one correct answer." They learn to continue inquiring to see what else they might discover.* ➤

After about twenty minutes, Iva decides its time for the students to share some of their groups—their categories—with each other.

She brings the students together again as a group; however, she does not ask them to return to their semicircle because she wants them to have easy access to their word cards. First, she helps Miranda, Jeanette, Tommy, and Ricardo, who had been working at tables, find a space so they can see the pocket chart, hear her and their peers, and still use their word cards. Then, she asks the other students to turn so they face her and the pocket chart.

[Iva] "Here we go! More tough stuff! As we share our groups, I want you to practice listening to each other very carefully. That means you have to do a lot of silent thinking. See what you can learn about our words from listening to your friends. Select your favorite group and get ready to share it with everyone: first, put the words in that group together; second, think about why you put them together; and third, be ready to share when I call on you."

While the students are organizing their groups, Iva places her set of word cards in one side of the pocket chart. Then she looks around to make sure everyone has at least one group ready, and calls on Ricardo.

[Iva] "Ricardo, would you read us the words in your set?"

[Ricardo] "*Tree* and *trees* and *ladder*"—as Ricardo reads his words, Iva places *tree, trees,* and *ladder* one under the other in the pocket chart— "have two letters just alike."

[Iva] "Hold on just a moment before telling us why you put them together and let everybody read and think about them. Study Ricardo's group and see if you can see some ways those three words are alike. Raise your hand when you have an idea." She gives them a minute and calls on Jessica.

[Jessica] "They all have *e*'s and two have two *e*'s."

[Iva] "That's right Jessica, all three words (placing her hand under each word) *tree, trees,* and *ladder* have *e*'s in them, and *tree* and *trees* have two *e*'s. Does everyone see the *e*'s? . . . Come up, Luis, and point out the *e*'s for us." Luis does so and returns to his seat, and Iva calls on Jeanette.

[Jeanette] "All have tall letters."

Iva says, "Jeanette, would you come up and show us?" Jeanette walks up and points to the *t* in *tree,* the *t* in *trees,* and the *l* and the *dd* in *ladder.* Iva responds, "Thank you, Jeanette." Pointing to the words and letters, Iva explains, "*tree* begins with tall letter *t,* so does *trees,* and *ladder* begins with tall letter *l,* plus has two other tall letters, the two *d*'s. When we are writing these letters, we make them taller than our *r*'s, *e*'s, and *a*'s."

Iva is teaching the students to attend to the formation of letters. Students see and hear the twenty-six letters of the English alphabet formed many, many times in these sessions. ➤

Luis bursts out: *"little trees* has five tall letters." There is much waving of hands, but Iva moves the students' attention on to other attributes.

[Iva] "Look carefully at Ricardo's group. Read them again for us, Ricardo. . . . Can you think of any other ways these three words are alike?" She waits a few moments, many hands go up, then she asks Ricardo to share why he put those words together.

[Ricardo] "Two letters just alike."

Iva goes back to the student who formed this category and provides Ricardo with the opportunity to formally share his reasoning. ➤

[Iva] "Come show us." Ricardo comes up and points to the double letters in each word. Iva says, "Super, Ricardo, *tree* has two *e*'s, *trees* has two *e*'s, and *ladder* has two *d*'s."

Iva **extends** *Ricardo's statement of "two letters just alike" by identifying the names of the letters.* ➤

"Did anyone else put words together for the same reason? Jan?"

[Jan] "I put *apple* and *teddy* together because one has two *p*'s together and the other has two *d*'s together." Iva places the word cards with *apple* and *teddy* in the pocket chart under *tree, trees,* and *ladder.* She calls on Kareem, who has been patiently waving his hand.

[Kareem] "Apples, too, *apples* has two just alike." Iva adds *apples* to the pocket chart and calls on Jessica.

[Jessica] "I put *tree, trees,* and *little trees* together because they all had *e e.*"

[Brian adds] "I put *teddy* and *ladder* and *teddy bear* together because they have two *d*'s in the middle."

Iva uses Ricardo's category of "two letters just alike" to find out how many other students had a similar category. Then she has students share the items in their categories—both from students who could recognize that there were two letters just alike, side-by-side, to those who recognized and named the two letters. ➤

Iva is enthusiastic: "Umh! What good detectives you are. Look at this list of words with two letters just alike, side by side. Look over at our word chart and see if you see any other words that belong in this group."

Students identify words and Iva adds them to the pocket chart. This is how the list looks now:

tree	sitting
trees	grass
ladder	ladder
apple	tree trunk
teddy	apple core
apples	half-eaten apple
little trees	apple with a leaf
teddy bear	The bear's sitting.

Iva says, "Now watch closely. I am going to put together some small groups like those I saw you put together. Sometime today—when we have snack time or if you finish your center time early—see if you can read these words and figure out why I put each set of words together." Iva forms these groups and leaves them in the large pocket chart:

tree	ladder	apple	sitting
trees	teddy	apples	little trees
little trees	teddy bear	apple core	The bear's sitting.
tree trunk	ladder	half-eaten apple	
		apple with a leaf	

Day Six

Monday's lesson opens with the students again sitting on the floor facing the picture word chart. Iva says, "Who can read all the words on our chart?" Hands go up. "Great! What good readers you are. First, let's all practice reading them silently, then I'll call on someone to read all of them aloud." Iva quickly moves around the chart, placing her hand underneath each word, tracing the line back to the picture, while students practice their silent reading. Then she says, "OK, who's ready?" She calls on Jordan, who reads them all correctly, except for a little help with *apple core*. Then she calls on Luis, but asks him to wait a few minutes before he begins reading the words.

Again, Iva provides her students with constant practice and repetition in order to build sight vocabulary. ➤

Iva tells the class, "When Luis reads a word with two *p*'s in it (she writes *pp* on the board), I want you to raise your hand." Luis begins, but proceeds a little differently: where Jordan simply pointed to each word as he read it, Luis points to the word, traces the line back, and returns to the word before he pronounces it, imitating what Iva has been doing with the group. Even with all this going on, she has to slow Luis down a bit to make it work. And she notices that Jeanette and Bruce are still confusing *pp* and *dd* occasionally. When Luis has made it around the chart, Iva claps and says, "Good reading, guys, and great work spotting those words with two *p*'s. Now, let's look at our groups of words and work on our classifying."

ᗡoints to note . . .

1) *Iva diagnoses what students' notice and do in relation to one of the patterns in one of the groups they have been working on.*
2) *She reinforces a group (those words with* **p p**) *that she thinks represents a useful generalization. This reinforcement supports further work in and understanding of the classification process.* ➤

"Who remembers what that long word *clas/si/fy/ing* means?" Iva slowly pronounces it as she writes it on the board. Miranda blurts out, "It has two *s*'s just like *grass*." Iva responds by saying, "It does have two *s*'s just like *grass*. When we spell *classify* (pointing to the *ss*) or *grass* we use two *s*'s side-by-side. But think some more, you're thinking about how it's spelled, can anyone tell us what it means?" A few hands go up, but Iva decides to demonstrate instead of risking a series of guesses. "Watch closely." She looks at the word cards and selects *leaves, apples,* and *trees,* placing them one under the other in a small pocket chart. "I just classified these words—out of all our words, I chose these three words and put them together for a reason." Hands are waving and students are commenting. "Study them a minute, see if you can discover why I put them together." She waits, then calls on Jake.

[Jake says proudly] "You put them together 'cause they all have *s*'s at the end."

[Iva] "You're right, Jake. That is one of the reasons I put them together." Then she calls on Jan.

[Jan] "They're all **some**."

[Iva] "Can you say more about that Jan? What do you mean when you say '*some*'?"

[Jan] "Some leaves, some apples, and some trees, not just one."

Iva: "Good thinking, Jan. That is also one of the reasons I put these words together." Iva points to and reads *leaves, apples,* and *trees,* "I put these words together—I classified them into one group—because they all have an *s* at the end that tells me they mean more than one leaf, more than one apple, and more than one tree. Just like Jake and Miranda discovered. Let's study these *s*'s a bit more." Iva finds her word cards for *leaf, apple,* and *tree,* and places *tree* and *trees* one under the other in the small pocket chart. Let's look at *tree* and *trees.* How are they the same and how are they different?" Several children volunteer, and she calls on Jeanette.

[Jeanette] "They're spelled the same except for the circles on the end."

[Iva] "Which one has the circle, Jeanette, *tree* or *trees*?

[Jeanette shouts] "*Trees!*"

[Luis can't stand it any longer] "*S, trees* has an *s*. And *tree* is just one tree and *trees* are lots of trees."

Points to note . . .

1) *Iva provides another example of classification and leads students to analyze the characteristics of the group, and*
2) *she takes another opportunity to work on plurals and on how -s works to form plurals.* ➤

They look at *apple* and *apples* in a similar fashion, then they get to *leaf* and *leaves.* Students easily note that both words begin with the letters *l e a* and that they both have to do with leaves, one or more. Iva writes these words on the board:

tree	apple	leaf
trees	apples	leaves

"What is different about *leaf* and *leaves* from *tree/trees* and *apple/apples*? When you have an idea, raise your hand." Iva waits a long minute, then calls on Miranda.

[Miranda] "*Leaf* has an *f* and *leaves* has no *f*."

[Iva] "Miranda, come up and point out the *f* in *leaf*. . . . Everyone watch closely. . . . Thanks, Miranda. For many words, when we want to make them mean more than one, we can just add an *s*." Iva writes *girl* and *girls* one under the other and some of the students shout out "girls"; she writes *boy* and *boys* one under the other and some shout "boys." "Think hard. Who can come up and point to the one that means more than one girl and tell us why." They work quickly through *girl/girls* and *boy/boys*.

Then Iva says, putting her hand on the small bookcase beside the board, "Look at our bookcase, what do we call these (putting her hand on the bookshelf)?" "Books" shouts someone; "shelves" shouts someone. Iva smiles and writes *shelf* on the board. Then she says, "I heard someone say the word that means more than one shelf," and she writes the word *shelves* on the board beneath the word *shelf*. "*Shelf* is one of those tricky words like *leaf*. We can't just add an *s* to make it mean more than one . . . we have to change some letters." She takes a minute to let them notice that *leaf* and *shelf* both end in *f* and that both *leaves* and *shelves* end in *ves*, then has them practice reading *tree/trees*, *apple/apples*, *boy/boys*, *girl/girls*, *leaf/leaves*, and *shelf/shelves*.

Points to note . . .

1) *Iva continues to have students work on how words are alike and different.*
2) *She has them work on plural and singular forms.*
3) *She uses the words **leaf** and **leaves** from the chart to begin teaching one of the common generalizations about forming noun plurals (adding **ves** instead of just adding s).* ➤

Iva decides the lesson has lasted long enough, "You've been such good listeners and had so many good ideas about how letters and words work that we did not get to our word lists. We'll come back to those after center time. Let's stand up, get some wiggle room, and have some music and exercise." She turns on the train song, one of their favorites.

It has taken Iva a while, but she has learned to stop at appropriate conceptual loop or lesson loop times, to stop when the students have been engaged for a long time (30+ minutes), and to stop when they get too squirmy because they know it's time for the fire truck, or lunch, or Sam's mom to bring in the gerbils. ➤

Day Six Continued

Iva moves the lesson on. "How many of you studied our word lists yesterday or this morning?" (Of course, all hands go up, even Paulo's who was absent for three days.) "Look at our first list (she points to *tree, trees, little trees,* and *tree trunk*). Who knows why these words are together?"

[Tommy] "*Tree, trees, trees,* and *tree trunk* all start like *truck.*"

[Iva] "What a good detective you are Tommy. I could have put them together because *tree, trees,* and *tree trunk* all have the same beginning sound, like *truck* (she writes *truck* on the board and underlines the *tr,* but that's not what I had in mind." Hands are waving eagerly, and Iva calls on Jeanette. "Jeanette, could you come up and show us something else that is **alike about these** words?" Jeanette comes up and points to the two *e*'s in each word and says "*e*'s, have *e*'s."

[Iva] "Good thinking Jeanette. I put these words together because they all have two *e*'s."

[Jordan pipes up] "And they all have *tree* too."

[Iva] "You're right, Jordan. Now everyone watch closely, I am going to add a new word to our picture chart." All the other words were written with a black marker, so Iva picks up a green marker. She walks over and looks at the picture chart, puts her hand on something in the air that looks like a bee. The students shout "bee," "bug." Iva says, "It could be a bug, but I think it's a bee. . . ." and writes *bee* on the board. "I am going to put *bee* in my group. Now, what do you think, Jordan?"

[Jordan] "They all have two *e*'s."

Iva says, "Let's look at our second group." She points to the list with *ladder/ teddy/teddy bear/ladder*. The students quickly identify the two *d*'s, and Miranda notes that *ladder, teddy, teddy,* and *ladder* all have "two parts." Then Iva has them take their words out of their envelopes and match the third list, takes a few responses from the group, and does the same thing with the fourth list, then has them read each list aloud.

Iva brings this segment of the lesson to a close by saying, "In the morning, I want you to study our picture and think about what you see in it. And, later, we'll write some sentences about what you see." She does not try to explain the meaning of *sentence,* but uses the term intentionally.

> *Iva wants the students to study the picture and think about what they see. She uses the word **sentence** but does not belabor the term. She will model what **sentence** means tomorrow.* ➤

Day Seven

The students are on the floor near the picture word chart. Iva has set up an overhead projector near the chart and taped a large piece of white paper on the wall. She says to her students, "Today we're going to write sentences about our picture. Instead of telling us what an object is in our picture, like *apple* or *one red apple,* you can tell us something more about the picture, like (she picks up the word card with *The bear's sitting.*) we have here. Who can read this sentence? Ricardo?" Ricardo reads, "The bear's sitting." Iva says, "Watch while I write another sentence about our picture." She turns on the projector, looks at the picture momentarily, and writes "There are two ladders, a large one and a small one." She pauses and asks, "Who sees some words in my sentence that they can read?" Hands go up and she calls on several students who identify *ladder, two, one,* and *one.* Then she reads the sentence, and follows this with having the students read it with her. "Now, who has another sentence for us? Everyone listen carefully."

> *Points to note...*
>
> *Working on the concept of sentence:*
> 1) *Iva begins by using the short sentence that was already a part of the data set.*
> 2) *She creates a new sentence as a model for the meaning of sentence.*
> 3) *She provides an opportunity for students to practice reading their sight words within the sentences and to celebrate their growing skill in reading.*
> 4) *And she continues to help students "notice" that letters make up words and words make up sentences.* ➤

As a student shares her or his sentence, Iva listens, repeats it orally for clarification and volume, writes it pronouncing each word as she goes, and finally has all the students read it aloud with her. Here are some of the responses that Iva writes on the transparencies:

"The bear has two eyes."

"The bear has two ears."

"The teddy bear has on blue coveralls."

"The bear has a red handkerchief around his neck."

"A black nose."

[Iva] "Who or what has a 'black nose,' Jordan?"

"The teddy bear has a black nose."

Iva helps Jordan extend his descriptive phrase into a sentence. ➤

"The teddy bear is leaning against the tree trunk." (Tommy actually said "ginst" but Iva transformed this to "against" as she wrote and read the sentence.)

"The teddy bear is in the middle of the field all by himself."

"The bear is leaning on a big tree."

"There's lots of tall, green grass."

"I see some yellow flowers beside the fence." (Miranda actually said "side the fence" but Iva transformed this to "beside the fence.")

Iva transformed both Tommy's "ginst" and Miranda's "side the fence" into standard English, both in pronouncing it and before writing it for all to read. ➤

"I see a little gate in the fence."

"The bear is sad."

[Iva] "How do you know the bear is sad?"

[Ricardo] "He isn't smiling and he's all alone in the field."

[Jake] "Who ate the apple? Can teddy bears eat apples?"

[Iva] "Jake gave us two sentences."

"Our bear is brown and furry."

"Our bear's head is round."

"His ears look like furry triangles."

"One tree has lots of apples on it, red apples, big ready-to-eat apples."

"Blue sky."

[Iva] "Helena, what do you want to say about 'blue sky'?"

[Helena] "I see blue sky."

[Jeanette] "Dirt."

[Iva] "Jeanette, what about the dirt?"

"Some brown dirt."

[Iva writes] "There's some brown dirt."

"How did the teddy bear get in the field?"

[Jessica] "Whose bear is it? I wish it were my teddy bear."

[Iva] "Jessica gave us two sentences."

Jake and Jessica gave two sentences. For both Jake's and Jessica's responses, Iva simply comments aloud that here we have two sentences, helping students begin to notice the separation between sentences and preparing them for future study of terminal marks that signal the end of a sentence. ➤

"The basket has five apples in it."

Iva calls a halt, "Whoa! My hands are tired. I know you have more great sentences, but that's enough for now. Can you work just a little bit longer? We need to think about a title for our picture." Iva picks up *The Rain Drop, At the Seashore,* and *Somewhere Today,* all informational books she has shared with the students. As she holds each one up, several students say the titles, almost in unison. Iva smiles and says, "Yes, *The Rain Drop, At the Seashore,* and *Somewhere Today* are all titles that tell us something about the sentences inside these books. Can you think of a good title for our picture? Look at it and think about our sentences. Raise your hand when you have an idea." She gives them a moment to think, then writes the first few responses on a transparency: The Teddy Bear, The Teddy Bear in the Field, Apples, The Lost Teddy Bear, Outside.

Iva is working with the students on inferential comprehension—can they look at the picture, think about their sentences, and figure out an appropriate "big idea." Sometimes, Iva has students think of a title before they write sentences, especially later in the year when she is working more on writing. She uses the students' thinking about the title to help focus the group paragraph they will write, and reminds students that once a title has been selected, they need to think about what it promises the reader as they select or write their sentences. ➤

Iva turns off the projector and says, "I have asked Ms. Roberts if some of her sixth graders can help me tap your sentences into the computer and write them on sentence strips. We'll work on reading these sentences (Luis pipes up, "It'll take a long time to read all those!") for several days. Sometime today or in the morning, I want you to practice reading all the words in your envelope, because your sixth grade buddies are going to come in after breaktime tomorrow and listen to how many words you have learned to read."

At 1:00, four sixth graders come to help with the sentences. Iva organizes them by showing them some examples of sentence sheets and sentence strips from last year, finds out who has the best penmanship, and gives them the transparencies with the sentences. They organize themselves for work. Iva gives Davida, who's setting up the computer file, a handwritten title and format for the first two sentences and asks her to be sure to put the file in 16-point font, saying "It'll save me a lot of time later, not having to reformat."

When Iva was writing each sentence, she jotted down enough of each student's name on the opaque strip of the transparency. The beginning of the sentence sheets looks like this:

The Teddy Bear in the Field
Sentences Written on October 22, 1996

1. "The bear has two eyes."

   by Jan Fisher

2. "The bear has two ears."

   by Ricardo Sirvan

Points to note . . .

1) *Iva has "published" the students' ideas/sentences.*
2) *This publication is a celebration of what they have developed.*
3) *These sentences become part of the language curriculum for the class:*
   - *students will practice reading the sentences,*
   - *students will practice their sight words, and*
   - *students will read their names, the names of their classmates, and begin to understand the idea of authorship and audience.*
4) *They will begin to recognize connector words such as* **The, the, on, in**—*and their likenesses and differences.*
5) *They will begin to recognize verbs such as* **has, is, did, see,** *and Iva will comment about* "**There's**" *and how the apostrophe works to replace the* **i** *in* **is.**
6) *Some of these common words will go on two pieces of poster paper (cut in half) posted in the room so students can use them if they wish in their own writing. One half-sheet will be labeled "Verbs." Iva will not hold forth or try to define "verbs" for these five-year-olds, she simply labels the chart accurately and tells the students "We call words that work like this in sentences 'verbs.'" The other half-sheet will be titled "Connectors." (For first and second graders this sheet would become several half-sheets labeled "Articles" and "Prepositions" and "Conjunctions.")*
7) *The students will eventually classify these sentences, studying how they are alike and different; noticing punctuation—as in the period, the question mark, and quotation marks; noticing aspects of syntax—"All these sentences begin with* **The**," "*All these begin with* **The bear**," *these with* "**The bear has**,"

and so forth; and noticing other characteristics of how words work to gether to make sentences.

8) *Eventually, Iva and the students will develop group paragraphs using their sentences as they are, or with any modifications necessary to put several together into a paragraph. She will use these modifications as content for instruction, and she will also use the group paragraph as a demonstration of classifying the sentences by content instead of structure.*

9) *By this time, which may be four to six weeks into the picture word inductive model (near the "end"), students will classify the sentences by topics they come up with, such as the teddy bear (all sentences will be about the bear; or only about how the bear looks; or about where the teddy bear is). Sometimes they will use their sentence strips and sometimes Iva's. As they work as individuals or as a group, they will be working on an advanced composition skill in informative writing—the focus and organization of a piece around a major idea.* ➤

The sentence sheets end up printed front and back on light pink paper, four pages in all. While the class has written several picture books together— one on animals, one on letters and colors, and one on the days of the week and classroom and home activities—this will be the first primarily print book they have created. As they continue to work with the picture word inductive model, short paragraphs will be added to their book. For example, a paragraph describing the teddy bear, a paragraph describing how to find the teddy bear. Eventually, each student will contribute at least one page, that he or she has written. (Illustrations are the child's choice; they are not required.)

Day Eight

Iva opens the lesson by saying, "Let's take a look at some of the titles you recommended yesterday." She turns on the projector and asks for volunteers to read each one. When this is done, she places an asterisk (*) by "The Teddy Bear in the Field," and talks briefly about why she selected this title, relating her comments about each suggestion to the picture, the words, and the sentences they generated. At one level, she is conducting direct instruction on identifying the main idea by having students consider and discuss "what's our picture about" and "what's our word chart mostly about" and "what are our sentences mostly about."

Points to note...

1) *Iva is engaging the students in a metacognitive activity in which she "thinks aloud" to them about why she selected this title in terms of its more comprehensive nature, relating this to the picture and their sentences, and to the idea of what titles promise to the reader in informative prose.*

> 2) *From her university courses and knowledge of the research in reading comprehension, Iva knows that many people at all age levels have difficulty getting the big picture or "determining the main idea," so she is laying the foundation for her students to be successful in this major communication skill, both as readers and as writers.* ➤

Then she moves the lesson on. "This morning, let's just have fun reading our great sentences." She switches the projector back on and leads the students in choral reading. Then she smiles and says, "Now it's your turn to practice reading them by yourself and here they are." She gives each of them a booklet, provides time for them to look at each, share their comments, and asks question about how it is set up. Then Iva tells them to find some space and practice their reading. As they find their space, she reminds them that they can use the chart or ask the author if they cannot read a word.

Points to note...

1) *Iva wants students to learn to use the chart as an illustrated dictionary because*
   - *she wants use of it to become routine;*
   - *she wants them to develop an awareness of when they do not know a word; and*
   - *she is teaching good reference skills, using the dictionary and looking up information when you need to.*
2) *Iva also encourages students to politely ask the author if they have trouble reading a word. However, she will watch these interactions carefully at first, because while she wants to support seeking of assistance from the author when needed, she does not want any student to become dependent or lazy as a reader/learner.*
3) *The class will spend many days on these sentences, reading together from Iva's large sentence strips and engaging in the activities described above. By the time they leave these sentences, most students will be able to read all of them.* ➤

Later in the picture word inductive model, after most of the students can read many of the sentences, the students will classify them. They will come up with many categories, with attributes ranging from those that focus primarily on the mechanical and concrete aspects of language—such as length of the sentences ("long ones" and "short ones"); these all begin with *The;* these all begin with *Our;* these sentences all have five words in them and a dot at the end; these all have little canes (?) at the end; these begin with the same first letter—to categories that focus primarily on meaning and content, such as "These sentences all have color words"; "These sentences are about apples"; "These are about things you see outside"; "These tell about the bear and the bear's body"; "These are all asking stuff."

Day Eight Continued

The sixth grade buddies come in at breaktime and Iva orients them to the tasks. They know the students because they have worked with them once a week since the second week of school as part of the school's **Literacy Together** campaign: sometimes reading to them, sometimes listening to them read/share a picture book, putting their animal booklets together, and tapping their stories into computer files. She has collected the students' word envelopes and asks them to make certain that they all have the thirty words on the list in their envelope. She says, "As usual, make it a fun shared experience. We'll take about thirty minutes, or more if we need it. I'd like to know, by the time you finish, which word cards your buddy can read quickly by simply looking at the card (sight words), which ones can be read independently using the picture chart, and which ones they have trouble finding or reading even when they use the chart. If you finish quickly, play word games with the cards, read, write, do whatever seems appropriate. Thanks for your help. Have fun!"

Points to note . . .

1) *For her kindergarten students, Iva wants this to be a celebration of what they can read and what they have learned; for the sixth grade students, she wants it to be a pleasurable social experience, and she wants them to feel the satisfaction of using their more advanced literacy skills as they work with the kindergarten students.*

2) *Iva also wants a more precise diagnosis of how many words each child knows. She has the buddies assist with this formal assessment of exactly how many words each student has in his or her sight vocabulary. Of course, the role of the buddies could be performed by parent volunteers or community volunteers; year before last, she had a dozen regular volunteers (eight women and four men) from the retirement home a few streets away.* ➤

As breaktime finishes, the buddies get to work, scattered throughout the room. Iva walks around keeping her eye on things, but spends the bulk of the time jotting down anecdotal records as she observes students using the picture chart or reading their word cards.

That afternoon, Iva summarizes the sheets from the sixth graders. Briefly, just in terms of sight vocabulary for these twenty-six kindergarten students: twelve students (six boys and six girls) had mastered all thirty words; eight students (five boys and three girls) could read all the words but went to the chart to "check" a few; three students (three girls) had mastered fifteen to twenty words and went to the chart for help with five or more words; two students (one boy and one girl) had mastered ten to fourteen words and were able to use the picture chart to read the others except for help with sections of *The bear's sitting, half-eaten apple, apple core,* and *apple with a leaf* (they could read these cards as a unit, but had difficulty with *sitting, half-eaten, core,* and *leaf* as individual words); and one student (Jeanette) had mastered nine words (*teddy bear, ladder, ladder, grass, apple, apples, one apple, tree, trees*).

Points to note...

1) *Iva knows which students have mastered which sight words from the chart.*
2) *She has a number of ideas about how to help everyone move toward the goal of reading all the words on sight.*
3) *She knows that, developmentally, her students are at many levels of language development. At the same time, she knows that the reading of these words is within the conceptual reach of all her students.*
4) *Thinking about a few of her students and Jeanette, she remembers one of her professors, in a class she took last year, talking about how some students just need more time to get there, and Iva knows from her own experience that this is true.* ➤

Overall, Iva is very pleased. Almost half her students come from families in which Spanish is the native language. And Jeanette, the student who has mastered the fewest number of words, just moved to the United States in August from Martinique with her family. While Jeanette is fluent in French, she speaks no English and Iva speaks no French. Iva is pleased that Jeanette has mastered nine words, but wants to facilitate her progress. (The district has bilingual programs for Spanish/English and English/Spanish that parents can select, and Iva speaks Spanish at a basic level.) But Iva has been very concerned about providing an optimum program for Jeanette—whose mother is struggling to make a go of it, is working days at a hotel, and is struggling to learn English herself. Iva, working with the principal, has been searching for someone who speaks French who will come in regularly as a volunteer tutor for Jeanette. A parent called last night and said her neighbor would be willing to come in three times a week until Christmas. Iva has set up a meeting and hopes she has found an "assistant."

Scenario Summary

We have been visiting with Iva and her class during the weeks of October 14 and October 21. Iva was using a teaching strategy called "The Picture Word Inductive Model," a device for eliciting words in the children's listening/speaking vocabulary so that those words can be studied and mastered and, through classification, be a basis for the early exploration of phonics, spelling, punctuation, and composition. Iva will continue with this same picture chart for at least two more weeks, having students add more words, classify them, play with them, and write stories with them. By the time the four weeks are up, most students will have mastered at least fifty sight words and will be able to articulate many concepts about how the English language works.

Using the Picture Word Inductive Model with Beginning Readers and Writers

In this section, we define the picture word inductive model, review its conceptual and operational framework, explicate the sequence of the model, and provide some general teaching tips. While the model has uses from primary through secondary school, the focus thus far in this chapter has been on its use with students at the emergent and beginning stages of literacy, especially those students in kindergarten through second grade.

Definition

In the preceding scenario, we hope you could feel the inquiry orientation that is so essential to using this model. Providing instruction that places students continuously in the roles of seeking to understand how language works and using the information they generate to move themselves forward as language learners is the primary purpose for extended use of the model. Formally, although a bit wordy, we define the picture word inductive model as:

> an inquiry-oriented language arts strategy that employs photographs containing familiar objects, actions, and scenes to elicit words in children's listening/ speaking vocabulary; leads classes, small groups, or individuals to inquire into those words, adding them to the sight reading vocabulary, adding them to their writing vocabulary, and discovering phonetic and structural principles present in these words; and teaches students how to use observation and analysis in their study of reading and writing and of comprehending and composing.

While we have used the model primarily with English and supported its use with Spanish, PWIM appears to work basically the same in any of the Indo-European languages, the same with older students and adults who are beginning readers, and those who are just beginning to learn English.

Briefly, the instructional sequence of the model cycles and recycles through the following activities: The students study a picture selected by the teacher; identify what they see in the picture while the teacher labels these items on the picture word chart; read and review the words they have generated; use the chart to read their own individual set of words and classify them according to the word properties they can identify; and develop titles, sentences, and maybe even informative group and individual paragraphs about their picture (see Figure 4.2). The full sequence of a PWIM unit may take three days—or two months; it depends on the richness of the picture and the age and language development of the students.

For most students, whatever their ages, the strategy is a satisfying and pleasurable activity: they enjoy observing, seeing the words they generate and the sentences they express come into print and becoming part of the "studied curriculum," categorizing words and sentences, and discovering useful language concepts and generalizations. Most participants are naturally motivated because they are successful learners.

Conceptual and Operational Framework

Here we discuss the approach to literacy, learning, and teaching at work in PWIM. One of our goals is to help you develop cognitions about language, learning, and teaching that will guide your decision making when implementing the model. Much of the discussion focuses on the nature of instruction, the role of the teacher, the role of the students, and the interactions among these three.

The picture word inductive model uses an integrated language arts approach to literacy. By this we mean the teacher arranges the events in the sequence of the model so that students work on developing skills and competence in reading, writing, listening comprehension as a tool for thinking and learning, and sharing their ideas orally with others. The primary instructional emphases are learning how the written language works, and using this information to read and write. In many ways, PWIM is a formal group language experience approach, with much structure and many metacognitive activities on how language works built into its sequence.

Throughout the model, students experience the association of oral language with written language—they see it happening, see their words and ideas (phrases and sentences) go into print. The symbolic associations begin to be understood: pictures represent real things, words represent real things, sentences and longer pieces represent stories and reality as seen by oneself and by others. PWIM is designed so that students use the speaking/writing/reading connection and the reading/writing connection continually as they participate.

While the picture word inductive model can be used to help students attain many of the language arts goals in our curriculum guidelines, at prekindergarten through second grade these three goals are constant:

1. building sight vocabulary;

2. building confidence in one's ability to learn; and

3. learning how to inquire into language and using what you know/find to read and write and participate fully in one's education.

	The Sequence of the Picture Word Inductive Model
FIGURE 4.2	**for Beginning Reading and Writing**

Learning about Symbols and Communication
(the relationships among "real things," pictures, words, letters, and sentences)

1. Select a picture.

2. Have students identify what they see in the picture.

3. Label the picture parts identified. (The teacher draws a line from the picture to the word; says the word; spells the word with her/his finger or the marker pointing to each letter; says the word again; students spell the word with the teacher.)

4. Read/review the picture word chart.

5. In grades kindergarten through three, and with beginning readers of any age, have students classify the words into a variety of groups. Identify certain common concepts in the words to emphasize with the class as a whole. The students "read" the words by referring to the chart if the word is not in their sight vocabulary.

6. Read/review the picture word chart. (Say, spell, and say.)

7. Have students add words if they wish. These words are then added to their word bank.

8. Have students think of a title for their picture word chart. (The teacher leads students to think about the "evidence" and information in their chart and about what they want to say about this information.)

9. Have students generate a sentence, sentences, or a paragraph directly related to their picture word chart. The teacher models putting the sentences together into a good paragraph.

10. Read/review the sentences.

Grammar/Mechanics

1. Students hear the words pronounced correctly many times, and they have an immediate reference source to use (the picture word chart).

2. Students hear the words spelled correctly many times and participate in spelling the words correctly.

3. In writing the sentences, the teacher uses standard English usage (transforming student sentences if necessary) and uses correct punctuation and mechanics (commas, capital letters, etc.). As different mechanical and grammatical devices are used, the teacher mentions why she is using this device. After many lessons in which the teacher has modeled these devices, she can ask students what needs to be done.

(continued)

Reminders

1. Keep the picture word chart posted prominently and ensure its easy access as a reading/writing resource for students.

2. Encourage students to create their own picture/word charts on plain paper or construction paper.

3. Most picture word/inductive models take at least five to ten days. They can take twenty to thirty days depending on the number of words generated and the conceptual richness of the list. Students master all words for sight reading. Modules can be used throughout the year and are great ways to integrate all areas of the language arts (listening, speaking, reading, writing). Pictures also can be chosen to strengthen students' understanding of science and social studies concepts.

4. Date the chart.

Developing the Learning Community

When the picture word inductive model is first used, the teacher will need to help students learn the format and sequence of the model and the social routines that will facilitate lots of children working and learning together. Thus, we teach students how to participate—teaching them explicitly by explaining and demonstrating, or through role-playing the moves yourself, or by "rehearsing" specific actions with a small group of students and then demonstrating it to the class.

For example, students may need explanations and demonstrations of any one or all of the following actions:

- studying each new picture as it goes up so they will be ready to contribute (some teachers put the picture up a day before they are ready to "shake" the first set of words from it);

- knowing the signal and coming efficiently to their space near the picture chart (many teachers use this model early in the day, right after their morning getting-the-day-started routine, and at the beginning of the year, some teachers put strips of tape on the floor);

- speaking loudly enough to be heard by their classmates and the teacher;

- learning to listen to each other;

- learning to raise their hands;

- learning to listen while they wait their turn;

- reading silently and orally;

- thinking "silently";

- responding appropriately in relation to the task at hand;

- keeping up with their word cards;

- sharing space at the picture word chart, especially the first few days of a new chart when students are busy practicing their reading; and

- finding and sharing workspace around the room when they are classifying words and sentences or putting together sentences.

As always, use your common sense and your sense of humor. Many of these demonstrations and initial learning experiences can be grand fun for you and your students.

Part of what we strive for with this model is helping students learn that they are responsible for thinking things through and for applying what they are learning. For this to occur, students need time to think, listen, and build on each others' ideas and on "remembrances" from previous lessons. Teachers often find they need to move the lessons more slowly than they are accustomed to, especially the first time or two through the model. From the beginning, try to consciously balance thinking time and a cheerful learning pace. Short, intense lessons of twenty to thirty minutes are often best for pre-kindergarten through first and second grade students, for this is not the total language arts program.

Both group and individualized instruction occur throughout PWIM. However, all students participate in all the phases of the model at the same time. When words are being elicited from students, you want everyone attending the event; for example, all students are seated around the picture chart when words are being shaken out. When it's time to practice reading/matching words, everyone practices reading. When it's time to classify, everyone classifies: from the student who puts a set of word cards together because they all have one word, to the student who groups *apples, trees,* and *leaves* together because they all mean "some not one," to the student who groups *ladder, leaves, ladder,* and *little* together because they "all sound alike at the first, they all begin with an *l* and it looks like the numeral *1*."

The range of accurate responses described just above is common and one of the curriculum advantages of the picture word inductive model: there is no curriculum or academic limit on what students can learn about language and how it works. Anything they can "see," articulate, or verify can become content for individual and/or group instruction.

Another general curriculum and instructional advantage is the opportunity for constant assessment of progress. Because so much of what is generated by students is visible, and because there is time to listen and think built into the model, constant diagnosis of student progress in language arts becomes a less-stressful task than it usually is for most primary teachers. Results are immediately useful for modulations in the next example or set of examples provided, the next question asked, or the next lesson planned.

Within each class, students' language development will vary, as will their confidence in participating. Given time, many experiences with the model, and a nurturing and joyous learning environment, most students—not just the quickest or most language-agile students—will make rapid progress. From the beginning, the teacher models the provision of thinking time and being patient when listening to others. Teachers find that even with four- and five-year-olds, they can say, "Hold on, we need to make sure everyone has time to think, share, etc." However, you do not insist that every student volunteer a word for the chart, although you may invite anyone who has not contributed a word or comment to the lesson by saying something like, "Maybe you'll have something for us later." Some students are simply shy, and some students have already—even at age five—come to think they are not "star learners," "not as smart as their classmates," or that their comments or answers are not "as welcomed" as those of others. When you feel this may be the case—whatever you speculate in terms of its origin (circumstances at home, overcrowded day care centers, the student's personality)—you want to address it in as many ways as possible: helping these students re-establish their faith in their natural learning ability.

We want success for everybody. And PWIM has been designed to help students develop as independent learners and as independent readers and to foster confidence based on knowledge that they secure for themselves as learners.

Selecting Pictures

The pictures are the basic materials necessary for teaching this model. They are tangible, concrete, and attractive, and they provide an excellent stimulus for common work in language development. Equally important, the students generally enjoy working together on them.

With preschool, kindergarten, and first grade students, we use large pictures of scenes that will be somewhat familiar or include many representations or objects that will be familiar to most students: scenes with children, scenes with animals, scenes inside the house or school, scenes outside. There are many reasons for using pictures or photographs that are easily understandable and accessible to these young children. One is so students will be immediately successful with their visual "reading" of the picture and its details. Two, as they read, or identify and label, the details or actions present in the picture, everyone will have something to offer to the word list they are generating. This word list will form part of the class's language curriculum for at least a week and maybe much longer.

The use of reality-based pictures (photographs or posters that are of real scenes or scenes that students can easily relate to) has many advantages. In most schools and districts, we do much more with fiction and narrative in our primary curriculum than we do with nonfiction and the development of informative, high-quality exposition. The picture word inductive model can be used to offer a more balanced approach in teaching written communication. Just in terms of the pictures used, you can help students develop skill in beginning research and basing what they say and write on evidence. You can help them learn to use their observational skills as a source of information when writing—an available skill waiting right there to be tapped by us and by our students. In general, using one's observational skill as a source of information when writing is a far underused resource. And, finally, the concrete and common stimuli of the picture and the picture word chart allows the teacher wonderful specificity and common examples as she "thinks aloud" about writing informative sentences and paragraphs; thus, we have ample opportunities for metacognitive activities on the formation and shaping of ideas we wish to communicate.

Sources for Pictures. Photographs are great! Sources include calendars, posters, book companies, stores, old magazines such as *Instructor* and *Life,* newspapers, enlarged photographs. Sometimes you will find public libraries, book stores, card shops, and so forth, getting rid of (culling their files or selling for a drastically reduced price) picture photographs of an area or of some topic relevant to your curriculum. Ask parents and other caregivers to keep their eyes open for appropriate posters and photographs.

For pre-kindergarten through first grade (maybe even second grade), twelve good pictures are all you will need for a year, and you may wish to laminate them for re-use. In fact, for most kindergarten and first grade classes, six to eight good pictures will take care of the year because of the amount of time needed to build sight vocabulary; to "see" and learn the generalizations about how letters and words work that are present in each set of words generated for a single chart; and to read, write, and play with the language the students have generated around the picture.

An Illustrated Dictionary. The picture word chart is an illustrated dictionary created by the students and the teacher. This dictionary supports language use by the class as a group and by individuals; it needs to be posted and remain posted where students can use it to support their reading, their writing, and their independence as learners. Because they can pronounce the words by using the chart, children as young as four or five will begin to "notice" and comment on spelling and phonetic structure. Until the words are part of the student's sight vocabulary, they are anchored in their representations on the picture chart.

Identifying Content for Instruction

Students volunteer the words that will be studied. While the teacher can always add words, you want most (more than 95 percent) of the words to come from the students' speaking vocabulary or from their investigations. The formality and extent of these "investigations" range from a more thorough exploration of the picture, to discussions with each other, to adding words they find from reading picture books or having books read to them.

How many words do you write on the chart? There's no magic number. Many teachers who are skilled in using the model in kindergarten and first grade often stop at the first round (the first time words are shaken from a picture) when the students have generated around thirty words. If students only generate fifteen words, go with fifteen for the first sequence of lessons. Use your judgment, and keep the lesson moving briskly while still providing adequate "thinking time."

The teacher—while still the obvious adult authority, instructional leader, and curriculum expert—does not know which specific language concepts will be emphasized until she looks at what the students generate: what they "see," what they can do, and what they can articulate about what is happening. However, the following communication processes and specific skills are always being developed: **reading** (sight words, phonetic analysis, structural analysis, contextual analysis, literal and inferential comprehension), **writing** (the relationship between oral language and writing; sharing common meaning through words, the essence of communication; composing sentences and paragraphs that convey ideas for ourselves and others; spelling; punctuation; letter formation; grammar and usage), **listening** (for comprehension, identifying and discriminating details, gathering and organizing information; and as respect for others), and **oral language development** (sharing ideas clearly, responding orally to the ideas of others and blending ideas together, "publishing" orally). But until the words are elicited, the teacher does not know which sight words, which phonetic rules, which aspects of structural analysis (compound words, inflected endings, plurals, contractions), of spelling (final -e rule, doubling the final consonant, capital letters for proper nouns), of punctuation (hyphens, apostrophes, terminal marks) will be developed.

For young children and beginning writers of any age, the following mechanics receive constant attention and are a natural part of the model: the correct formation of letters; the formation of words, where one ends and another begins; the formation of sentences, signals for where one begins and one ends; and the formation of paragraphs, where one begins and ends and what belongs "inside" it. Hundreds of repetitions are built in for reading and spelling, but also for these mechanics of writing.

As words, sentences, and paragraphs are generated and analyzed, the teacher and students make continual curriculum and instructional decisions about what will become the focus of brief or long-term study. Much of the instruction about the mechanics of written language and the process of analysis is informal, and the modeling and explanations are constant. For example, a student identifies and says "post office," and the teacher may write and spell *post office* on the chart; another student volunteers "U.S. Post Office," and the teacher may write and spell *U.S. Post Office.* Then she may say, "Does anyone know what capital *U,* capital *S,* stands for? . . . It stands for the *United States,* the name of our country. We call it (pointing to the *U.S.*), an abbreviation. *U* dot, stands for *United,* and *S* dot, stands for *States.*" At this point, the teacher may add *United States Post Office* to the chart. Now, there are three correct labels representing the building in the picture, and the students have had a quick overview of the complexities of language and communication, not counting the specifics of spelling, capitalization, and punctuation.

Anytime during a lesson, even when the initial word list is being generated, the teacher can comment about compound words, punctuation marks, sentence structure, whatever seems worth "noticing." Through this informal format, this running-but-not-constant-dialog about how our language works, the teacher helps students develop the foundations of cognizant control of language and of standard written communication. From the very first lesson with the model, students are invited and expected to comment on what they see in the words or sentences: they are developing clues and general rules about how our language works.

A Final Reminder on Using PWIM

Inquiry with a purpose. From the beginning of the picture word inductive model to the end, the teacher models seeking, thinking, and utility of learning and provides instruction that engages her students in seeking, thinking, and using their accumulating knowledge.

chapter 5

Literacy across the Curriculum

$\mathcal{N}$ow we move from kindergarten to sixth grade. We provide a rationale for using the picture word inductive model to support student inquiry into content area domains other than language arts, followed by a six-day scenario in a sixth-grade class, and conclude with an explanation of the moves of the model and the uses of multiple forms of media as resources for inquiry.

Rationale for Using PWIM with Students in Grades 3–8

There are three related parts to the rationale for using the picture word inductive model with students in grades three through eight: one part deals with stages of reading development; another with the uses of multiple information sources as the curriculum advances into topics that are new to the children; and finally, with uses of the model to stimulate inquiry in any substantive domain.

A New Stage of Reading Development

Jeanne Chall contends that there are different stages of development in reading that need to be considered as we build curriculum for the primary and upper grades (1983). We agree with her. Partly the differences in stage are due to the fact that many—we hope virtually all—of the children have, by the end of grade two, acquired a very large sight vocabulary and have learned many of the phonetic and structural conventions of the language. They can use dictionaries and contextual clues to identify the meanings of new words. While attention to the development of sight vocabularies continues, the emphases on phonetic and structural analysis shift to the reminders of the principles and their application to words that are new to them. As the children mature as language learners, the instruction provided needs to assist students in acquiring knowledge and skill with more complex syntactical structures and more complex devices for expressing ideas and structuring essays and stories.

However, if a student cannot read fluently by the end of the primary grades, then PWIM is used in the same form as described in Chapter 4, because developing a solid sight vocabulary and learning the phonetic and structural conventions of language are incredibly important to further development.

A Change in Curriculum

For most of the children in most school districts, the materials of instruction change somewhere in the span of the third/fourth grade. Print materials become longer and contain words and ideas that are new, requiring assiduous attention to comprehension and the development of vocabulary that stretches beyond the listening/speaking vocabulary. In fact, from this time on, most people will add to their listening/speaking vocabulary through reading. They will have already learned to read most of the words they hear in their normal social context. Also, most of the primary curriculum stays close to the students' known world. Now, the curriculum is designed to bring new information into their world and to teach them to synthesize information from multiple sources and express their thoughts in more highly structured and complex written forms.

Stimulating Inquiry into Any Substantive Content Area Domain

A major principle for using PWIM with older readers is that **the engagement with pictorial material is a tremendous stimulus to inquiry.** Reading about the unfamiliar puts the student in the hands of the writer; viewing pictures of unfamiliar settings puts the student in the hands of the photographer. However, pictures confront the student with vivid images that often arouse curiosity immediately. Unfamiliar things become stimuli to inquiry—"What is that?" "What is it used for?" become questions to answer. Thus a major difference in the use of the model with older children is that the print material often pushes them beyond the familiar. They will be able to make observations with their developed vocabulary and conceptions, but new ones will be just around the corner of the inquiry.

Another principle underlying the use of PWIM is **the provision and use of balanced informational sources that enrich learning.** Students explore topics via pictures, the printed word, and videotapes from multiple sources produced from different perspectives and with different intentions. *The model helps them move into the level of information processing needed by the literate world citizen*—a level essential to full understanding of the world around them and critical to their full participation in society after their schooling is over, if not before.

Now let's visit a sixth grade classroom where the picture word inductive model is being used to teach social studies.

PWIM in the Sixth Grade: Developing Communication Skills and Teaching Social Studies

In the following scenario, you will watch Ron, a sixth-grade teacher, and his students use the picture word inductive model as they begin their inquiry into ancient and modern Egypt.

Day One—The First Week in October

Ron has selected three enlarged photographs and a five-minute video clip of Cairo and the Pyramids of Giza to use in opening up the study of Egypt. One photograph shows a current scene of downtown Cairo that includes the Nile River, a modern bridge spanning it—over which a number of vehicles of various sorts are moving—with large buildings and mosques in the background; and far in the distance, if one looks carefully, are the tops to two pyramids (Figure 5.1). The second photograph shows one of the Pyramids of Giza and the desert; and the third photograph shows the statues in a temple. The video clip begins with the same scene that is depicted in the first photograph, then moves around that area of the city from the same perspective, moves in closer to the street scenes, and then to different areas of the city. It includes all the richness of the city sounds of inner Cairo.

As the lesson begins, Ron says, "We are beginning the study of another area of our world. We will study early civilization in this region, and we will study what life is like there today. We'll begin by looking at several photographs and some videotape clips. We'll use sources like these, as well as books and other print materials, to gather information throughout our unit—using the pictures, the videotapes, and print or textual information to build and clarify our knowledge about the region and its culture, present and past."

The three photographs have been lying facedown on the table. Ron takes the first photograph (Figure 5.1) and says to the students, "Look carefully at this picture. Think about what you are seeing." He moves slowly around the

FIGURE 5.1 The "Mystery City" and Its Body of Water

u-shaped configuration of his classroom, allowing students to take a close look at the scene, then props the picture on the whiteboard shelf and asks the students "What do you see?"

Here are some of their responses with the words underlined that Ron selects to write on the chartpaper:

"A <u>city</u>."

[Ron] "Why do you say this is a city, instead of a town?"

"All the buildings, <u>many buildings</u>."

[Ron] "What kind of buildings?"

"<u>Tall buildings—skyscrapers</u>."

"One of the buildings is a <u>stadium</u>."

[Ron] "Which building and why?" (Ron picks up the picture and takes it closer to the student.)

"This <u>domed building</u> looks like a stadium, maybe a <u>big football stadium</u>."

[Another student volunteers] "Or a lot like a <u>temple</u>."

"A nice blue sky."

"The sun is very bright. It may be setting . . . maybe a lot of the glowing light is the sun shining off the buildings."

[Another student adds] "There's lots of smoke or smog, though."

[Ron] "How does this relate to the idea of 'city'?"

"Lots of people, maybe lots of businesses creating smog."

[Ron] "Are you saying that the amount of smoke or smog indicates this is a large city?"

"Yes."

"There's a bridge."

[Ron] "What do you notice about the bridge?"

"There's lots of traffic—cars, trucks, lots of small white cars."

"A lake."

[Ron] "Why do you think it's a lake?"

"It has houseboats on it like Lake Shasta."

"An ocean."

[Ron] "What makes you think it's an ocean?"

"Well . . . it's so big. I think it's a bay."

"I think it's an ocean, too, but this is the harbor."

[Ron] "Are we agreed there is a large body of water in the middle of the city?" He adds the phrase to the list.

Ron is amazed that no one has said "river." To him, it so obviously looks like a river, but as always, what his students "see" and do not "see" and how they use the bits of knowledge they have fascinates him. ➤

One student pipes up and says, "I think it's a lake too, because I visited my uncle in Michigan one summer, and there was a lake, and a bridge, and lots of boats in it just like this."

Ron does not want the students to become vested in exactly what the body of water is yet. So he says, "We're agreed that there is a large body of water in this city. Let's move on to other things you see. As we look at video clips and more photographs of the region, you will be able to determine the nature of this body of water."

"Let's look now at this video clip of the city." Ron shows about three minutes of the videotape. Students recognize and comment on the bridge, on the building that looks like a stadium, and that part of the city looks "old" and "poor" and the other part looks "modern" and "businesslike." Later, Ron will draw from them the reasoning behind these labels.

Ron turns off the VCR and says "What can we add to the list we're building about this region?"

"This could be <u>a city in Egypt</u>, because I think I see <u>pyramids in the background</u>."

"There's a really tall building. I think it's the <u>Empire State Building</u>.

[Ron] "Where is the Empire State Building, what city?"

"<u>New York</u>."

"Lots of traffic in the streets."

[Ron] "What can you tell us about the traffic?"

"<u>Mostly cars in the city, not many large trucks for a city this size</u>— doesn't look like the traffic we have in L.A., except there's lots of it. And the cars look small and not so good."

[Ron] "Say more, Randy."

"Well, <u>maybe it's a poor country, maybe people can't afford big cars or new cars</u>."

"The city is <u>probably Cairo</u>, because that's <u>the only place with pyramids</u>."

"The building I thought was a stadium . . . Now I think it's a <u>monument or a temple</u>."

[Ron] "Why?"

"Well . . . it reminds me of pictures I've seen of monuments in Washington, you know, like the Lincoln Memorial. It could be a temple, though, because we saw some like that when we studied <u>Israel</u> in Ms. Hamlin's class."

"The city is <u>Las Vegas</u>. I know. The <u>pyramids are a hotel</u>."

[Ron is a bit startled by this assertion/hypothesis but does not show it. He simply says] "Say more, Robert."

"Well . . . Las Vegas is in the desert, and there's this big hotel shaped like a pyramid—

[Katrina chimes in and says] "That's right, it's the <u>Luxor Hotel</u>—and there's this bridge there, you know, like the <u>London Bridge</u>."

Ron continues to add information to the chart based on what students say in the videotape, items such as *trees line some streets, strange horn sounds,* something that *sounds like chanting.* Then he says, "Let's revisit the videotape. We'll watch those first three minutes again, then move outside the city. See what else you can discover about this city, this area." After the first three minutes, the camera zooms out toward the Pyramids of Giza so students can see their relative closeness to the city, then breaks away and the next scenes show close-ups of the three pyramids. Ron turns off the VCR and continues to gather ideas from his students.

"The water is a <u>river</u>."

[Ron] "Why?"

"It just looks more like a river. You know, <u>river banks</u>, and it's sort of <u>long and narrow</u> and it has this big bridge and there's <u>lots of traffic on the river, several kinds of boats</u>. So I think it's a river."

[Ron says] "You're right, Jay. I'll confirm that the body of water is a river, and it's a very important part of life in this region of the world."

"Those are big pyramids. This is probably <u>Mexico City</u>. It's a big city and they have pyramids from the Aztecs, and Mexico has a lot of desert."

"That <u>white domed building</u> that Francesca was describing, I got a better look at it. It's a <u>temple</u> just like those we studied <u>in Israel, in Jerusalem</u>."

[Ron] "Do you remember anything in particular about those temples?"

"Well, they had to do with religion."

"There are <u>several pyramids, three I think, and one is larger than the others</u>. This is <u>probably Egypt, because they have lots of pyramids</u>."

[Another student responds] "No—it's Israel, Paulo. Didn't you notice that the people on the boats and some of the people in the streets had things on their heads—remember they have to cover their heads when they go outside."

[Ron asks] "Did everyone have them?"

"No, but lots of people did."

[Ron] "Men and women, or just the men or the women?"

"Both."

[Ron writes <u>"coverings on the head of some men and women"</u> on the chart and asks] "Do you remember why some of the people in Israel wore head coverings?"

[There's no response from Clay. Ron asks] "Can anyone help?"

"It has <u>something to do with religion</u>."

[Ron] "Can you say more about that?"

"Umh . . . no."

[Sandy says] "Well, it could be <u>India</u>, too. They wear things on their heads."

[Ron] "Can you say more about that Sandy?"

[There's no response, so Ron asks] "Do you have any idea why people in India might cover their heads?"

[Zeke responds] "Because it's what they do there, like here we wear lots of jeans and tee-shirts and baseball caps."

[Ron says] "Well, you're right, Zeke, a number of people in Israel and in India do cover their heads. Later, we'll explore why—partially in this unit and as we study other regions of the world."

Now, I want you to look at another photograph. He shows them the second photograph (Figure 5.2) of the single pyramid in the rocky desert. He takes it slowly around the room. "What new information do we have or what can we confirm?"

"It's definitely <u>a desert country</u>."

"We can see a city in the background, through the dust or smog, a big city because I can just see the tall buildings."

[Ron] "So <u>the city and the pyramids are relatively close</u>?"

"Yes."

FIGURE 5.2 The "Unidentified" Pyramid

Points to note . . .

Ron uses both photographs and videotapes to take his students to the regions they are studying. He has a number of reasons for using and beginning with the photographs. One is simply technical, the photographs can be studied in depth; the action is "frozen"; and they can be placed around the room for study and reference at any time. Also, he can carefully diagnose how well his students can "read" a photograph, gather information from it, and use evidence provided by it to support their statements, generalizations, or hypotheses; and he can diagnose their awareness of when they need more information to support an idea. Watching the students use the photographs as a tangible medium—a concrete source of information they can actually see and touch—helps Ron know when they are guessing and helps the students learn the difference between guessing and knowing.

Students are more accustomed to viewing videotapes and using them as a source of information than they are to studying and discussing pictures, but that is not why Ron uses them. He uses them to bring a massive amount of information about an area or subject to his students in a brief amount of time, then listens to their thinking in terms of how they use this information. Their ideas help him decide what picture or other material to use next—and, as is often the case, he may need to find new information or direct them to sources that contradict a false concept they have formed. He always finds surprises as he opens up an area of the country or the world for conceptual exploration, as in the Las Vegas example. ➤

The lesson has taken about an hour so far. Ron decides not to use the third photograph today. He gives the students a writing assignment to help them synthesize what they are thinking about the area: "Think about the two photographs your have observed and the video clip. Jot down what you know about this place." He gives students a few minutes to write, then collects their papers.

"For homework or during study time, I'd like you to find out which countries have pyramids and why they were built. If you can, bring in the source you use; if not, just write the source, its author and date, and what you find out."

Amy comments, "They were built as burial grounds for the kings."

Ron says, "Just check it out, see what you can find."

Points to note . . .

Ron wants all of them to do a little research, even those students who feel certain they know the region. He knows that if they dig around in this topic, they will add something to their knowledge base. He also wants to remove the concept that "only the Egyptians built pyramids" and to have students begin to think about why the people of this and other regions built pyramids. ➤

That afternoon, Ron looks over their responses in order to more formally diagnose where they are as individuals and as a group in thinking about the region and to help him think about which materials—which photographs, videotapes, or print material—he should bring them into contact with next. Here are a few of the students' written responses:

> "We have been looking at a large city that has a river running through it, lots of traffic, and lots of religious people."

> "The city is Cairo, Egypt, and the river is the Nile River. There are pyramids and temples from the pharaohs. And the country has lots of desert."

> "This city is surrounded by a hot, rocky, dusty desert. It would be hard to grow anything there except in the area near the river."

Eight of his thirty-one students feel certain that the city is in Egypt, and they provide varying amounts of evidence; eight believe it's in Israel, mostly because of the desert, the head coverings, and the domed buildings—three of these students identify the city as Jerusalem; four of the students label the city and country as Mexico City, Mexico; the other students primarily describe the city and/or the terrain. As always at the beginning of the year with each new group of students, Ron ponders how we have managed to teach and how students have managed to learn so many "pieces" of conceptually disconnected or lightly-connected information.

Day Two

Ron and his students will continue their exploration of ancient and modern Egypt via pictures and videotapes. The pace of the lesson may seem slow to some, but Ron is still working on helping his students behave as members of a learning community. They have come a long way in these five weeks: they have learned to talk to each other and not just "respond to the teacher"; they are gradually learning—in science, language arts, and social studies—to be ready to explain their reasoning or how they came up with an idea; they are learning to be more thoughtful about what they say and what their classmates say—not always, but they have improved. They still need much support and guidance in forming useful and accurate concepts, in noticing the relationships among ideas they hold, and in "seeing the big picture"—as in the relationship among head coverings, religions, and climate or as in the idea that the city had to be Jerusalem, without once thinking about where Israel and Jerusalem are located in terms of the larger geographical/political region.

Today's lesson opens with Ron saying, "Let's take a few minutes and hear what you learned about the pyramids. As you share your information, show us the location of the pyramids on the world map. In fact, use some of my post-its and flag the location on the map."

"Oh, before we get started, did anyone other than the Egyptians build pyramids?" Ron grins as a number of students give a resounding "Yes."

"Here we go." He has the LCD panel set up on the overhead projector and is seated at his desk, facing the students. As students volunteer information, Ron taps it in and all the students can read it on the screen:

Egypt—most of the pyramids we can see in Egypt today were built by the Egyptians between 2600 B.C. and 1900 B.C., over 4000 years ago. The Pyramids of Giza are close to the capital city, Cairo. Sixty-seven pyramids "stand in the open land around Cairo." They were tombs for the pharaohs.

Guatemala and Honduras—where the Mayan civilization flourished in   —Pyramids that served as temples to their god were found at Copan and along the Rio Copan. Can still be seen today.

Yucatan—where the Mayan civilization flourished in   —The Temple of the Warriors at Chichen Itza is a pyramid, has about eight terraces, and serpent columns. (Zeke brought in a great photograph.)

Mexico—especially near Mexico City, where the Toltec and Aztec civilizations flourished in   —The area has many examples of temple-pyramids. "The Temple of Quetzalcoatl at Teotihuacan was already old when the Spanish conquistador Cortes climbed its steps around 1520."

Ancient Assyria and Babylonia (Modern Iraq)—had staged pyramids called ziggurats. The Tower of Babel, with the Temple of Marduk near the top, was a ziggurat. It was built around 300 B.C. Only saw some reconstructions and ruins, no "really good photographs" that looked like pyramids we could see today.

Why were pyramids built? Egyptian pyramids were tombs for the pharaohs, like a burial place for kings; in other regions of the world, the pyramids were religious temples, built either to honor the god(s) or as a place to worship the god(s) or both.

Several of the students have more to share, but Ron asks, "Did anyone find pyramids in regions of the world other than those mentioned?" No one did, so Ron saves the file and prints it. "I'll give you a copy of this for your notebook tomorrow."

Three or four students are discussing how close we are to the pyramids in Mexico and Central America. Ron says, "All right, guys. Talk to all of us." He allows the interchange to last about five minutes because the students are discussing the geography of the world, talking about distances and how the pyramid as a structure came to be used in places so far apart—speculating on whether it had to do with the lack of equipment for building large structures and how people without cranes moved such large stones.

Sam wants an additional point to be added to the discussion. He says, "I think many of us thought pyramids were only in Egypt because there is so much more information about those pyramids. They're a big part of Egypt's tourist attraction. It was a lot harder finding information about pyramids in Mexico and Central America—and they're so close to us!"

Ron says, "How many of you agree with Sam? Was it more difficult finding out about pyramids other than those in Egypt? Raise your hand if you agree." Many hands go up, and several students comment that the easiest was Egypt, then those from Mesopotamia (Ancient Babylonia and Assyria, current Iraq). Ron wants to keep this idea alive, "This year, as we study ancient and modern civilizations that developed in different areas of our planet, let's remember Sam's idea. Is it accurate, and if so, why?"

Ron moves the lesson forward, "Today we are going to study two more photographs. One taken about a hundred miles from our city, and one taken in the city." He picks up the first photograph (See Figure 5.3.), leaving the other facedown on the table, and passes it around for the students to study. Again, he records the phrases shown in underline.

Some of the students notice the <u>hieroglyphics; the bodies of the statues somewhat in profile, no muscles in the figures, the shape of the hair; the deep</u>

FIGURE 5.3 The "Headless Statues" That Fascinated the Students

red color of the stone. There is some discussion of whether this is <u>a temple</u> or not. A few students believe it cannot be a temple because <u>the heads are off the statues</u>. Some students feel the heads were broken off over time; some feel they were designed that way. (Ron allows a brief interchange between students who believe that no one would have headless gods in a temple and those students who believe this is possible and intentional.)

𝒫oints to note . . .

As in Day One, Ron writes ideas that relate to the picture and the region on the flip chart. He wishes he could just tap them into the file, but he feels he needs to move around among his students. Some of them still need his proximity to help them stay focused. They are not yet ready for sustained discussions with him sitting down as "discussion leader"; later in the year, when they are more practiced at listening to each other, building on and contradicting each other's ideas appropriately, and putting ideas together, they can participate in such discussions—and his life will be technologically easier. Also, right now, Ron does not want them taking lengthy notes: they must learn to listen to each other, so he takes the cumulative notes on the chart. Later, he will tap the words from these first two days into a computer file and make some duplicate files for students to use as they build an information file on this region. ➤

Ron picks up the second photograph, a close-up of a street scene (Figure 5.4). Students comment on the <u>construction going on in the city; the grayness of the building materials</u>; how <u>many buildings look so much alike in structure and material, maybe the city is in a poor country that cannot afford to build more interesting buildings like those in the United States</u>; the <u>policeman</u>; a man they believe to be a <u>soldier</u>; the <u>group of women</u> talking, <u>some wearing modern dress and some wearing traditional dress with the head covered</u>; and so forth.

Now Ron wants his students to formally process part of the information they have been gathering during these two days. He gives them this writing assignment: "Write a few paragraphs explaining how life in this city/country is like life here around Los Angeles."

In studying cultures and regions of the world other than their own, Ron wants his students to begin thinking of the likenesses first. ➤

While the students are writing, Ron taps their ideas from the flip chart into the computer. Here's the result:

FIGURE 5.4   Street Scene That Prompted Speculation among Students

Region: Modern and Ancient Times

1. A city: many buildings, tall buildings (skyscrapers)

   large city, lots of smoke or smog

   lots of traffic

   mostly cars in the city, not many large trucks for a city this size

   lots of small white cars, not many new or big cars

   maybe it's a city in a poor country where people can't afford big or new cars

   trees line some streets, especially those near the river

   strange horn sounds

   something that sounds like chanting

2. Architecture: a large domed building, looks like a stadium, maybe a football stadium; or a temple; or a monument

3. The bridge: has lots of traffic, looks like four or six lanes

4.   A large body of water: could be a lake (houseboats)
     could be an ocean bay or a harbor

     a river: riverbanks, long and narrow river, lots of traffic on the river, several
     kinds of boats

5.   Climate: nice blue sky

     the sun is very bright

     a desert country

6.   Hypotheses, with reasons, about location:

     a)   Cairo, Egypt—the city and the pyramids are relatively close

          a city in Egypt—pyramids in the background

          probably Cairo, the only place with pyramids

          a city in Egypt because there are several pyramids, maybe three, and
          one is larger than the others, probably Egypt because they have lots of
          pyramids

     b)   New York City, U.S.A.—Empire State Building

     c)   Jerusalem, Israel

          the white domed building looks like a temple, like the buildings we saw in
          a picture of Jerusalem last year

          coverings on the head of some of the men and women, maybe has some-
          thing to do with religion

     d)   Las Vegas, Nevada, U.S.A.—the pyramids are the Luxor Hotel

          the bridge is the London Bridge

     e)   Mexico City, Mexico

          a big city

          big pyramids from the Aztecs

          Mexico has a lot of desert

     f)   India

          people wear coverings on their head

They end this day's lesson with Ron showing them the next two or three
minutes of the videotape, which includes a lengthy scene panning the Sphinx
with the three large Pyramids of Giza behind it. Most students feel they now
"know" that this is Egypt and that they are no longer guessing or speculating,
but their homework is to find out for certain by finding sources relevant to the
Sphinx.

Day Three

As yesterday, Ron has the LCD panel set up, and he records the students' major findings about the Sphinx. This time he has them identify their sources of information. After some discussion about why, when, and for what purpose the Sphinx was built, Ron moves into the next segment of the lesson.

As he pulls the cord to roll up the world map so it will be out of sight, he says, "Number from one to seven on a piece of paper. Write a response to each question":

1. What is the country?

2. What is the city?

3. What is the body of water?

4. What is the name of the pyramids near the city?

5. Name as many countries as you can that adjoin this country.

6. Does it have access to an ocean or sea? If yes, can you name it?

7. On what continent is it located?

> Ron gathers their responses orally. "Enrique, what is the country?"
> "Egypt," says Enrique.
> "Raise your hand if you agree with Enrique." All hands go up.
> "Pauline, what is the city?"
> "Cairo," responds Pauline.

Ron proceeds through each item in a similar fashion. Here are the results he tallies on the whiteboard: Items 1 and 2: all 30 students present responded correctly; Item 3: 18 identified the Nile River as the body of water running through Cairo, 4 students identified it as the Amazon River; Item 4: 20 students identified the Pyramids of Giza; Item 5: 2 students correctly named two countries adjoining Egypt (both students naming Sudan and Israel), 8 students correctly named one country adjoining (4, Saudi Arabia; 2, Israel; 2, Sudan), no one identified Libya, a number of students identified "Africa" as the country adjoining, and several identified Iraq; Item 6: approximately one-half of the students believed there was an ocean or sea on one boundary and the responses in terms of naming it were all over the place, although 3 students did identify the Red Sea and 2 the Mediterranean Sea; and Item 7: 11 students identified the correct continent, Africa, the other 19 responses ranged from the Middle East, to South America, even a few for Europe.

Ron pulls the class map down and says, "Look at this region carefully as we go over your responses." He confirms their knowledge of the country as

Egypt and the city as Cairo. He labels the body of water as the Nile River and foreshadows its importance to the region. He confirms the Pyramids of Giza and indicates their approximate location on the outskirts of Cairo. Then he gives the students a couple of minutes to study the region and correct their responses to Item 6 before he points out and names the adjoining countries of Libya, Sudan, Saudi Arabia, and Israel. He does the same thing with Item 7, allowing them to see and correct their response if needed before he points out the Mediterranean Sea and Red Sea. Then Ron points out Jerusalem and reminds the students about their hypothesis that the city in the photographs and videotapes was Jerusalem. He tells them that the two cities are about 400 miles apart, about as far apart as Los Angeles and San Francisco, and that there has been much strife in this region of the world for centuries, including the past 60 years. He asks them to begin a section in their notebook in which they will record notes about the nature of the turmoil and its reasons.

He says to them, "Now, study the region for a couple of minutes. . . . Close your eyes and try to 'see' it. What is on the northern boundary, the western boundary, the southern boundary, and the eastern boundary? You want to develop in your mind a picture of Egypt and its region. The implications of this picture are important in understanding its past and its present."

Anne-Marie can't contain herself, "Yes, Egypt has the only river in that part of the continent!"

Ron brings the lesson to a close. For homework, he assigns two tasks: One, find an atlas and study Egypt and its region, the Middle East. Two, he passes out the notes accumulated from the flip chart during the first two days of their exploration and the notes he typed in about the pyramids. He tells the students to look over the items from the first two days and put a checkmark beside those they now know represent accurate information about Egypt; mark through those items that represent inaccurate information; and put a question mark beside those they are uncertain about.

Day Four

The lesson begins with Ron passing out a blank world map with the countries outlined. (See Figure 5.5.) He says to the students, "Label Egypt, the countries around it, the Mediterranean Sea, the Red Sea, and draw in the Nile River. When you have finished that, engage in a quick review by labeling the seven continents, the United States, and Los Angeles." He turns on the overhead projector, so students can refer to these directions in writing if they need to.

Ron walks around the class, glancing at the papers and jotting down a few notes. He notices that all except two students have labeled Egypt correctly and have the Nile River in approximately the correct place, with the main inaccuracy being its length. All except five students have labeled Israel correctly, with about half the class correctly labeling Libya, Saudi Arabia, and Sudan.

FIGURE 5.5 Unlabeled Map Given to the Students

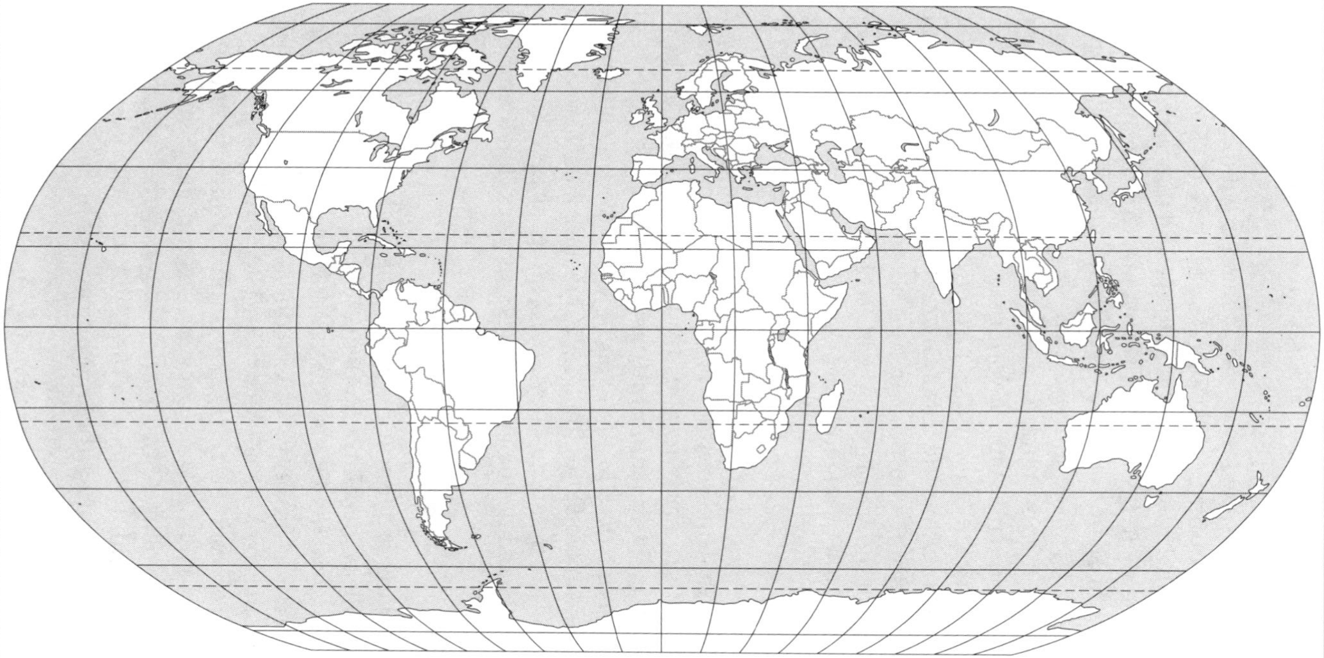

About half a dozen students are still having trouble with the Red Sea and the Mediterranean. After about five minutes, he pulls down the world map, "All right, check your work." He leads them through the task quickly, beginning with Egypt.

Ron moves the lesson on, handing out a map of the Middle East that includes the countries and cities clearly marked. (See Figure 5.6.) He tells them to add to their notebook new information they accumulate about Egypt. They begin adding items about the Sahara Desert, the White Nile and the Blue Nile, the Aswan Dam. Next, he gives them a map of Egypt with a statistical data base from *PCGlobe,* and says "See what you can add from these sources." After about fifteen more minutes, he says, "Work with your partner, compare notes, then we'll discuss some of your main points as a group."

The last fifteen minutes of the hour, Ron leads a discussion about their ideas, concluding the lesson by saying, "When we are in the library today, find something you want to read about Egypt or the region. It can be about ancient or modern Egypt. Begin to check out some of the questions we have generated about religion, dress, and so on."

Day Five

Ron has students continue to study the maps and the statistical data from the region. His students are already forming questions for further research as they accumulate information in their notebooks. They are particularly interested in the differences in life expectancy between Egypt (males, 59; females, 60) and the United States (males, 70; females, 78). He asks them to begin keeping a list of the questions they are forming, as periodically the class will discuss these lists and decide which ones will be explored mutually.

Day Six

Ron begins the lesson by presenting and providing an overview of six resources he wants all the students to read and gather information from during the next few weeks: six paperback copies of *Gods, Graves, and Scholars: The Story of Archeology* by C. W. Ceram; six paperback copies of *The New State of the World Atlas* by Michael Kidron and Ronald Segal; six copies of the textbook *A Message of Ancient Days* by Houghton Mifflin; five encyclopedia volumes with extensive sections on Egypt (a mixed package including two *Encyclopedia Britannica* volumes, two *World Book,* and one *Compton's*), plus the *Grolier* on CD-ROM; and six issues of *The New Yorker* which has a long essay on Egypt.

As they explore these resources—along with those they self-select from the library or find from other sources—they will gather information around different components of Egyptian culture, past and present: languages, social organization, beliefs and values, customs, foods and clothing, shelter, and the history of the people.

FIGURE 5.6 **Map of the Middle East**

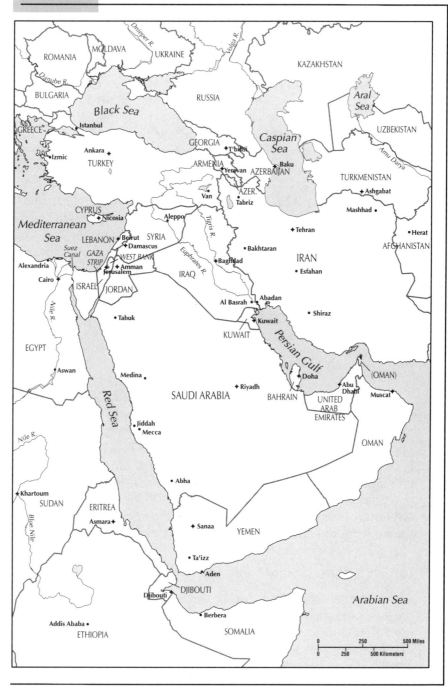

And the Days Continue

Ron will continue to shape the exploration of Egypt past and present by listening to his students comments and using that information to select other pictures, print material, and videotapes.

In Ron's school district, ancient civilizations (Mesopotamia, Ancient Egypt, Ancient India, Ancient China, Ancient Greece, and Ancient Rome) have been assigned to sixth grade in the curriculum framework. Ron and his class will spend four to eight weeks on each area; at least three regions will be studied in depth (around eight weeks each) from the perspective of ancient and modern times. The class will explore each region in terms of time (differences, similarities, heritage, and cultural transmission) and space (location, similarities, differences, topography and climate and how it affected early and current life).

Moving into his social studies content and beyond the students' skills in gathering information from visuals, Ron can diagnose what the students have learned about an area or subject, both from studying the subject in earlier grades or in units earlier in the year and/or from their general life experiences. He also quickly discovers some of the stereotypes or misconceptions they have acquired about people and regions. He listens carefully to his students' ideas: to determine how much they know, the accuracy of the information, and any "false concepts" they have developed. He juxtaposes this diagnostic information with his social studies goals and objectives—together they indicate the most appropriate materials and activities for the next stage of the inquiry.

Using PWIM to Develop Social Studies Literacy

This section reviews applications of the model with students who already have basic beginning reading and writing skills, addresses the use of multiple photographs in exploring a domain, and provides a brief overview of the functions of the different forms of media. Different aspects of the model receive more or less emphasis depending on the grade level and the abilities of the students and on the curriculum objectives toward which it is aimed.

Moving "Up" the Literacy Curriculum

As the model is used in grades three and above, many of the learning processes and applications of knowledge and skill in the language arts that are present in kindergarten through grade two implementations simply advance in breadth and depth, as well as becoming tools for learning in science, mathematics, and social studies. The model itself becomes an instructional vehicle for integrating the curriculum areas. For example, the study of composing and comprehending expository, descriptive, and informative prose advances and is used to support information processing in every subject. The inquiry into written communication continues to focus on the clarity and accuracy of the intended message and on using standard conventions to convey this message; however, the amount of information gathered and synthesized, the variety of audiences, the variety of purposes for writing, and the length of the compositions all expand.

The gathering of additional information from nonfiction books generally increases at each grade level, as do the length of group compositions and individual compositions developed around different aspects of the picture. Using Bonnie Brigman's end-of-second grade unit on the mission as an example, some paragraphs might be developed that describe the tools in the picture and their use, the clothes worn by the missionaries and the Indians, or the construction of the mission.

We expand and deepen the students' study of the complexities of communication, and we broaden their exploration of the curriculum topics, generally using more than one picture. The teacher moves the students toward more sophisticated information processing: they gather information from a greater variety of sources; they engage in discussions about the consistencies and inconsistencies among these sources; and they learn how to investigate the accuracy of these sources in terms of time (dates), special interests, varied perspectives and biases.

The amount of data classified by students also expands as the model is used in the upper grade levels, as does the amount of research and investigation of the events or situation depicted in the picture. Classification by content often leads to identifying key concepts and supporting details that form natural paragraph content about the subject(s) being explored. As in, for example, "these sentences all describe items found in the pharaoh's tomb; these describe why certain items were placed in the tomb; these describe the sarcophagus; these describe how the tomb looks, and so on." Classification and synthesis of their information and the information they collect from other sources provide many opportunities to teach students relevance of data for supporting a main point, the elimination of irrelevant information, and the expansion of a detail into a major point when warranted.

The phonetical, structural, and contextual analysis that does occur is often focused on:

1. patterns of need diagnosed from what students say or write;

2. exceptions to general rules (if the plural of *house* is *houses* and *blouse* is *blouses,* why isn't the plural of *mouse, mouses*? and what about the plural for *rice*?); and

3. language conventions that simply must be memorized, such as the difference in meaning and pronunciation between "the *capital* city" and "the *capitol* building."

Also, from third grade up, the teacher or class can designate certain words for inclusion on the word list or in the word bank, while continuing to have all relevant terms and descriptions on a flipchart or printout.

Students engage in reading multiple sources of information in the area of inquiry, in writing to process and synthesize this information so that it is more likely to become part of their knowledge base for use—reading and writing to learn are at work.

Using Multiple Pictures (and Other Media) As Resources

Beginning around the end of grade two or the beginning of grade three, the pictures begin serving other disciplines along with the language arts. Many of the pictures/photographs selected need to support the social studies and science units being taught. Most often, they are used to open an area of study and become a focal point for discussions, examples, and the gathering of additional information as students explore a domain or subject. For social studies, pictures of the neighborhood, the community, the town, or events and special sections of any of the above help to simultaneously anchor and expand students' explorations of the characteristics of these settings. In science, pictures could be of animals in their "natural" settings (from dog house, to rain forest, to ocean), or plants in their many settings (from window sill, to desert, to ocean), or the variety of businesses and services (of a dairy at work, of lunchroom workers cleaning the kitchen, of a dental hygienist at work). The list of possibilities is as extensive as the concepts and topics within those curriculum areas.

The pictures continue to be used to promote the expansion of students' vocabulary, the mechanics of spelling and language usage, and the use of observation in providing content and evidence in oral and written discourse. However, there is far less emphasis on phonetic and structural analysis and far more emphasis on content analysis of the picture and what it depicts.

Through the pictures selected by the teacher, students advance up the curriculum ladder, using the pictures as a stimulus and source for in-depth study and for practice in gathering evidence to support assertions and generalizations. Although teachers can always use a great general picture, the use of multiple pictures within a social studies unit or science unit helps students clarify similarities and differences among cultures, regions, and environments. For example, in social studies, using pictures related to Westward expansion; to colonial America; to depictions of Indians in their native setting, on the trails as they were displaced, and on the reservations; to photographs allows students to compare life and culture in the countries they are studying.

These pictures of distant times and distant places will help in making the curriculum objectives and textbook content **real** and meaningful. As instructional materials, they help students extend their thinking about other periods of history and other cultures, and begin to clarify the similarities and differences among different times in history and different groups of people.

In science, pictures could be of forests at different stages of development; of mountains formed from volcanoes or earthquakes, and pictures of both at different stages of formation and erosion; of chickens in the farmyard and chickens in the large commercial pens. Again, much of the focus on pictures will be observing characteristics, determining similarities and differences, making speculations about actions and consequences, forming hypotheses, and gathering and synthesizing additional information related to those hypotheses.

Using Various Media: Symbolic, Iconic, and Enactive Materials

Symbolic material is largely the printed word, but also maps, charts, and graphs that contain information in the form of symbols—words and other things that stand for something else. Our students need to learn to mine print material for information and understanding.

Iconic material takes the form of pictures and drawings that depict reality—they bring visual representations of real things to us. We cannot take all the students to India, but we can bring pictures of India to them.

Enactive material takes the form of moving pictures and reproduced sounds that "act out" events and interactions that are at a distance. We cannot take all the students to Congress, but we can show a videotape of Congress in action.

As students study a topic that is new to them—let us use the example of life in India—they need balance in the three types of sources, rather than relying on symbolic material alone. The reason is not for vividness alone ("a picture is worth a thousand words"), nor a matter of learning style (developed preferences for certain kinds of material), although both of these considerations are important and useful. Rather, it is that the three sources provide genuinely different kinds of information.

Consider students who are being introduced to life in India. As they read about Indian homes, they bring to the printed page their own concept of "home." Pictures can help them see the variety of homes in India, enlarging their concepts in ways that are very difficult with print material alone. Enactments via motion pictures or video or audio tapes can show the Indian families in action. Print descriptions or passages of dialogue are important, too, but the balance is critical to full understanding.

To inquire thoroughly, we (our students and us) need to get as close to the object of study as we can. When we are studying something that is "right here" or when we perform an experiment, we can inquire firsthand. As we study other cultures and the history of science, we have the problem of assembling material that will let us get as close as possible without really being there. Pictures reduce the distance between us and something that is outside of our immediate perceptual experience. Although they are not reality, they are a window to the far away and long ago. By scrutinizing them carefully, we can inquire realistically into people, places, and events that are far away. Moving pictures (tapes and film) enable us to see things in motion, again allowing us to inquire—not firsthand—but surely they bring us closer to the action and scenes than if we don't have them available.

Original documents—letters, proclamations, and newspaper accounts—also bring us closer by enabling us to see the products of other minds. (Thus, a biology class that studies Louis Agassiz' notebooks takes us closer to his mind than if we simply repeat some of his observations.) Textual material and reference books provide information as well, but in summarized form; inevitably, the writer is between us and his/her experience. Thus, we balance print reference material, original documents, pictures and photographs, and film to stimulate inquiry and provide an appropriate range of sources for our inquiry.

Summary

The picture word inductive model in grades three through eight is designed to intensify inquiry into substantive curriculum domains, inducing the students to mine pictorial material intensively, enrich textual material by providing information about areas and concepts the printed words represent, and build a real, understood vocabulary about the domain being studied. It induces categorization with better understanding of what is being categorized, and it induces synthesis and consolidation of new material by shaping written expression so that the "writing to learn" effect occurs.

chapter 6

Building the
Learning Community

Throughout the book, we have stressed learners inquiring alone and together. In this chapter, we address the development of the learning community that supports such inquiry, including the tending of individual differences. We take the position that the development of the learning community is a natural part of the teaching/learning process. In most elementary school classrooms, the teacher represents the society—in this case an inquiring, democratic one—and the social climate of the classroom needs to prepare young citizens for thoughtful, cooperative life within this society.

Nearly all teacher candidates experience some degree of anxiety when they think about how they are going to organize students for instruction, how they are going to build a productive learning community. We certainly did, and nearly every teacher we know has also. And, as near as we can tell, hardly any experienced teacher ever stops trying to figure out how to start the year strongly and smoothly. We want to take some of the mystery out of the process and provide ideas you can experiment with as you organize your classes.

We'll explore how to build a community that can work cooperatively and inductively, including bringing the parents into a partnership with you. If you learn to do that, you can solve most "classroom management" problems.

Let's think about those three teachers in Chapter Three. How did those teachers work with their students? Think for a moment about Evelyn Burnham's class during the first 20 minutes of the day. . . .

The class assembles, pulling books and notebooks out of their backpacks.

They spend the next twenty minutes organizing themselves for the day. The computer crew for the week turn on the eight old 286 computers that Evelyn has scrounged from local businesses (adding memory and CD-ROM drives to them) and the Pentium, with its modem and classroom-size monitor.

The students bring their Just Read files up to date and several add items to the class "I Recommend This Book" list.

Working on the Pentium, one of Evelyn's "assistants for the month," using slips of words handed to her by the other students, enters words on the "Words We Need To Know" list that will be used at 9:00 A.M. The list comes from the students' scan of encyclopedia articles on several of the United States. For homework last night, all students read articles and identified words that were new to them and whose meanings were not apparent from context.

The science crew for the week sets up paper and instructions for making a variety of experimental paper airplanes that will be used to open a new stage of a science unit.

Another student assistant prints out one of Evelyn's files that contains sentences using adverbial words, phrases, and clauses, a data set that will be used in their study of writing.

While the students work at their organizational tasks, Evelyn has conferences with two of them on books they are reading, concentrating on comprehension of plot and character and assessing their needs in reading comprehension.

Note the variety of things that students have learned to do. Evelyn has organized them into teams around the learning tasks that they engage in. They participate in setting up the learning environment, rather than passively waiting for Evelyn to do so. They are *busy*, rather than milling about. They are engaged in action research over their "Just Read" program, studying what they read independently. They have learned to use computer technology productively as a natural part of their inquiries.

Active inquiry is the norm. By teaching the students to work cooperatively and inductively, Evelyn has ensured that these students see the learning process as one in which they continually collect data, organize it, reflect on their information, and write about what they are studying. This is a sharp contrast to classrooms where students primarily respond to learning tasks, get through their assignments, and depend on the teachers' thought processes rather than their own. Their parents, too, are closely connected to the classroom, both in Just Read, in which they, too, study what the kids are reading, and in curriculum. For Evelyn makes sure they are aware of the curriculum content being studied and of the progress their children are making.

Note, too, that Evelyn has organized the day so that she has time to teach reading in a way that tends individual differences. She has conferences with individual students as they read material at their level. All of this occurs in a context where she has no need to provide "busywork" to the class while she meets with small groups and individuals.

With the learning community established, Evelyn's students can transition smoothly from one learning session to another. Not only that, but the class can transition from teacher to teacher.

Real-Life Example

Recently, we (your authors) had the pleasure of making a set of videotaped demonstrations in a class whose teacher, Linda Wyant, has built a learning community similar to the one Evelyn has developed. We entered the classroom to set up our equipment and materials just before a scheduled "recess." Well, the kids were organized to take their recess helping us get ready for the lessons. Two were cleaning the overhead projector and approached Bruce, who was to teach the lesson, to find out where he wanted the screen. A couple of students helped Emily set up the tripods and arrange the microphones. A team had run off the handouts, actually notebooks containing about one hundred pages of material on the Middle East, and distributed the material after checking with us that we wanted it passed out before we began. These students let us know that they would handle our duplicating and distributing needs and could make overheads instantaneously, should we need their help. Several other students asked if we wanted the chairs and tables rearranged and made the changes we asked for. We found that we had thirty-five teaching assistants, ready to help and, you can imagine from what we have said, how ready they were to participate cooperatively in a series of lessons taught by a total stranger! Linda's class is a learning community ready to cooperate with her, with one another, and with other teachers who are introduced to them.

We have had many opportunities to observe Linda. One of the striking things about the way she works with children is the very direct, economical way she approaches the job of organizing them. She never says, "This will be on the test and to get a good grade you will have to learn it." She says, "We'll start with a pretest to see what you know and then have periodic tests so you and I can measure what you're learning." She sets up a "duty roster" for her task groups, and the students manage the roster and divide up the tasks. She radiates an adult persona: she has a clear understanding that she is the adult who is to teach the ways of the society. As a mature adult, she treats the children with respect and warmth, letting them know she has confidence in them. Those of you who are just entering teaching out of college think of yourselves as young and wonder if the students will follow you as an adult leader. They will, if you radiate that you know you are an adult. Most children respond to adulthood. The teachers who have "management problems" generally have created them by acting as an enforcer of learning rather than a natural social leader.

The Role of Our Beliefs about Children and Teaching and Learning

Beliefs have much to do with what we can do confidently. We all start with beliefs that undergird our approach to the development of learning communities. As you review the following beliefs, think about which ones you currently hold. Are your beliefs conducive to building a learning community? Do you have some you need to let go or modify?

On Student Capacity

First of all, let's believe that all children can learn well. Can learn *everything* we teach, not just enough to get by. How do we radiate this belief? Largely by how we interact with them. We *talk* a language of confidence: "Let's consume this area! Let's learn everything in sight! Let's get going! You can become the best-educated kids anyone ever saw!"

Teachers who radiate confidence in their students generate more learning than teachers who give in to popular myths that only a few are really capable and the rest just have to settle for second best (Good and Brophy, 1986). The reason is what is called, technically, an "expectations effect." Essentially, if we expect to find that the students are highly capable, we convey that to the students and they respond by allowing their intelligence to work. If we expect to find that they are not capable, they respond by acting dumber; we have given them permission not to learn. Students in the optimum learning environments actually increase their performance on intelligence tests.

An Experiment to Try. There are some things we can do to show students how capable they are. Suppose that on the first day of school we give them something to learn, something new to them, but of a small enough size that it can be feasibly learned in a short time, an hour or so. Have them study it and take a test. Then have them study it again and retake the test. Then have them study it again in cooperative pairs, with each member trying to help the other master the material, followed by another test.

The students will learn that *each* of them can learn a given amount of material to 100 percent mastery or close to it. Note that we are saying that *all* the students learn that they *all* have learning capability. They are also learning that you expect complete mastery and won't settle for less. They are also learning that they can, and *must,* in your classroom, help each other learn and that classroom goals will be set and all members of the class are responsible for seeing that they are achieved. The vast literature on cooperative learning, some of which we will review in the next chapter, shows unequivocally that students in cooperative learning environments learn more, feel better about themselves (increase in self-esteem), and develop better social skills.

A few years ago we were involved with a middle school that was plagued with disciplinary referrals. The kids squabbled with each other, the teachers squabbled with the kids, little things became big things, kids were "sent to the office" and, for repeated infractions, ended up being suspended (about three students out of five in the course of each semester!). We persuaded the faculty to experiment with "cooperative learning days." They were very skeptical because they thought that the students would just end up quarrelling all day. Nonetheless, they tried it, and, lo and behold, the squabbling diminished, the referrals dropped accordingly, and that fall, the suspensions fell from over 300 to about 50. Note that the effect was immediate. Students can learn new ways of behavior very quickly.

On Individual Differences

There are many beliefs in our culture that work against learning and make it difficult to build the learning community. Going right along with our view of capacity to learn as a characteristic of all students, we need to believe that the possession of learning capability is not hindered by variables such as gender, socioeconomic status, ethnicity, or learning style, but rather that the richness of individual differences is an asset to a learning community. Whatever their learning capability—"gifted, normal, less than gifted, below average," whatever the label—students can be taught to learn more powerfully, and we are capable of helping them enhance their learning capability. As you will see in Chapter 7, a major effect of inductive inquiry is to increase the capacity to learn, and there are other models of teaching that provide additional learning tools.

Currently in U.S. schools, many students learn that they cannot learn, either in general or in specific areas. Thirty percent of our students leave school without graduating; many who graduate believe they have learning disabilities in reading, writing, arithmetic, art, music, foreign languages, and virtually everything you can think of. These students, and our entire society, are paying a horrible price for those beliefs. We have to work together to eliminate these tragic outcomes. An important factor to keep in mind is that the basic curriculum of our schools is within reach of virtually every child who has an intact brain.

Our job is to teach students how to learn in the fullest sense, in their cognitive and emotional development, their ability to get on top of learning, controlling it affirmatively and reaching for a high quality of life. The job includes helping to develop literacy in the fullest sense: the ability to read and write powerfully, of course, but also the literacy of the fundamental disciplines and knowledge of the world and how to navigate it.

Questions for You to Ask.   Can intelligence, or part of it, be taught? Which age group can learn the fastest: eight-, twelve-, or sixteen-year-olds?

Skillful, experienced teachers like Evelyn, Bonnie, and Bruce study individual differences and develop the learning community simultaneously. As they study student learning, they identify those differences that need to be tended in order to help individuals and the group move forward.

These differences among students quietly manifest the richness of the human scene; they should not inhibit learning, but enhance it. Students come with a myriad of differences. They will learn various kinds of things at different rates and approach various learning tasks with different degrees of confidence. They will be rigid and flexible at the same time. They will come from happy and unhappy homes and, improbably, some from happy homes will be unhappy and some from unhappy ones will be cheerful and sunny. Gregariousness and shyness manifest themselves, often in the same body and mind. They will change at different rates while they are with us, spurting ahead and falling behind, sometimes gaining in one area while losing in another.

On Learning Histories and the Therapeutic Dimension of Teaching

As humans try to do things, they experience different degrees of success and a complex of emotions about performance. A student's performance and feelings become a personal learning history. He or she will carry that history into schools and universities and courses, greatly affecting how learning tasks are approached. In any given class, there will be children who feel great and approach the course of study with great confidence and an upbeat feeling. In the same class will be children who feel okay, as well as those who approach the tasks with dread. And, there will be children who come with a positive learning history in one area and a negative one in other areas.

Think of yourself. Are there areas where you enter a learning situation feeling confident and filled with positive affect and others where you are uncertain and anxious? Most people have a mixed learning history.

As you teach, you will need to become well-acquainted with students' learning histories. If they have poor learning histories and the phobic behaviors that attend such histories—"I can't write," "I'm no good at math"—we have to work to cure these phobic behaviors. In life-and-death curriculum areas like reading and writing, we cannot afford to fail. In some ways, radiating confidence and making safe spaces for changing these phobias is easy, but for many teachers it appears to be difficult.

In some teachers' classrooms, virtually everyone has success. Studies of "referrals" for discipline are one example. Some teachers literally never refer anyone, while some others refer as much as thirty percent of the class during a year. Similarly, some teachers never refer a student as a candidate for "special" education because their students all learn to read, the primary cause of referrals for attention to special needs. In some classrooms, the symptoms of attention deficit disorder rarely appear. In others, the symptoms are present in many students. Thus, how we teach, and the kind of learning community we develop, has much to do with the kinds of learning history the students will carry with them.

Curing a poor learning history takes a great deal of determination and kindness. Evidence about the necessary labor comes from the studies of special education, where the "cure rate" is only about four percent per year. Similarly, students referred to programs for "English as a Second Language" often fail to acquire independent competence in English; the rate of success is about five percent per year.

A major reason for these poor "treatment rates" is that success depends on overcoming the poor learning histories that were developed so early in the schooling experience. One of the most upsetting statistics in U.S. education is that, by the end of the third grade, we can predict the place of the children in their high school class by quintile. In other words, we can tell with accuracy which students will be in the top twenty percent, the next twenty percent, and so forth. Success, or lack of it in the first three or four years of school, predicts success in the following nine years.

Essentially, students need to believe in the effectiveness of hard work: "If we work, we will learn." If anyone needs more time than someone else to get something done, then so be it. And some content is more critical for mastery than other content. In curriculum terms, that means students must learn to read with good comprehension and decent speed, to write coherently and be able to synthesize information and ideas into readable and lucid pieces, to read widely and regularly fiction and nonfiction, to understand our mathematical system and solve everyday problems by using it, and to have basic literacy about the sciences and how they work and the social sciences in relation to understanding the political globe, the nation and how it works, and the state and community and how they work. That's all. And just about everybody can accomplish that much by working hard at it. It is *after* that has been accomplished that one can worry about whether one has the talent to make world-class contributions.

As you read this, you may find yourself thinking that there are curriculum areas that are beyond *your* reach—that you can't learn languages, or to play the piano, or. . . . Put that behind you. Yes, you can! And, if you teach in the primary grades, upper grades, or the middle school, give your children the gift of believing in themselves and don't let them give themselves permission to slack off in any area because they are not "talented." It is we who will eliminate poverty in our society and we who will help the flowering of all of our youth.

Experiments You Can Do with Primary Kids. This experiment is built around the "ring-toss" game, where participants throw plastic rings in an effort to hook them over a low pole. Provide a number of ring-toss sets. Have the children try to find a distance from the pole where they can get all their tosses hooked around the pole. They will find that they need to stand very close to the pole to get all their tosses hooked around the pole. Then, have them stand about five or ten feet away and throw ten rings and tally a score. How many hit the target? Then, have them practice and tally the scores again and again, watching the improvement occur. The class can tally the improvement for the whole group, as from one in ten tries to three, then four, and so on. They will learn that they can all improve, and that practice is what does the trick.

Experiments to Do with Upper Grade and Middle School Students. Ask the students to think about the four major curriculum areas (language arts, mathematics, science, and social studies). Then have them pick one of the areas where they have the least confidence and plan a brief project in that area. After they have completed the project, ask them to report their experiences and discuss how they feel.

A variation also begins by having the students reflect on each of the curriculum areas. Then, as the work in each curriculum area begins, and they have to engage in the study of those areas where they feel least confident, have them express their feelings. By allowing these feelings to surface, you and they working together can figure out ways to control their anxiety and help them perform better.

Teach the students about avoidance behavior and how to attack it by direct action. For example, when you teach students material that you know triggers anxiety, stay with it. Teach the kids that they can master material thoroughly. Use the inductive model to target areas of difficulty. Many students report that problem solving, often in the form of the dreaded "word problems," gives them serious trouble. So . . . have them classify word problems, developing categories that connect problem types with methods of solving them. In other words, help the students get conceptual control over the areas they tend to avoid.

Our opening lesson in Linda Wyant's class taught students the names of the Middle Eastern countries, connected to the map. In the course of thirty minutes, those students went from where they could only stare helplessly at a map to where they *all* could fill in the names of the countries and possessed a few items of data about them. They *asked* if we would teach them the rest of the globe.

On Intelligence and Time

How long does it take to do something?

Time is always on our minds as we teach. You'll probably never meet a teacher who doesn't talk "time" and how little there is of it. How we think about time and manage it is of utmost importance in dealing productively with individual differences.

We're going to focus on the problem of time that is caused by the fact that *there is literally nothing that children do in school that they do at exactly the same rate.* This fact is a normal part of the human condition, but the difference in time that people need to do things can feel like a plague if we don't learn to deal with it. And, bless them, particular children are speedier in some areas than in others, and at different times, and with different partners. And—they change all the time, learning to do some things faster and, when they are reaching new plateaus of learning, suddenly getting ponderous where they have been fluid.

Consequently, when thirty or more students are doing any given thing, they will do it at different rates and different degrees of richness and have different emotions called up by it. In some learning environments, these differences literally cause chaos and create terrible problems for students who find themselves unable to complete tasks or with time on their hands or with things half-learned or with bad feelings about the whole class. In other learning environments, there is plenty of psychological space in which individual differences roam productively. The teachers who create the environments where individual differences are a problem are generally frantic. The folks who create environments in which individual differences are managed productively have a fine time teaching.

We're not going to solve the problem by eliminating these differences! We can't pour the kids into a mold and recast them so that everybody does everything at the same rate. So we need to find productive solutions and then design teaching/learning transactions and courses so that individual differences are not a problem. Let's begin by looking at some aspects of the nature of intelligence.

Why begin with intelligence? Because there is no aspect of education where there is more confusion than in the areas of human capacity that we group under the term *intelligence.*

In the second decade of the twentieth century, psychologists in the United States made a concerted effort to develop tests that would predict rates of learning so that conscripts into the armed services could be classified for various kinds of training. In time of war, training is compressed into the shortest periods possible, so that the trainees can be sent to duty as soon as possible. So if a given program of training was organized to be accomplished in, say, a four-month period, the services wished to, as much as possible, select trainees for that program who could complete it in four months. Persons who would need five months would not fit into the program very well. The Army General Classification Test was developed, a pencil and paper test (most training required the ability to read at some speed, if not to write) that took just one hour to complete, and on the basis of that test inductees were classified into training of various durations (the more complex training was given longer time periods). The test worked fairly well, partly because the results were interpreted conservatively (it was okay if someone could have completed the course more rapidly than the allotted time, but not more slowly).

The educators of the time had great interest in the concept of testing for the length of time needed to complete educational tasks, for the curriculum of the time was a "lock step" one, with lessons assigned daily. It had been noted that there were students who had trouble "keeping up," and who fell farther and farther behind as the year—and years—went on.

A good many psychologists were searching for ways of measuring what was called "intelligence," an inborn capability to learn and solve problems. Gradually, the results of the scores on those tests that measured speed to accomplish learning tasks came to be seen, in the minds of psychologists, educators, and the public, as tests of "intelligence." The results were interpreted to be indications of quality of thinking as well as speed in responding to training.

Forty years later, John Carroll, a psychologist and linguist, was to point out that in these tests, which were administered in specific periods of time (many in just one hour) *rate* or speed was a major factor. What would happen, he wondered, if people were given more time to take them? Well, sure enough, more time allowed scores to rise, challenging the notion that the tests measured quality.

Benjamin Bloom, a psychologist and specialist in measurement from the University of Chicago, applied the concept of time to instruction. He suggested that school performance might change dramatically were persons given the time they needed to accomplish learning tasks. For example, the average student might need one hour to perform a task, but some students might need an hour and ten minutes. If we allow only the one hour for the task, the student needing more time would fail to master the material and would look like a poor student. Were the student to have just ten minutes more, average performance would result. Seen from this perspective, students needing more time, rather than being poorer students, would just be people who needed more time for a given task. Bloom suggested that we, as teachers, could solve much of the time problem simply by arranging things a little differently. Students needing more time would just have to work a little longer, rather than seeing themselves as stupid.

In recent years, other psychologists have pointed out that the traditional tests of "learning ability," a term that has become more politically correct than "intelligence," measure only one facet of learning, the one most associated with speed in taking multiple-choice tests, but that in reality learning ability is many-sided, and the concept of multiple intelligences (Gardner, 1983) has been developed. The concept has two important uses for teachers. One is that it draws attention to the need to develop many sides of the human being rather than just a few. The other is that it makes clear that children/ people are all many-sided and may differ in capacity. Learning may come easily in one domain but not in another.

Let's begin with the task of providing time to learn. About two-thirds of the population have measured "ability indices" or "Intelligence Quotients" between 90 and 110. Essentially, the difference in time to do a task requiring reading and writing is not great within this range, about ten minutes altogether for an hour-long task. So, if we provide a task that requires about an hour to complete it, we can manage quite well if we allow about an hour and ten minutes for the task. Now, about 92 percent of the population have measured ability indices between 80 and 120. A person scoring at 80 requires about five to ten minutes more than one at 90 to complete a task requiring reading or reading and writing. So, if we allow 80 minutes for the students to complete the task, virtually all of them will have enough time to complete it.

Put another way, students who need more time may have to put in more time, whether in school or at home. The really good news is that if they do, indeed, put in that time, they will master the material about as well as the kids who needed only an hour for the same task.

On Collaboration

Students can work together productively. The school is a training ground for democratic behavior. Learning to cooperate in small groups and in classes gives students the building blocks for long-term, productive interaction with others.

Teach students how to work together, if necessary. Begin by organizing the class into work groups of two, the easiest size group to manage, and provide tasks where cooperation is productive. (Not *everything* is done in groups. Individuals do the learning and much of it is independent.) Teach the students ways of balancing tasks when working together. For example, when consulting resource materials, such as books, both members need to read and both need to record, rather than having one read while the other records. *Both* members of the work group are responsible for the product of any given work session. *And* students need to know that everyone has to be ready to work productively with everyone else. Thus, the work group membership needs to change, so that the students adapt to new people regularly and, incidentally, get to know everybody in the class.

Students need to learn to listen to one another when anyone is speaking to the entire class. Class discussions are largely wasted time when students talk only to the teacher or give a report to peers who are sitting in stony silence. Class decision making is impossible or fruitless unless there can be discussions where everyone contributes and everyone is responsible for hearing what is said.

Teach students to participate in tending the learning environment as they did in Evelyn Burnham's, Bonnie Brigman's, Bruce Hall's, and Linda Wyant's classes. This social participation helps prepare them to be responsible for the health of the community in which they live and work.

Build the cooperative classroom from the first day of school on. The cooperative learning community provides much advice on how to do this, and you will surely want to read two or three of these books:

Johnson and Johnson—*Circles of Learning (1993)*

Also, there are a number of handbooks that discuss cooperative learning strategies that we can teach ourselves. For example:

Spencer Kagan (1990) *Cooperative Learning Resources for Teachers.*

Now let's move from beliefs and time into thinking about how these ideas relate to the first week of school, to our three cooperative learning classrooms, and to the inductive model of teaching.

The First Week of School

The most effective (and happiest) teachers waste no time building the learning community. Let's look in on the first days of the year in Evelyn's, Bonnie's, and Bruce's classes and see some of the things they do.

Evelyn Burnham's fifth grade class enters the classroom on the first day of school. They find all the computers turned on. On each screen is the same message: "Please check a book out of the classroom library. Select a desk, which will be yours for the time being, and begin reading the book silently. If you come across a word you can't figure out, write it on a card in your **Words to Learn** box."

The kids are a bit confused, but, looking around the room, they sort out from the tables of science paraphernalia and video equipment, the bookshelves which are labelled **Classroom Library**. They find cards on one of the shelves and sign out their books, locate a desk, and begin to read. Evelyn moves about the room, introducing herself to the students and making name tags for them.

Bonnie Brigman's second grade enters the classroom on the first day of school. They find that their desks have been labelled with their names. A note on the blackboard asks them to find their desks and to begin reading a set of sentences that are on the desks. They are to write down any words they have trouble pronouncing or understanding.

Like Evelyn, Bonnie moves about the room, introducing herself to the children. She invites parents who have brought their children to stay, and asks them to read a description of the Just Read program which she has run off for them.

After about twenty minutes, Bonnie asks the students to share any words they had difficulty reading. When a child indicates a word, Bonnie asks how many others had difficulty reading that word. She has her clipboard on her knee, with a list of the kids' names, and she records the words they have trouble with. Bonnie constructed the sentences in this data set to include words representing most phonetic combinations. In each sentence, there is a word that she is fairly sure will be new reading vocabulary to these beginning second graders, so that they have to use context clues to comprehend the word.

Bruce Hall's eighth grade social studies class enters the room on the first day of school. They find name tags on the desks and locate their seats. Bruce gives them a minute to get settled, introduces himself, and turns on the video recorder. A scene from the film *Gandhi* appears, and they watch while Gandhi delivers the famous speech on passive resistance. When the scene is over, Bruce asks the students to write their impressions of the scene. "I want us to get started on our study of the world. I also want to get a look at how you write."

"Is this an English class?" asks one of the students.

"Well, it's called social studies, but all classes are about literacy. We'll write a lot this year."

Points to note . . .

All three teachers, working with students of quite different ages, do some quite similar things:

1) *All three let the students know, by the tasks they give them, that they are in a learning environment. They provide instructions and get the students cognitively engaged with worthy content or skills immediately. They do not spend time telling the students how to behave, they assume that the students will follow their instructions. And they are right; the students get to work.*

2) *In addition to taking the students into the learning process without delay, they are kind and affirmative. They use their adult presence with students. Their adult presences and social skills are a part of their teaching repertoire.*

3) *Evelyn, Bonnie, and Bruce study the students from the moment they enter the classroom. They are preparing to modulate materials, lesson sequence, grouping, whatever—as they get information on what the students can do and how they do it.*

4) *All three assume that the students can manage their own activities: checking out books, reading independently, writing on demand.*

5) *All three expect independent reading and writing. They begin their Just Read programs the first day of school. They see the central importance of literacy in the teaching of all curriculum areas. Literacy is not just the process of reading and writing but is also the development of the key concepts in each curriculum area—the ways of thinking that carry understanding.*
6) *All three radiate confidence in themselves and in the students. They make it clear that they are the adults in the teaching/learning transaction, but do not pretend to be gods or to be all-knowing. If the students get stuck, they say, "Well, let's try something else and see if it works." They let the students see them as learners.* ➤

Modeling As a Learner

The confidence of these three teachers is based on their own habits as learners and their own confidence in the learning process. They have taught themselves to use computers as learning tools, and the students observe them as they teach themselves more skills regularly. They read widely and study the areas they teach intensively. They *never* suggest that learning is anything but a product of effort.

How can you radiate this confidence? The same way they do. Read a lot, study what you teach, study the kids, and let them know you are doing so.

Helping the Students See What They Learn

Nearly always, our three teachers study what the students know as they begin a unit of instruction, and they assess gains regularly. Frequently, they give tests at the beginning of a unit of study and again, periodically, throughout the unit. At some point, they have the whole class work together to master basic content that all the students need to learn.

Progress is noted and communicated, preferably by the students themselves. For example, suppose that the students are trying to master the "multiplication and division facts," of which there are 45. The students begin with a range of from 22 to 45. For two days, the work groups study the facts, test one another, and individual students are able to track their progress as they move from, say, 22 to 30, then 30 to 35, then 35 to 40, and, finally, a mighty effort to reach 45.

Some models of teaching can virtually eliminate dispersion in a distribution. For example, a colleague of ours used mnemonic devices to teach his fourth grade students the names of the states and their capitals. *All* his students learned all of them and remembered them throughout the year. Thus the distribution of his class's scores on tests of their ability to supply all the names on a blank map had no range at all. The average score was the top possible score. Time and opportunity to learn, plus persistence, makes for many successful learners.

Teach the Students How to Respond to the Inductive Model of Teaching

Far and away the most important aspect of teaching students to be a learning community is to make clear what they have to do as learners. Let's see how this works within the structure of the inductive model.

In Phase One: Mastery of a Domain

First, the students need to learn that their job is to master the data of the various domains that they explore in units of study. They need to know that superficial coverage is not enough. Their job is to build conceptual control over those areas and to master the skills that they need to profit from the study.

How do we accomplish this? Essentially, by providing students with a lot of relatively short experiences where they master domains.

In Phase Two: Collecting Data

The students need to form the concept of *data sets*. Essentially, they need to understand how to approach a set of arrayed data. How do they learn this? They do it by experiencing many data sets that are presented to them and learning to collect more information that rightfully belongs in the data set.

For a while, we need to keep telling students that the data are the basis of all concept formation, that we will give them data and they will add new information to those data. As they gain experience, they will develop a set for learning and mastery. They will know that when a unit begins, their job is to pounce on the available data and be ready to add other information to it.

In Phase Three: Scrutinizing a Data Set and Learning about the Attributes of the Items in the Set

At the beginning of a unit, the students learn that their first job is to examine the data set and become familiar with the characteristics of the items in the set. Whether letters, rocks, businesses in the community, information on states, nations, or the American colonies, the foundation of the house of inquiry is built on the careful study of the material. Many teachers and students have a tendency to rush this phase of the model and then find that the classification phase falls apart because the students are not familiar enough with the data set.

In Phase Four: The First Passes at Classifying

The first attempts to classify are done generally by individual students working alone, or by groups of two. The kids begin to group the items. We might ask them to make one subset of the data set or to make several groups, but the process is the same: the students bring together items according to their characteristics or attributes.

Then they share what they have done with the other students. Extremely important is that the sharing experience be a sincere provision by the students of what they have learned and not simply a report to the teacher which the other students can ignore. The students not only identify the group; they also provide the reasons for their classification.

Let's imagine a kindergarten or first grade class that has been given a set of letters to sort. There are six *H*'s, five *L*'s, and eight *A*'s in the set. The children have assembled their letters into groups. Now they show their groups. Mary reports that she has put the *H*'s and *L*'s together because "their lines all go straight up or straight across." The teacher questions the students to make sure that all of them understand why Mary put these letters together.

George reports that he has put all the *A*'s together because "They are all exactly the same." Again, the teacher questions the children to make sure they all understand what George has done.

In a few minutes, the possibilities in this limited data set will be exhausted. Then the teacher provides labels for the sets of identical letters: "We call this the *H*, that the *A*, this the *L*." She then provides more letters, including some *H*'s, some *A*'s, some *L*'s, and some other letters as well. She is teaching the children to inquire into letter shapes.

Some Simple Principles for Establishing the Learning Community

We could have written for you a hundred pages on theories and studies of classroom management. Instead, we have decided to try to develop a straightforward approach built around the cooperative and inductive processes. We summarize this section with some principles that we think will work for you.

- Treat students as thinking beings, and they will act thoughtfully.

- Treat them as responsible, and they will act responsibly.

- The tasks of teaching/learning are the key to building the learning community.

- Cooperative classrooms engender respect and self-esteem.

- Cooperative/inductive processes engender intrinsic motivation.

- Active learning equals rapid learning.

- Teach students how to learn, how to respond to the teaching/learning tasks.

- Use teaching models that have plenty of room for individual differences.

Reflections and Ideas for Inquiry

We suggest that you approach the building of a learning community directly and in a relaxed manner. You are creating a mini-school with high standards. You are studying your students and bringing them and their parents into the inquiry.

Avoid the "Don't smile until Christmas" advice that some will give you. Avoid the belief that kids only behave when they are under threat of penalties. You are a **TEACHER**, not a prison warden. There are few children you cannot reach if you study that child, make a partnership with the child and his/her parents or caretakers, and make it clear that you will introduce that child to our culture and how to build a high quality of life in it. We have included "Tips for Teachers from the Behavioral Stance," Figure 6.1, to help further your thinking about the social system of your classroom.

FIGURE 6.1 Tips for Teachers from the Behavioral Stance

Here are a few ideas from social learning theorists, ideas that can help you build the learning community.

Classroom Rules

Which is best, a list of behaviors to avoid and negative reinforcers (a one-time violation results in the "name on the board," a two-time violation results . . .), or a list of desirable behaviors and rewards (a certificate proclaiming "You are the Greatest)?

Tip: The high-probability bet is the positive rules and positive reinforcers or nurturers.

Off-Task Behavior

If twenty-eight students are on-task and two are off-task, which teacher behavior has the highest probability of succeeding in bringing the two into an on-task mode: reprimanding the off-task students or praising the on-task students?

Tip: Praising the on-task students (positive rather than negative reinforcement).

(continued)

Instruction or Self-Instruction

In the computer lab, when introducing a new word processing program to students who can already use another program, one teacher takes the students step-by-step through the manual. The other gives the students the program and, after a brief orientation, asks them to teach themselves to use the program. Which works best?

Tip: Controlling your own learning schedule arouses positive affect. Also, pacing is under the control of the individual, who can move rapidly or slowly according to individual needs.

Itchy Students

A kid just doesn't seem to sit still or pay attention for more than a few minutes at a time. Do you: give the kid extra homework when he/she wanders off-task, or teach him or her a relaxation exercise and how to use it when the hyper feeling rises?

Tip: The first solution is a negative reinforcer that also uses academic work as a punishment, which can produce an aversive response. The second solution provides effective control, makes the student a partner in regulating his or her behavior, and provides the opportunity for positive self-reinforcement as well as external reinforcement.

Motivation

Following a test at the end of a unit in mathematics, one teacher has the students correct their own papers and figure out their gain scores. The other teacher scores the test and provides the students with an analysis of items missed. Which is the best bet for motivating the students?

Tip: Self-scoring, emphasis on progress, and setting of new goals will win almost every time.

chapter 7

Selecting Topics for Inquiry: The Constructivist Dilemma

$\mathcal{W}$ ell over a hundred years ago the English philosopher Herbert Spencer wrote a challenging essay entitled "What Knowledge Is of Most Worth?" in which he made the serious point that the period of formal education is very short when we consider the amount of knowledge in our cultural storehouse. Deciding what will pay off for our students—the topics that will open up that storehouse—is a considerable intellectual task. Clearly, everything that is available cannot be taught in the years of childhood and young adulthood. So we have to ask what will get the most emphasis in the curriculum.

And within the curriculum, there is a perennial dilemma revolving around the question of whether relatively few topics will be studied in depth or whether a large number of topics will be covered superficially. The position taken on this question is of great importance, not only because it speaks to what subject matter will be taught, but also to how the teaching/learning process can be conducted. To bring students into the process of constructing knowledge, we have to confine ourselves to fewer topics that are fully explored. To enable students to consolidate knowledge and skills, we have to stay with topics until mastery has been achieved.

Yet, there is considerable pressure to pack the curriculum with information that is regarded as the mark of the educated person. Recent public criticism of schools includes considerable attention to whether students know what are considered essential details of, for example, history. Books like Ed Hirsh's *Cultural Literacy: What Every American Needs to Know* are filled with thousands of bits of information that the authors regard as cultural essentials. And the public, with good reason, recoils with horror when it is discovered that a large percentage of graduating seniors cannot identify Ulysses S. Grant or Robert E. Lee. To make the situation more complicated, there is considerable—and appropriate—pressure to redress the neglect of the history of African American people in the United States and the neglect of the cultures of our recent immigrant populations.

As we consider the question of selecting topics for students to inquire into, we need to balance simultaneously the questions about what will be taught with the questions about how we will teach, because the teaching/learning transaction will have as much to do with intellectual and social development as will the material that is dealt with.

Teaching As Social Custom

Most relevant to us in present context, the entire society teaches. Socialization is inseparable from culture itself. Long before there were written records, humankind gathered itself into little societies, learning essential and significant patterns of behavior just by figuring out how to live together in groups. Each little group proceeded to invent all sorts of things to enhance their quality of life, including ways of passing their cultural patterns along to the young. Those ways of teaching became an important part of the culture.

Over time, institutions devoted to aspects of socialization were developed and, thus, schools came into existence. Within them, patterns of education were developed and became known to everyone in the society. Those patterns were (and are) how we teach. *Everybody* knows how to use those patterns. They are transmitted along with the rest of the culture and become part of us. The style of church schools was a powerful influence. The step from reciting the catechism to reciting lessons was a very short one.

From the middle of the twentieth century, researchers began increasingly formal studies of how teachers normally behave and, by the late 1960s, the research community had formal knowledge that the "recitation" was the normative teaching method in the United States.

Essentially, students are presented with material through textbooks, lectures, laboratory, or field experiences. The teacher then questions the students over the material they have been exposed to, clarifying points and providing the students with feedback about their responses. With the exception of a small percentage of teachers, questioning and then responding to student answers is the mode observed in American schools. In Bellack's (1962) terms, the teacher would solicit answers, the students would respond to the questions, and the teacher would react to the student responses. In some studies, such as Bellack's investigation of secondary teachers of the social studies, *no* other pattern was observed. Hoetker and Ahlbrand (1969) and Sirotnik (1983), after analyzing dozens of studies of American classrooms, confirmed "the persistence of the recitation," and Goodlad and Klein (1970) reported that it persisted even in schools where considerable resources had been expended to disseminate very different approaches to teaching. Over the past fifty years, repeated studies of teachers' educational philosophies confirmed the position of most that highly direct teaching, with consistent questioning and prompt feedback, was the best way to teach (Clark and Yinger, 1977).

We have little doubt that the dominance of the recitation is a broadly cultural phenomenon, rather than an invention by a subculture of professional educators. Essentially, it is a major part of the process of socialization in American culture.

A mother asks her infant baby, "Who's that?"

"Da," replies the child.

"Oh, wonderful, sweetie. Yes, that's Da. Oh, George, she's so wonderful! She's *talking*!"

"Now, who's *that*?" chimes in Da, pointing to the dog.

"Da!" shouts the baby.

"No, dear, that's Rover, the Wonder Dog. Now, let's say 'Rover' together."

These good-hearted folks are winding up to spend innumerable hours quizzing their child. Most schools will provide them with many fine opportunities in the form of homework assignments requiring a little reading followed by a set of questions to be answered.

The Recitation Mode of Teaching

Think about your own experiences in school for a moment and the proportion of time when your teachers conducted their classes by asking questions, often directed toward one student at a time. If your experience was typical, the questioning mode occurred a great deal. The reason is that the recitation pattern is massively institutionalized in the conduct of schooling. An enormous testing industry questions children and lets the schools know whether their students can read, understand science, and so on. Testing by asking students to write is regarded suspiciously as "subjective." Most of the public, and many teachers, believe that qualities such as intelligence can be measured by brief quizzes and that the results are fixed; the quiz identifies a quality that cannot be improved.

The recitation appears in a surprising number of adult activities. We get driving licenses by answering questions and following directions. Our tax forms are questionnaires. The armed forces use a one-hour test to classify us for training.

The media loves the extension of the recitation into adult life. Televised "quiz shows" are enormously popular, as are talk shows, which are essentially public interviews filled with short-answer questions about, incidentally, what are often private matters. Sports commentators quote statistics (asking and answering their own questions in the manner of the skilled teacher) to the point where it's sometimes difficult to find out who's playing or winning the game being shown. Adults as well as children gain status by knowing the names of rock groups, singers, and popular songs and demonstrating that knowledge in much the same way that they sang the ABC song in kindergarten.

In interaction, we are, to a substantial degree, a "recitation culture."

Creators of innovative models of teaching have to deal with the cultural dominance of the recitation. Both philosophers and psychologists have to learn whether they have, in fact, created a model that will accomplish their purpose better than the recitation would.

The cultural norm of teaching in the recitation mode is the massive control group against which all other models will be measured, as we will see in the next chapter.

Very few people will believe there is an educational knowledge base worth considering unless that knowledge, applied on a large scale, is demonstrated to make a difference in the critical assigned functions of the school—teaching reading and writing and literacy across the curriculum areas. ➤

As an aside, the recitation is so ingrained that much of the public is suspicious of any model of teaching that does not resemble the recitation. However powerful it may be, a model for teaching reading will arouse negative affect if it does not include provision for the children to be quizzed over the letters and their sounds. A mathematics curriculum that does not include the recitation of the "three plus fives" will have hard going. Any alternative model has to be convincingly superior to be defended successfully, despite the manifest limitations of the "tell 'em and quiz 'em" approach. Keep this issue of recitation in mind as you proceed to the next topic.

In Chapter 8, we will explore the inquiry into the efficiency of inductive teaching in comparison to the recitation, and introduce lines of research on the assumptions of the model. Here, because it is plain that in writing this book we are suggesting that you make inductive models one of the first promi-nent tools in your repertoire, we need to think with you about the selection of domains for inquiry with your students and some of the rationales for select-ing curriculum topics.

Thinking about Curriculum

Most scholars of the basic curriculum areas of the school—we will deal with just the language arts, social studies, science, and mathematics—grapple with the "what knowledge is of most worth" problem. Most agree that the process of inquiry is itself the major content of the disciplines. In a book published in 1995, Carl Sagan stated his position in a pithy sentence: "The method of sci-ence, as stodgy and grumpy as it is, is far more important than its findings." His position is that we cannot even understand the findings without experi-encing the method, because the content of the findings is inextricably inter-woven with the method. Writing a hundred years ago, the mathematician Alfred North Whitehead made the same point in a ringing declaration:

> Let the main ideas which are introduced into a child's education be few and important, and let them be thrown into every combination possible. The child should make them his own, and should understand their application here and now in the circumstances of his actual life. From the very beginning of his ed-ucation, the child should experience the joy of discovery. The discovery which he has to make is that general ideas give an understanding of that stream of events which pours through his life, which is his life. (Whitehead, 1929)

Yet, we ask, "How do we find those general ideas?" The scientists, mathe-maticians, and social scientists who have propelled the modern movement to update the curriculum have come to a conclusion that is startling to many laymen. Their conclusion is that the concepts that form the intellectual struc-ture of the disciplines are relatively few and that they are within reach of chil-dren in an "intellectually honest form" if we will teach few enough things in sufficient depth that the children can discover them (Bruner, 1961).

Let's consider a practical example of what these folks are saying. Suppose we provide middle school students with an anthology of forty poems and lead them to classify them in "every combination possible." They will discover the various ways the poets use imagery, the forms and structures of poems, the types of messages that are conveyed with the various voices poets use: they will find many of the ideas that are used by advanced scholars and they can check their ideas against those of the professional students of poetry.

Also, as a practical matter, you need to select domains that will pay off for your students through inductive inquiry. Note that we don't advocate that you teach *everything* with the inductive model. However, selecting and developing units of instruction is one of the most demanding intellectual tasks we face as a society, as members of a faculty, and as individual teachers.

Locating Domains in the Basic Academic Areas

In this section we will provide rules of thumb that you can use to identify important domains for study, ones that are amenable to inductive teaching.

Language Arts for Beginning Readers and Writers

The domains for beginning readers and writers differ from those for students who are further along in their learning.

Letters.   The letters of the alphabet need to be learned, and two types of data sets are easily built. One type of set comes from the development of sight vocabulary words. If you review the scenario in Chapter 4 that describes the picture word inductive model in action, you will note that the children are learning a set of words as they shake them out of the picture. That set of words is classified, and one basis for classification is by the letters they contain. Thus, these kindergarten students can put together the words that begin with the letter *b* at the beginning and at other places in the word, the *br* combination, and so on, clarifying their perceptions of the letters.

Another type of set contains the letters by themselves on cards. Such a set of twenty cards might have six or eight *h*'s, *z*'s, and so forth. As the children classify them, they will concentrate on the shapes of the letters, making an *h* category, a *z* category.

Sight Vocabulary Words.   Lists of words grow on the "words we know" charts around the room and the students keep their copies of words in their vocabulary boxes. We can select sets of words from this storehouse and the students can classify them by meanings and by structural and phonetic characteristics as described in Chapter 4.

Titles of Books.   As they learn to make titles, those titles, plus titles from books, become sets. By classifying these titles (and the covers of books), they can learn how writers announce their books, introduce topics, and combine illustrations with words.

Making the Reading/Writing Connection.   The children study how expert writers open books and chapters, introduce characters, structure sentences and paragraphs. They classify those devices (such as opening sentences) and experiment with the resulting categories.

Language Arts for Developing Readers and Writers

The Reading/Writing Connection. The study continues, but the devices become broadened to include imagery of various forms and more complex sentences and the use of more intricate clauses and phrases. Grammatical forms become more advanced as children study the uses of the colon, semicolon, and ways of reading and writing definitions and explanations in complex prose. Persuasive writing is gradually introduced.

Studying Literature. The children study stories, poems, and plays, learning categories of literature. The structure of the library becomes apparent. As the students progress through the middle school, they study ways of synthesizing information from multiple sources.

Vocabulary. The analysis of words never stops, but expands to data sets reflecting the origins of words and phrases, connotative as well as denotative meanings, and the advanced study of prefixes and suffixes. Scientific and mathematical vocabulary is studied, as metric expressions, elements and their structures, equations, and terms from geology, astronomy, and meteorology.

The Social Studies

In all areas, literacy is a major goal, and the social studies provide data sets that are operated over from a language arts perspective.

In the primary grades, the students study human activities in the home, local businesses, the school, and community, using observation (field trips, interviews, and observation schedules) and information from books.

As the children mature, the states of the United States, information about Native Americans, the structure of government, current events—all provide data sets that are amenable to classification. Newspapers and magazines provide sets for inquiry into the nature of advertising, the content (and structure) of editorials, and current happenings and problems. Historical documents (letters written by settlers, contemporary newspaper accounts, treaties and speeches) provide rich sources of information. Biographies of important historical figures and descriptions of important events are available.

The entire globe becomes available as the children classify nations and cultures. They compare and contrast the characteristics of the regions of the world. The history of civilization is really the history of culture, and the children study and classify the characteristics of the ancient cultures and try to learn which of their elements have become part of the contemporary cultural scene. Human ecology is also a rich source, as in the study of climate on human behavior and institutions.

Increasingly, our contemporary social issues can help define topics as studies are built around the history of racial and ethnic groups in the United States and the nature of the cultural groups who mingle here.

Science

Again, literacy within the discipline is the major objective. The development of vocabulary is critical. "Hands on" direct observation and experimentation should be the primary source of data from kindergarten through the middle school.

In the primary years, students can classify leaves and the shapes and structures of the flowers, vegetables, bushes, and trees that are around them, expanding to the study of flora and fauna brought to them through reference books and data sets. Examine the data set on animals in Appendix B and see how many similar sets could be developed over other material, such as flowers.

As the children mature, they can conduct experiments and more elaborate observations (as in the case of the House Plant unit in Chapter 3). We have used the Sunset Books, which are really enormous data sets on flowers, trees, and ornamental bushes dealing with their characteristics and ecologies.

The children can also conduct elaborate experiments with levers, pulleys, and simple machines. They can build electromagnets and study the objects around them using those magnets. The geology of the earth provides infinite information that can be applied to the study of the local geology (How did our ecology develop?).

There is an enormous storehouse of books that provide experiments for upper grade and middle school students, with titles like "1001 Experiments You Can Do in Your Kitchen," and "Learning How Things Work."

The human body and how it operates is an ever-rich topic. Computer programs like *Bodyworks* open up all manner of inquiries, and the kids' bodies are right there for observation.

Note that the types of domains we are suggesting for science are ones where there is firsthand observation and experimentation as a major part of the study. Topics where students cannot experiment are worthwhile (atomic structure, for example) but cannot be learned inductively, as fascinating as they are. Children love to study prehistoric animals, but they are not around to observe. The local zoo is, however, and contains many animals to categorize.

Mathematics

Arithmetic is often thought of as deductive, but is actually a rich source of inductive sets. If students classify the numbers 1–100 they will discover odd and even, prime, and a number of factorial relationships (alternative expressions of the same quantity).

Geometrical shapes can be classified early on, and if the classification continues through the grades, most principles of geometry can be discovered.

Through the grades, the "number facts" can be classified, the properties of 9 discovered, as well as a number of computational skills.

Problems make wonderful sets. The dreaded "word problems" can be classified by type and by type of solutions, helping students acquire conceptual control over the area of mathematics (problem solving) where achievement has traditionally been lowest.

Equations make great sets. Through induction, the students can discover the communicative, associative, and distributive properties and learn to use them.

And, again, **VOCABULARY**. One of the major problems U.S. students have in learning arithmetic is the arcane vocabulary used by mathematicians. So let's have them master it! Classification is a powerful tool for learning to control the vocabulary of any subject.

Where Did These Curriculum Topics Come From?

We had three criteria when we selected the above topics as guides for your study of the curriculum. The first criterion is that they lead to the understanding of some of the major principles of the academic disciplines. The second is that they reflect important cultural knowledge: things people should be familiar with as members of the society. The third is that they are easily amenable to inductive inquiry. Our goal was to provide a relatively simple guide for your planning, but one that fits topics in the curriculums of most school districts and has reasonable fidelity to the current opinions of the best scholars in the academic curriculum areas.

Learning Resources and Inquiry

From a teacher's perspective, we have more access to rich materials than we have ever had before. When a child's sight vocabulary approaches 500 words, more than 15,000 books now in print are within conceptual reach, books on myriad topics and containing a rich variety of human stories. Sitting here at our computers, we have materials now possible to access in every classroom. We can call up four encyclopedias ranging from ones young children can use to the most complex information sources ever written. Several data bases on the United States and the nations of the world are in our CD-ROM bank. We have a picture dictionary for children and an enormous "talking dictionary and thesaurus," as well as a program that will translate Spanish into English and vice versa, "talking" to us in both languages. We have an art gallery, several literature anthologies, a number of interactive human anatomy programs, an astronomy simulation, and programs of science experiments we can do in simulated form or replicate in our kitchen. All of this in a stack of disks less than a foot high. The Worldwide Web is a keystroke away. Last week we watched NASA's enormous collection of photographs and video programs about space exploration. The Library of Congress catalog is free to us, as are the growing resources of the Smithsonian. We can access one of our daughters' Web Pages where she leads a dialogue on U.S. poets and artists from her home in the college town where she teaches. And then, of course, there is our conventional library. And all this is in an ordinary middle class home!

The resources available in schools are dizzying. Never before has it been so clear that the materials are there for ample in-depth inquiries. Nor has it ever been more clear that conceptual control is essential to the productive access to those resources and the wondrous joys of discovery that give rise to our students' social and intellectual growth. In any North American school setting, we can ensure that our children become richly educated and leave us knowing how to become even more so.

chapter 8

The Study of Teaching: Inductive Inquiry into Inductive Inquiry

*L*earning to teach opens the doors to the study of children and adolescence, teaching and curriculum, and the academic disciplines that provide content to the curriculum areas. We study as we teach, watching the students respond to the tasks we give them, building a picture of their minds and how they think. We study as we examine formal research on children, on the teaching/learning complex, and on the academic disciplines.

In earlier chapters, we have suggested ways that every teacher can conduct informal research while teaching with the inductive model. In this chapter, we discuss the nature of educational research and how lines of research emerge and are carried out. We begin with some clarifications about scientific inquiry and its role in education (Section One), move into how administrators and teachers in one district engaged in action research as cooperative inquiry (Section Two), then look at some of the studies of the inductive model of teaching and its effects on students (Section Three).

We hope this chapter provides models for inquiry and serves as an invitation to inquire—to join us and the professional colleagues cited here in the never ending search for better understanding and better ways of teaching.

Thinking about Inquiry

Basic and Applied Science

As science, education is *applied science*. The term does not imply second rate. Rather, applied sciences are fields where we are trying to improve how we do things. We draw on relevant *basic* sciences for ideas, and those ideas are tested in *applications*. Basic and applied sciences feed each other, trading ideas and problems. Biochemistry is a regular supply system to medicine, generating medicines and diagnostic tools in profusion. Medicine provides problems that stimulate biochemists—the observations of physicians generate ideas that can lead to long lines of research. Physicians engage in applied science as they invent and test techniques, directly contributing to the body of knowledge of their field.

The field of education is not as tightly organized as is medicine, nor is it as closely tied to basic research. Many teachers have not been steeped in educational research as a source of external information to explore or as an individual tool to use in developing more powerful classroom practice. The pipelines to bring research to the classroom have not been well-laid, meaning it has often been time-consuming to find relevant research. However, the ERIC system has been established to accumulate studies and is easily available on CD-ROM disks, and in regional laboratories and centers around the country a number of researchers work assiduously to scan and summarize research findings. The *American Educational Research Journal* and the *Review of Educational Research* are available, as are the yearbooks and other publications from the National Society for the Study of Education and the Association for Supervision and Curriculum Development. Handbooks of research on the curriculum areas are published regularly.

In a rough fashion, the research community and teachers bear something of the same relationship that medical researchers and practitioners have—the connections are just much looser. But, when they are made, educational research can improve practice greatly. For example, during the past ten years researchers at Johns Hopkins University were distressed that only seventy percent of U.S. children were learning to read effectively enough to comprehend upper-elementary grade textbooks and other resource materials by the end of the primary grades. They went to work. Drawing heavily on prior research and development, the Johns Hopkins' team created a curricular/instructional approach that effectively reaches more than ninety percent of the students (Slavin and Madden, 1996). They have demonstrated its effectiveness in more than 250 schools. The product of their work is available to schools around the world. Other researchers have developed different, but equally effective, approaches to the same problem.

Tightening the connection between research and educational practice can make a big difference to the effectiveness of schooling and teachers.

Scientific Study

Scientific study belongs as much to education as it does to biochemistry.

The stereotypic view of scientific study is one where we act on some aspect of the environment in two or more ways, controlling all variables that might affect the interactions, and study the outcomes with precise instruments. The sample is selected so that it exactly replicates the population of any material being studied.

When studying objects that are not alive, that have no will or memory, such an ideal can sometimes be approximated, but, very little research actually proceeds in such a clean fashion. Scientists continuously work to reduce the "error bar" relative to any given finding or belief: that is, they try to increase the confidence they can have with regard to any assertion of what is "true." To get the error bar so small that they are virtually certain about something requires many studies, and even then a new idea or new bit of evidence may require another long line of work.

Most of you are probably familiar with the search for an explanation of why the dinosaurs and many other large animals disappeared, and with the hunt for evidence that a large meteor set off a chain of events that tremendously affected the ecology of Earth, thus destroying the environment that supported the dinosaurs. In the last couple of years, new evidence has been found but the error bar remains wide enough that there is still room for debate. Eight other hypotheses continue to be discussed, although some of them are supported by only flimsy evidence.

Research related to human beings is often regarded as messy because the "classical experimental study" is rarely possible in the study of human beings. Actually, "messy" refers to how it *feels*, rather than what it *is*. With patience and diligence, teachers and formal scholars have learned a great deal that can help us. Educational practice is just not like a game of billiards, where calculating angles and force can achieve precise results. The very complexity of the human scene is, as we have pointed out repeatedly, a matter for celebration rather than dismay, and humans can do much to understand humans and use the knowledge thus gained to help all children thrive. The variety and complexity of human beings and their social environments are there to be celebrated; however, the educational models that work will not be like formulas for guiding billiards players or gamblers, and the error bar will be much larger than in the physical sciences.

In fact, the nature of the human being and the size of our "confidence limits" is such that we are very suspicious of folks who proclaim that they have simple and certain solutions to educational problems. We can create some very useful education models without having an error bar of close to zero, learning to live without certain, universal solutions to educational problems. We just have to be sure to keep a close eye on our students' progress and be ready to modify and augment the model when it is not getting the desired results with some of the children. Also, we, the agents of education, vary considerably as we interact with children and colleagues. The models of teaching whose use are warranted by substantial bodies of research depend on good implementation to get their effects. If someone uses them half-heartedly or with little skill or understanding, those models lose power.

As a general reminder, the "hard" sciences do not proceed in quite such a linear fashion as much of the public assumes. The mind of the scholar restlessly probes problem areas and recognizes that new solutions require fresh thinking as well as orderly programs of research. New ideas rarely spring forth from the data. The mind of the researcher creates those ideas by paying attention to information or patterns that were previously neglected.

Nonetheless, educational research often feels *extremely* messy compared to the sciences that study inanimate objects or the physiological dimensions of organic creatures such as ourselves. We cannot select random samples of the world population of students, gather them into an isolated setting where they will not be subject to outside influences such as parents or friends, and then proceed to study the effect of educational procedures on learning of various kinds. Also, think for a moment of the complexity of measuring the processes and intended outcomes of the inductive model: studying the students' collection and organization of information; the categories they generate; the hypotheses they develop; the ways they test those hypotheses; the outcomes in terms of whether they can do those things better and how well they acquire and retain information, concepts, and skills; and the transfer of those concepts and skills to new learning situations and new events. In addition, students change in cognitive complexity, conceptual flexibility, self-esteem, and in many other ways, *while we are working with them.* They also have lives outside of school. While we are teaching them to write, some read voraciously out of school while others do not. Some have nurturant parents and others have abusive ones. Random events occur continually. They may slip in the bathtub the night before the test or fall in love the week we are asking them to develop hypotheses about the prospects of stability in the Middle East.

Because of the messiness—really, the complexity—of the human world, some people come to be so skeptical about the possibility of reliable research that they refuse to believe there is any research-based educational knowledge. Or, they contend that unless there is one hundred percent agreement among researchers, we do not have a "knowledge base." That is a terrible error because, despite the complexity of carrying out educational research, thousands of reasonably good studies have been done. Although probably none of them have been "perfectly" controlled, we can scan across them and learn a great deal. We can find areas where there are consistent findings and use those findings as we teach and see if we get the same results.

As a homely example of how much can be learned about human beings, think of your closer friends and acquaintances. You do not interact with your friends in order to study them, but, notwithstanding, the scientist in you has learned to predict many aspects of their behavior in many situations. You have noted the consistencies in their behavior (and inconsistencies as well, for that matter). Your pictures of your friends are not completely accurate, for your observations have an error bar of their own, but your judgments are not worthless; you are right more often than you are wrong.

In scientific inquiry we try to narrow the error bar, using multiple measures and observers and testing varieties of explanations to give us more confidence in what we see, create better explanations, and, in the case of education, develop better ways of helping students learn. What distinguishes research from informal observation in daily life is the degree of disciplined inquiry that is brought to bear and the continuous battle against self-deception. A major task in learning to teach *professionally* is learning how to reach into the knowledge base so that one's conceptions of teaching are tested against the products of scientific inquiry, to ensure that one's ideas are in the process of continual testing. The size of the "error bar" does not depend on whether an idea is right or wrong; it is the degree to which it has been tested objectively. Remember that the methods for teaching reading that succeed with only seventy percent of the students are *believed* to be good methods by the teachers who use them—but who are unfamiliar with the research into curriculums that do a better job.

Professional Inquiry and Conventional Wisdom

In many vocations, the necessary knowledge and skills can be learned on the job or with relatively short periods of specialized training, building on the general education that is provided in the primary and secondary phases of education. In others, knowledge and skill are far-removed from the general knowledge we all share and are learned almost entirely in college and graduate study and in specialized workplaces. Engineering and medicine come easily to mind. Everyone learns something about physics and chemistry, but not enough to consider themselves a practitioner of civil or chemical engineering. We all know about "silicon chips," but the architecture of the computer is not known to those of us who have not spent long years in specialized study and learned things not provided by general education or socialization. Few of us who have not been specially trained or have not pursued a very strenuous self-education would believe they "know" how to be a chemical engineer or a computer architect.

However, as we discussed earlier, education is quite different from most professional pursuits. There is a body of general social "knowledge" about teaching. Parents know how to "teach" the culture to their children, how to socialize them. The society is full of wisdom about how to teach. Parents raise their children and, in doing so, come to believe that they have discovered good ways of doing so—and many have, for that matter. They may not be professionals of education, but they have had experience "teaching" children and have developed a body of personal knowledge that is relevant to education.

One of the reasons nearly everyone believes he/she knows how to "teach" stems from the fact that most of us have been to school and have observed teachers for years. We pick up teaching procedures throughout our schooling experience *without knowing whether these procedures have been tested or not, but they seem "right" because they are part of our cultural heritage.*

These normative ideas about parenting and about teaching are the product of experience; they can be strongly held and can greatly influence behavior. However, their existence as cultural heritage does not ensure that they constitute the best possible ways of parenting or schooling. In the 1930s, eighty percent of men and women believed that married women should not work outside the home because it would be harmful to children if they did so, and many married women felt that it was socially deviant to work. Today, eighty percent of the U.S. population believe women *should* work or that it is allright to do so and does not harm the children. An idea that seemed so correct to most people in the United States sixty years ago now seems to be incorrect to most members of our society.

Part of our job as professional educators is to be as aware as possible that ideas that are culturally pervasive because of social support (in other words, the conventional wisdom of our time) may not stand up as the best for children we teach. Education would be perfect were conventional wisdom perfect.

Just Read As an Example.   We have tried to focus this chapter on the process of inquiry—the process of applied research—rather than on a series of "answers" about what research says about good practice. To illustrate how inquiries into educational practice operate, let's look now at an example of a line of work into children's outside-of-school reading. We've selected Just Read as an example because the research was done in field settings, often with hundreds of children in many schools with many teachers; was done with a team of teachers, administrators, and professional researchers working together; and dealt with several issues and variables that need to be considered when any educational treatment is developed and studied. Also, we wanted you to see how inquiry worked to fashion a program we have mentioned several times in this book.

An Emerging Inquiry: The "Just Read" Program of Research

At several points in the inquiry we will invite you to ask questions or take positions on issues. Try to imagine yourself as a member of the research team and let your ideas unfold along with the studies.

Our setting is eleven schools and hundreds of homes whose students attend a unique school district in the country of Panama. The schools are operated under the auspices of the Department of Defense Dependents Schools (DoDDS) and are located on military bases. Many of the homes are on the bases, but many are in Panama City. The schools were opened to serve the children of United States Army, Air Force, and Naval personnel of all ranks during the terms of duty of their parents. The schools also serve the children of civilian employees of the bases, the children of diplomatic personnel, and the children of about 200 Panamanian citizens. The school population is fairly transient due to the reassignment of military and diplomatic personnel, but most of the children attend the schools for four years or more.

The teachers come from all over the United States, and many have taught in DoDDS schools in other parts of the world. Some of them have been in Panama for many years; some are new to the system; some transfer to other settings after only a few years. Some are the spouses of military personnel and will leave when their husbands or wives are transferred; some are Panamanian citizens.

Beginning of the Just Read Inquiry

The opening dialogue began one day at a meeting of teachers, principals, central office personnel (the director and curriculum coordinators), and two professional researchers who were consultants to the district. Someone began speculating about how much independent reading (reading of self-selected books at home) the students were doing. Everyone had an opinion, and everyone was surprised at the variety of those opinions.

As we list the opinions, please reflect on them and take your own positions on them, judging from children you know or children you have taught. In other words, do you agree or disagree with each opinion? ➤

  ▪ The estimates of independent reading ranged from
    a) the belief that most of the kids read widely, to
    b) the opinion that most read almost nothing except school assignments.

■ A couple of people thought that a "sustained silent reading" program in the schools had stimulated most of the kids to read widely.

■ Some of the teachers thought that "their" classes read widely, but that students in many others did not.

■ Some members of the group thought that the "good" readers read widely, but that the "poor" readers did not.

■ Some thought that girls read a lot, boys less so.

■ One teacher thought that the school's business is to teach the kids to read, but that whether they read independently or not is the responsibility of the children and the parents, but not of the schools.

■ Several members of the group thought that inducing the students to read widely is a major part of the language arts curriculum and is a very important responsibility of the school.

■ A good number of those present felt that the children of the wealthier parents would read more than the children of the poorer parents.

■ Someone differed, offering the opinion that the wealthier parents kept their kids so busy that they wouldn't have time for reading.

■ Several thought that television and video games were so attractive that kids felt that reading was comparatively dull and unattractive.

Remember to take a position on each of the above before we see how the group shaped their inquiry. ➤

Organizing a Task Group and Beginning the Inquiry. The director of the schools (equivalent to the superintendent in other school districts), the curriculum coordinators, and several of the teachers and principals became interested in the question of reading beyond the school day. They formed a task group to continue the dialogue above. In subsequent meetings, they turned the differences in opinions about students' independent reading into a series of questions that guided the first stages of their inquiry. Here are their first set of questions for exploration:

1. What is the national picture with respect to independent reading (self-selected titles read largely out of school and not as part of school assignments)?

2. And, importantly, how much do students in our district read independently outside of school?

3. Are there gender differences in independent reading nationally and locally?

4. Does the socioeconomic status of the parents affect the amounts of independent reading done by students?

5. Does competence in reading affect independent reading? Do the most skilled readers read out of school more than the poorer readers do?

The task group decided to study the research literature and to begin a careful study of the reading habits in one elementary and one high school. Let's see what they found in their initial inquiries.

Seeking External Information: National Surveys and the Professional Literature. Each of the questions raised above will be explored in turn.

Question 1: What is the national picture with respect to independent reading (self-selected titles read largely out of school and not as part of school assignments)?

The task force wanted to find out if there was a general picture of student performance in this area of reading behavior. They found the National Assessment of Educational Progress (NAEP) studies, sponsored by the U.S. Department of Education. The NAEP study (1988) they focused on examined reading competence of a large sample of fourth, eighth, and twelfth grade students in school districts across the United States and included surveys of reading habits. The study provided some fascinating information.

First, the National Assessment of Educational Progress Reading Report Card (1992) indicated that the average fourth grade student reads only four minutes a day out of school, including newspapers, magazines, and books. Over half of the students read nothing at all out of school. The amount actually declines by grades eight and twelve. In addition, about one high school student in seven visits a library, including the school library, during a given week for any purpose at all, and many do not visit the library at all during the school year. The NAEP assessment of reading competence indicated that more than a third of the fourth grade students were unable to read upper elementary grade textual material fluently and with high comprehension. Further, competence in reading rose little between grades four and eight and between grades eight and twelve.

In other places in the literature, task force members ran into the contention that wide reading is an essential component in developing competence in writing and that ensuring wide reading by students is a vital part of the language arts curriculum.

Think about these findings for a few minutes. Are you surprised? What implications come to mind? ➤

Collecting Local Data: First Empirical Inquiry.   The task force in DoDDS Panama collected data for fourteen weeks in one elementary school. They asked teachers and students to fill out a "reading record" at the end of each week. (See Appendix B for the record, which is one you can use in inquiries with your own classes.) Let's look at some of the baseline data and see what they found in response to their second question.

Question 2: How much do students in our district read independently outside of school?

The task force decided to organize the data to display trends for each student, each classroom, and for the school by week. Thus, trends could be seen at all three levels. For example, this is what the data looked like for five students in one fifth grade class at the end of a particular week.

TABLE 8.1 A Fifth Grade Class: Number of Books Read by Five Students during One Week

STUDENT	# OF BOOKS RECORDED
1	1
2	2
3	0
4	0
5	0

It is easy to see that three of the students recorded no books read; one student read one book; and one student read two books. Table 8.2 shows what the picture was for those five students over a four-week period.

TABLE 8.2 A Fifth Grade Class: Number of Books Recorded by Five Students over Four Weeks

STUDENT	# of Books Recorded			
	WEEK ONE	WEEK TWO	WEEK THREE	WEEK FOUR
1	1	1	0	1
2	2	0	1	0
3	0	1	0	1
4	0	0	2	0
5	0	0	0	0

From these types of tables, total books read and average number of books read could be computed for each week for each student, class, and school.

Gradually, the picture of outside-of-school reading emerged. Table 8.3 contains the data for the fourteen-week "baseline" period.

		Mean Number of Books Read per Student
TABLE 8.3		**During Fourteen-Week Baseline Period by Grade Level**

GRADE	MEAN NUMBER OF BOOKS
One	21
Two	35
Three	10
Four	4
Five	3
Six	3

The first and second grade students were reading picture-story books: the first grade students averaging about 1.5 per week, the second grade students about 2.5 per week. The third grade students were reading illustrated books, about 0.75 book per week, on average. The fourth grade students read, on average, about 1 book every five weeks; some reading juvenile fiction and nonfiction, others reading very simple books.

The data from each grade yielded something of interest to the task force. First, in the primary grades, where most of the reading was of picture-story books, the task force found that about one-third of the students were engaged in very little reading outside of the reading instruction periods, though most of these students had the skills to handle simply written books. Many of the first and second grade students read about one hour per week at home, enough for about two books a week, which did not seem like a lot to most of the members of the task force.

The task force watched grades three to six closely, where one would hope a habit of reading would have become firmly established, but where studies have actually shown that a slump is more typical (Chall, 1983). In grade three, about thirty percent of the students accounted for sixty percent of the books read. Several students did virtually no independent reading.

The fourth grade students averaged only four books for the fourteen-week period. The high was six books. Several students recorded no books read. The fifth grade students averaged less than three books for the fourteen-week period. The high was five (about a book every three weeks). The sixth grade students also averaged less than three books, and the high was five. In both grades five and six, many students recorded no books read.

The picture was worse in a second elementary school that joined the baseline study voluntarily. Twenty-seven percent of the students in this school did not read a book during the fourteen-week period. For those who did read at least one book, the average for grade six was 2.5; for grade five, 4.6; and for grade three, 7.0. Half of the second grade students did no independent reading.

The task force interpreted their data to mean that many, but not all, of the youngest readers become somewhat connected to the world of the picture-story book during the first two years of schooling, but that few of them are penetrating that literature extensively. During grades three through six, the next level of literature should be consumed by the students. If the data collected is anywhere near the mark, it appears that was not happening for many of these students. If the fourteen-week period is representative of the four years between grades three and six, then the average student would read about fifty books during the entire four years, with the highest consumers reading about seventy-five books. That is such a small sample of the books in our libraries that the body of literature as such would be virtually unknown to them. For the students who have virtually stopped reading outside of text-books, the picture was abysmal.

What is your opinion about these figures? Compare your opinion with that of the task force. ➤

Task force members were divided in opinion over the meaning of the data. Some members continued to maintain that reading is a function of the home environment. Others believed that the schools could and should take action. Nobody liked the picture, however.

Let's look now at what they found in response to their next question.

Question 3: Are there gender differences in independent reading nationally and locally?

The task force found that gender differences were considerable in the data from the national surveys, with females reading about twice as much as males. When they looked at the data from their own elementary schools in DoDDS, they found that female students read about twice as much as the male students. Judging from the data taken in the fourteen-week period, the average fifth grade female would read about nine books per year and the average male about four.

What do you think this means? Compare your opinion with the views of the task force members. ➤

Again, the task force members disagreed about the meaning of the data. Some asserted that the gender differences are just "what they are" and the school would have to live with them: "girls are just by nature more likely to read and enjoy reading than boys." Others believed that the school could make a big difference in behavior beyond the school, and that boys should develop a reading habit just as much as girls.

All members were disturbed by the reported amounts of reading by both boys and girls, but continued to differ about whether the schools could make a difference.

Let's look at their next question.

Question 4: Does the socioeconomic status of the parents affect the amounts of independent reading done by students?

The addition of the second school helped the task force with respect to this question. The national surveys had indicated that socioeconomic status was a factor, but that the economic status of a family did not guarantee that students would develop an independent reading habit. Some students from the most economically disadvantaged homes did, in fact, read widely. This second school served the children of many more high-ranking officers than did the first one the task force studied, as well as the children of some members of the diplomatic corps. Yet, students in the first school read more books and had many of the highest readers. This finding really puzzled some of the task force members, and they decided that the issue should be studied further as the inquiry progressed. Everyone agreed.

However . . . a number of teachers questioned whether the student reports were accurate. Some teachers suggested that the students would lie to inflate their reading records.

Here's another question for you to think about. Do you think elementary school students will probably report honestly? ➤

Responding to the concern about the accuracy of self-reports, the task force engaged in a series of case studies of students selected at random at each grade. The consultant/researchers conducted the case studies, in which each student was presented with her/his reading record and interviewed to try to find out whether the books had been read and whether they had been understood. Altogether, 36 students were interviewed. In 34 cases, the records appeared to be accurate. In the other two, the students had *underestimated* the amounts that they had actually read. The issue died for a while, but kept cropping up, and case studies were continued throughout the inquiry. Despite the evidence, many teachers remained unconvinced that the children would produce honest data.

Let's look now at what the task force found out about the relationship between reading skill and willingness to read.

Question 5: Does competence in reading affect independent reading? Do the most skilled readers read out of school more than the poorer readers do?

The case study students were administered, at the beginning of the baseline period, the Reading Power Test and the California Test of Basic Skills (CTBS) battery in reading and language, both of which are independent measures of reading competence. The results of these assessments were used to help determine whether amounts of reading were a function of competence in reading—as measured by those tests. The answer was "no." The distribution of CTBS scores was normal; the means somewhat above the national average; and the range of scores were from the low teens to the 99th percentile. The task force had to face the fact that they had students who were in the very top of the national distribution who did not appear to have a well-developed habit of reading. The coefficient of correlation between the number of books reported and the CTBS scores was just 0.15.

Put another way, the levels of reading competence and achievement of the students, judged by the tests, looked pretty good when compared with the nation as a whole. DoDDS Panama simply shared what appears to be a national problem: most of the students *can* read, but many do not exercise their competence much outside of required reading in school subjects.

Note that many "common sense" hypotheses were not supported by the evidence. Are you surprised by any of these findings? ➤

Making an Initiative and Studying Its Effects

Reflecting on the results of their inquiry thus far, the task force brought the issue to the schools and the "Just Read" initiative was born. They decided to design and implement an initiative in the elementary school that had first participated in the baseline study, examine its results, and see if they could devise an approach that could be used in all of the elementary schools. Their objective was to markedly increase the amounts of independent reading by mounting a campaign that would include the extensive involvement of parents.

The strategy to attain their objective contained three interacting components built on theses partially supported by past research: That a data-based study of student reading will unite the faculty–parent community and permit the continuous assessment of amounts of reading so that the program can be continuously improved. This thesis is based on studies of school improvement that indicate much higher rates of success by initiatives that built in continuous formative assessment of progress toward objectives.

Component One: The collection and use of data continued throughout the inquiry, helping individual students, classes, and schools measure progress and schedule celebrations of success. The data on amounts of outside-of-school reading were organized on a weekly basis so that building leadership teams and study teams of teachers could reflect on them, classes and teams of students could see their progress, and individuals could see *how much* they were reading and writing and *what* they were reading and writing. As a basis for offering guidance and encouragement, teachers used the data to study what types of books students were reading as well as how much the students were reading. Classroom libraries were augmented so that teachers could easily guide their students in book selection.

Component Two: The project began with an aggressive campaign to encourage parents and students to increase their amounts of at-home reading. Meetings were held to signal the beginning of the Just Read campaign. Newsletters, including samples of books read and writing produced by the children, were distributed. Paper chains, with titles of books read, hung from ceilings and doors. "T-shirt" parties, complete with "Just Read" logos and the like, were employed. The physical environment of the school was draped with writing, notes on books, and computer-generated advertisements for books. Parents were given ideas for reading projects, book clubs, trading fairs, and writing-at-home projects.

Component Three: Individual student, classroom, and school goals were set. Multiple ways of displaying progress were devised, from charts to chains of animals representing books read. Multiple ways of celebrating progress were generated for individuals, classes, and schools. These included certificates, notes sent home, announcements in newsletters, celebratory parties, and a host of other devices.

What is your prediction? Will this strategy work, and how well will it work? ➤

The Effects on the Quantity of Reading.   The first question, as the teachers and task force members counted the number of books read, was to estimate **whether Operation Just Read increased the quantity of reading by the students.**

Data from the fourteen-week period after the program kick-off (the first target period) was compared to data from the fourteen-week baseline period to generate the first estimate of impact (Table 8.4).

Before you look at the interpretation made by the task force, reflect on the table and develop your own conclusions. ➤

The increases in the primary grades were gratifying to the task force members, although the lack of increase in grade three was puzzling. In subsequent years, grade three increased as much as did the others. This pilot was the only time that a third grade did not respond to the initiative with substantial increases in amounts of at-home reading.

| TABLE 8.4 | Books Read by Grade and Period | | | |

	Baseline		First Target	
	MEAN	**RANGE**	**MEAN**	**RANGE**
Grade One	21	0–28	47	7–89
(Only one child read fewer than 28 books during the first target period.)				
Grade Two	35	2–71	50	8–104
(Only one child read fewer than one book per week during the first target period.)				
Grade Three	10	3–24	11	1–23
(The number of books stayed about the same, but the complexity and length increased.)				
Grade Four	4	1–5	8	3–29
(The mean doubled.)				
Grade Five	3	1–5	16	4–38
(The mean increased by five times. The lowest number was higher than the previous mean.)				
Grade Six	3	1–5	18	6–38
(The mean increased six times. The lowest number doubled the previous mean.)				

The increases in grades four, five, and six are what the task force members hoped to see as a first level of impact, though they were not satisfied. That the average fifth and sixth grade student increased to about a book each week is a productive increase from reading one book in five weeks. But half the students were reading less than a book each week, so the task force decided there was some distance to go. Overall, it appeared that the upper grade students were reading from three to six times the number of books they had read during the baseline period.

Task force members and district personnel decided to continue the initiative and expand it to include all nine elementary schools in the district. Important for their future planning, the task force discovered that individual differences among teachers affected the results of the initiative. Students in the classrooms of some teachers increased reading as little as fifty percent; while in other classrooms, the amount of reading by students increased four to seven times over the baseline. Task force members speculated that a thoroughgoing "all school" effort would gradually reduce the individual "teacher effect" as regular reading became an ingrained habit across the schools.

Adding Standard Test Results to the Picture.   One of the overall objectives of Just Read was to induce the students, with the aid of their parents and with cheerleading and counsel from their teachers, to increase their reading. The district wanted to build a culture of readers (and, not incidentally, writers). "Raising test scores" was not an objective. However, in the "pilot" elementary school, a study of standard test scores for the fifth grades indicated that the difference between student performance in the Fall and Spring administrations of the CTBS battery was substantial. The fifth grade mean had increased from the 48th national percentile to the 66th percentile.

The task force also wanted to see if there would be an effect on the quality of student writing. So, writing samples from the case study students were submitted to analytic scoring using an instrument developed by the UCLA Center for the Study of Evaluation. Comparisons were made between student writing samples collected during the baseline period and the first target period. For the elementary students, the average gain in quality of writing was about two and a half times the national average gain made in a school year. The gains cannot be attributed with certainty to Just Read. However, the task force decided to accompany the next year's effort with a thoroughgoing examination of the relationship between quantity of reading and writing and the results of standard test performances and quality of writing.

Why would quality of writing, which was not the primary objective of Just Read, increase as a result of the initiative? ➤

Moving into the Second Year.   The building leadership teams of the elementary schools oriented their faculties. Each school developed its own action plan. Data collection was introduced at the beginning of the year and followed, at the end of the first quarter, by the launching of the campaign and the development of the celebrations generated by each faculty. Data were organized and used as before, creating a formative–evaluation process that operated at the level of the student, the classroom, the faculty study group (clusters of teachers), the school, and the district (using the forms in Appendix B).

In addition, the California Tests of Basic Skills (CTBS) reading and language battery was administered to all fifth grade students in the district in September and March. Three standard writing stimuli were used to elicit examples of narrative, descriptive, and persuasive writing in September, January, and just before the close of school. The fifth grade classes were compared in terms of amounts of reading and writing generated and the results of the testing program in reading and writing. The fifth grade was chosen for the intensive testing program, though all grades were involved in the second year of Just Read.

Here are the results.

Amounts of Reading Generated. For the entire year, including the first quarter, the mean number of books recorded is shown in Table 8.5 for the students in grade two to grade six who were in school for the entire year. Altogether, the records of 1,553 children were included in the analysis.

TABLE 8.5	Mean Number and Lowest Number of Books Recorded for the Year by Grade	

GRADE	MEAN NUMBER OF BOOKS RECORDED
2	102
3	82
4	55
5	45
6	51

For grades four to six, the average student recorded fifty titles, or about 1.75 books read per week. This number is around ten times the national average, as near as we can tell from the various ways of estimating it. Grade two students read about twice as many titles, but, of course, these were shorter and less complex books. Grade three students were in transition to longer books, which is reflected in the figures. Task force members were pleased that grade three responded as well to the initiative as did the other grades. The trend was sharply upward from the first quarter to the second, and then continued a gradual upward trend.

Nonreading among students was greatly reduced. The results from fifth grade provide an example. During the first quarter, 11.4 percent of the fifth grade students recorded no titles. This was reduced to 3 percent in the fourth quarter. During the data-collection-only period (the first quarter), 16 percent of the males recorded no titles, dropping to 2.1 percent by the last quarter. Twenty-two students read fewer than ten books during the year. Only six children read fewer than five books. A quarter of the students averaged over two books per week during the year. The evidence appears clear to us that Operation Just Read had an enormous impact on the amounts of out-of-school reading done by the students. Yet it is, from a technical stance, a very easy initiative to implement.

Using the data they had, the task force asked a number of questions about the effectiveness of the program with different populations. They found that it was equally effective with boys and girls, whereas most studies of reading have shown that, in most settings, boys read independently less often than girls. They found that the gains were the same for students whose native language was Spanish as for native English speakers. They found that the program was as effective with the students whose reading skills were poorest as with those students with the better levels of skill, although the poorer readers read simpler books. They asked whether reading more affected the quality of writing of the students, and learned that gains in the quality of writing had enlarged to more than twice the national average gains. And, they found that tests of reading comprehension showed gains more than twice the national average gain. They also found the schools that had made the most gains in increasing quantity of student reading beyond the school day "pulled" the students who had previously done little or no independent reading into regular reading more quickly than those schools that started slowly.

By the end of the second year, Just Read had become routine in the district, with all classes and faculties inquiring on a daily basis.

Just Read in the Secondary School. A parallel study was conducted in the high school during the same period as the studies in the elementary schools.

Before reading the following section, speculate about whether the initiative will have the same or similar effect with secondary students. ➤

In the high school, approximately one-half of the students reported reading no books during the fourteen-week baseline period. Of those students who reported reading any books, the average was just two books during the period. Only five percent of the high school population read an average of seven books during the period.

After the high school kicked off its Just Read campaign, the average number of books read increased to one book every two-and-a half weeks (from one every seven weeks). The number of non-independent readers was reduced to zero, with no student reading fewer than two books during the first target period. Book-a-week regulars began to appear (no fewer than two per class). All students now knew that no one was avoiding the independent reading of books. Reading was not quite the height of fashion, but it was no longer in the category of deviant behavior.

The task force wanted even larger results. They were persistent. Soon, the effort became as routine in the secondary school as it was in the elementary schools.

Continuing the Inquiry. Do students who are induced to read with such programs continue to read a good deal after they leave school? Research on children who become avid readers has indicated that most of them read far more than the average through elementary and secondary school and college and beyond. However, Just Read attempts to build the reading habit in students who otherwise would not have joined the culture of readers. It will be interesting to see what emerges from long-term studies. And so the inquiry continues. . . .

Sharing and Extending Just Read beyond DoDDS Panama. Just Read is a curriculum-augmentation initiative that involves the community. Its implementation requires substantial "nurturant" staff development to help teachers, students, and parents learn to collect data on reading and to celebrate accomplishments.

Since the original inquiry in DoDDS Panama, the Just Read program has been disseminated to a number of school districts in the United States. These other districts range from inner cities, to affluent suburban districts, to isolated rural communities. Faculties and parents have been encouraged to conduct their Just Read initiative as a series of inquiries: not to just implement a program developed elsewhere, but to implement a program of research. Across all settings, building a community of readers has been a primary goal, which means, among other things, reducing or eliminating the phenomenon of "not reading" independently at home.

Here's a brief overview of what staff discovered and accomplished on one of these settings: In the fall of 1993, three school faculties in the Newport/ Costa Mesa Unified School District in California collected their baseline data and then began their community-involvement Just Read project. These schools were particularly interesting because they had been using for several years some of the more conventional programs to increase reading both in and out of school. However, Just Read brought the data-based action-research format to them. One school, in a community where many of the children were just learning English, moved from a baseline of an average of only one book per child per month to over 11 books per child per month. A second school, in a neighborhood of affluent families, discovered that more than half of their students were not reading at home at all! By March, that number had been reduced to 15 percent as students doubled the number of books read per week. By May, all students were reading regularly or somewhat regularly. Altogether, the 500 children in the school read 70,000 books that year. A third school, also in an affluent neighborhood, tripled the at-home reading in the first four months and nearly eliminated non-reading at home. As a side effect, quality-of-writing gains were four times what they had been the year before Just Read came to town. Both teachers and parents learned that goals could be much higher than they had been satisfied with before in the amounts of reading done by the average student, the number of children who could be reached, and in the quality of writing.

Having read about Just Read, do you think the research warrants the claim that it can increase independent reading by students? ➤

This question leads to another point about inquiry. Is it possible to invent another program, comparable in purpose to Just Read, that might be equally or even more effective? The answer is almost surely "yes," which doesn't discount Just Read's achievements, but stands for the probability of progress if one continues to inquire.

A Synthesis of Just Read As an Example of Inquiry in Education.　The progression of research on Just Read is fairly typical of programmatic research that begins with a problem that is recognized by practicing teachers and administrators. The researchers began with the population that was at hand, verified that there was a problem, studied progress, and asked a series of questions about the overall achievement of the primary objective—increasing amounts of at-home reading of books selected by the students themselves; questions about the influence of gender and ethnicity, including primary language; and questions about the effects on quality of writing and performance on general tests of reading comprehension. Further action research studies expanded the settings in which the program was tried, with similar results.

As you can see, the task force in the DoDDS Panama schools dealt with the inherent messiness of the human scene in a straightforward fashion as they dug into the problem. They enlisted the students and parents to collect data, and then checked out the accuracy of the data. They used the techniques of applied science to inform their collective and individual actions.

When the task force made their initiative, they clarified what they wanted, how they would measure it, and made the decision to study amounts of reading on a frequent and regular basis. They studied the results on quantity of reading, but did not stop there. They studied effects on reading comprehension using two independent measures; they studied effects on quality of writing and compared the effects to the national sample. They studied high and low frequency readers, studied schools that had greater and lesser effects, and looked at whether ethnicity had an effect. Finally, they studied the effects of their initiative in other settings (Joyce and Wolf, 1996).

The task force not only studied how much the students were reading and how students were currently performing in reading and writing; they also looked for influences on student performance, such as socioeconomic status (SES), gender, and prior reading achievement—variables important throughout educational research.

Why is it so critical as you look at programs and/or models of teaching to ask questions about their results in relation to gender, to prior educational achievement, to ethnicity, and to students from homes and settings that represent a variety of income levels? ➤

We had three motives as we introduced you to the program of studies done on Just Read. First was to illustrate how practitioner–researchers can find their way through the inherent messiness of the educational landscape. Second was to bring the issue of independent learning by students prominently into our discussion. Essentially, students need to read regularly to establish the habit of life-long inquiry and to develop the information for their own independent inductive efforts. Failing to develop strong habits of reading has greatly curtailed the general knowledge of our students and indicates that the habit of life-long inquiry has not been developed. We need to fix this problem. Third, we hope to entice you into the community of teacher/ researchers, constructing knowledge as you build learning environments in your classroom.

We hope that you will see what the DoDDS Panama staff did as a stimulus to your own inquiry. Why not begin your teaching career with a parallel study? Find out how much your students read independently and ask some of the same questions the task force did. Then, implement Just Read or a similar program and study the effects, collecting data regularly and modifying your approach as you see the results.

We'll turn now to studies on inductive inquiry. We'll describe just a few studies, and again, invite you into the process. Thus, what comes next is a further invitation to study the literature on teaching and curriculum and to reflect on what we know and what we need to know.

Inductive Teaching and Curriculum— Assumptions and Effects

The assumptions of the inductive model have led to a number of investigations. Some investigations have focused on the broad goals of the model, while others have focused on its utility for attaining specific, discrete objectives. Broader goals and objectives, such as how to inquire inductively and gain mastery of substantial domains of subject matter, are expected to occur over fairly long periods of time through many experiences with inductive processes. Other objectives, such as the development of specific concepts in science, mathematics, and language arts, are expected to be accomplished quickly and efficiently. Thus, some of the research in the professional knowledge base was aimed at general tests of the ability of the inductive model to accomplish its long-term goals, while other studies have been directed at specific questions. With respect to the inductive model of teaching—and almost every other model—information is found in a complex of multiple pieces of research rather than in a single study that provides quick and definitive answers. For the last section of this chapter, we have taken several hundred studies—all we could find that appeared relevant to the study of inductive inquiry—and classified them according to the questions they addressed. Then we have examined their findings and classified those. The resulting information is organized in terms of the objectives of the model and the questions researchers asked in relation to each of those objectives. Thus, we attempt to model inductive inquiry over the studies of inductive teaching and learning.

Assumptions about Inductive Thinking and Teaching

We have selected a few of the available studies to share as you begin your personal inquiry and seek conceptual control of the inductive model of teaching. We will look first at studies related to the assumptions that underpin use of the model.

Why Would the Model Work?   "Why would the model work?" is the focus of some of the inquiries.

- **Assumption:** Concept formation is a natural activity.

  Question: Is concept formation a natural activity?

- **Assumption:** Practice in concept formation increases competence in inductive inquiry.

  Question: Does practice in concept formation increase competence in conducting inductive inquiry?

- **Assumption:** Increased skill in concept formation increases students general ability to learn.

  Question: Do increases in skill in concept formation affect the cognitive development of students, increasing their general capacity to learn?

Effectiveness in Learning.   "Effectiveness in learning in the core curriculum areas" guides the next series of questions.

- **Assumption:** Concept formation (one of the essential phases of the inductive model) is effective in generating complex skills.

  Question: How effective is concept formation in generating complex skills?

- **Assumption:** Concept formation is effective for acquiring and mastering information.

  Question: How effective is concept formation for mastery of information?

- **Assumption:** The inductive model of teaching is more efficient in terms of student learning and curriculum mastery than the more dominant lecture/recitation model.

  Question: How efficient is the model in comparison with customary teaching practice?

Try to place yourself in the role of these earlier scholar/researchers. How would you answer some of their questions? How would you go about gathering information on the effectiveness and utility of the inductive model? Use the work of these past and present colleagues as examples of applied science in our profession, as examples of how knowledge about teaching and learning can be expanded.

Question: How natural is concept formation?   Much of the argument that concept formation is a natural human activity is based on early language acquisition: that the development of fluency in listening and speaking is evidence that children come to school with considerable competence in concept formation ability. Linguists studying children's acquisition of language have repeatedly noted that language learning is not just a matter of making specific associations of words with objects ("Mom" with the real mother, "Dad" with the real father, "teddy" with the real stuffed animal), although such associations are necessary. What happens is a process of forming generalizations whereby distinctions are made that enable the child to obtain conceptual and verbal control over the environment more or less simultaneously. Many of these distinctions about how language and communication work are made rapidly. In the early stages, children note similarities between objects they recognize and have words for and new objects, and they generalize in relation to these similarities. We can see this when a child uses the name of the dog ("Harry") for another dog. The child has noted that the other dog and "Harry" have much in common and uses the word—Harry's name—for the other dog, or even for dogs in general. After a while, the child discovers the name for all "Harry's," and uses "dog."

Children also learn syntax through a process of generalization. When they begin to use sentences, they use the word order they hear used in their environment. If English is spoken, most children's sentences will place adjectives before the noun (big dog), rather than afterward (dog big). In some other languages, they place the adjective after the noun (perro grande). No one needs to give infants a course on the structure of the language spoken around them. They can't help learning it.

Building concepts about the world around them and learning language appear to be simultaneous processes for young humans. The skill and adeptness of most children in using these processes represent a strong argument that concept formation is both natural and is well-exercised by the time formal schooling begins. (Think back to Chapter 4; also see Anderson and Freebody, 1981.)

Other evidence supporting the use of inductive teaching focuses on whether young children can respond rapidly to instruction that depends on their ability to form concepts or learn to do so rapidly. Essentially, the argument is that if induction were not a natural activity, then primary students would find it to be foreign and have difficulty learning to respond to inductive tasks. A number of studies speak to this question. An extensive study (Almy, 1970) examined primary students who were in schools where nearly all the instruction was inductive—science, mathematics, social studies. Almy found that the children could respond productively to inductive tasks, forming concepts and testing hypotheses, using direct observation and concrete materials.

In the area of learning-to-read, there have been a number of studies in which children learned to develop sight vocabulary and build phonetic and structural analysis skills inductively; and, again, in all the studies, the students have been able to respond rapidly. Spaulding (1970), whose major study we will discuss later, used inductive approaches to the teaching of reading and social skills with primary students who came from abusive and deprived environments and whose prior language development was much less than normal. Within a year, these seriously "at risk" students were building concepts and testing hypotheses.

Now, if the assumption is correct that induction is natural and that young students can respond easily to tasks requiring data collection, concept formation, and the development and testing of hypotheses, what is your hypotheses about how well older students can respond to inductive tasks? We'll provide some evidence about this question as we examine the next assumption.

Does practice in concept formation increase the competence to carry on inductive inquiry? Researchers/scholars have tried to find out whether inductive curriculum and instruction facilitates and extends the natural ability to form concepts. Do students use inductive thinking more powerfully if they receive help in refining their inductive skills.

The best evidence in this area comes from the studies of inductive curriculums in science, social studies, mathematics, and the language arts. In these studies, students practiced versions of the inductive model as they studied the topics in the curriculum areas at the elementary, middle, and/or high school levels. During the twenty-year period from 1955 to 1975, a set of academically oriented curriculums in science and mathematics were developed and used. The theory of these academic curriculums was relatively straightforward: The teaching of science—and all other curriculum areas—should be as much as possible a simulation of the scholarly process within the discipline of science. The concepts of the disciplines should be studied rigorously in relation to their knowledge base; thus students' studies in reading, writing, mathematics, science, and social studies would be carried on as inquiry. Further, the information learned would be retained over time because it would be embedded in a meaningful framework and the student would possess the interrelated concepts that make up the structure of the disciplines. (The essence of the position was stated in *The Process of Education* (Bruner, 1961) and in Schwab and Brandwein's *The Teaching of Science* (1962).)

In the academic reform movement of the 1950s and 1960s, entire curriculums in the sciences (e.g., BSCS Biology), social studies (e.g., Man, A Course of

Study), mathematics (e.g., School Mathematics Study Group), and language (e.g., the linguistic approaches) were developed and introduced to the schools. These curriculums had in common their designers' beliefs that academic subjects should be studied with the tools of their respective disciplines; therefore, most of these curriculums required students to learn the modes of inquiry employed by the disciplines as well as factual material and major concepts. Process learning—learning how to work and how to think about a discipline as a scientist does, as a linguist does, as a mathematician does—was valued equally with content. Many of these curriculum approaches came to be characterized as "inquiry oriented."

Essentially, the evidence about the "practice effect" of the inductive model comes from those studies that followed students for several years. The research reviews by Bredderman (1983) and El Nemr (1979) cite several studies that looked directly at the question of whether concept–formation ability increased, and in all cases it did—at all age levels and for boys and girls alike.

A carefully controlled series of investigations by Joyce and Joyce (1968) asked whether elementary students could increase their concept formation ability rapidly through short periods of intensive instruction. The students were presented with a series of banks of data about communities around the world with which the students were unfamiliar. After observing the students inquire into those communities for some weeks, Joyce and Joyce presented them with a series of slide-tape lessons illustrating ways of collecting and organizing data and building concepts. The students immediately responded by asking more and broader questions that ranged over more aspects of the cultures, built concepts that integrated information about the dimensions of the culture, and were able to respond to questions asking them to solve problems requiring the assembly and reorganization of information.

Hunt and Joyce (1983) conducted a study in which they led conceptually rigid and conceptually flexible middle school students through a series of inductive exercises and then asked them to conduct inductive inquiries in small groups, independent of teacher leadership. The students, both those who were conceptually rigid and those who were conceptually flexible, were able to conduct the teacher-less activities successfully, examining and organizing data and striving for conceptual control of the topics that were presented to them. Now, if inductive activity and tutoring in the inductive process increase the efficiency and power with which students can work inductively, does that affect their cognitive ability in general?

Do increases in concept formation skill affect the cognitive development of the students? In other words, does increasing a student's skill in concept formation also increase her/his capacity to learn?   Research on this question calls for providing students with intensive experience with inductive curriculums and using measures of cognitive development or intelligence to determine the effects of the inductive experience.

Bredderman (1983) reviewed those studies where students were exposed to inductive curriculums for three years or more and where tests of intelligence were given at intervals over the several years. He found that IQ scores rose an average five points when students were taught inductively for three years or more. He estimated that, were our schools organized around inductive teaching, IQ scores might rise by as much as twenty points in the course of schooling!

Spaulding had a similar finding in his three-year study with primary students who had failed to learn to read and had been expelled from school because of problems in social behavior (1970). (Can you believe that—students at age six or seven had actually been thrown out of school!) Spaulding used a complex of instructional models, but most of the instruction was inductive. The students learned to read and, perhaps most interesting, their scores on IQ tests rose about five points as well during the three years.

However, perhaps the most dramatic study was done with primary students in the Almy study mentioned earlier. Here, several curriculum areas were designed around inquiry–oriented models. Almy asked whether the cognitive development of the students was affected.

(As you know, children pass through conceptual developmental stages that have to do with their ability to understand and process concrete information and more abstract information. For example, using the frame of reference developed by Jean Piaget, young humans develop increasingly more complex levels of thinking in stages. Children pass through what are called pre-operational and concrete-operational stages toward the stage of formal or abstract operations (Piaget, 1952, 1960). Most primary students are in the early phases of the stage of concrete operations.)

Almy found that practice with inductive thinking did, in fact, accelerate the cognitive development of students, enabling them to reason more fully in concrete terms or begin to phase toward formal abstract reasoning.

What is your reaction to the idea that we can design education to increase capability in thinking? ➤

We'll now turn to investigations of the effectiveness of concept formation in learning the content and processes of the core academic curriculum areas.

How effective is concept formation in generating complex skills? In response to this question, we'll explore research on the development of skill in writing, one of the most complex and difficult areas for students. We concentrate on a recent study that we and our colleagues conducted in a school district in Iowa

(Joyce, Calhoun et al., 1994). The impetus for the study was twofold: one, students in the district, while writing better than the national mean (NAEP), were not performing at the level that test scores and grades indicated was possible; and two, a review of various approaches to the teaching of writing made by George Hillocks (1987) which indicated that inquiry-oriented approaches facilitated gains in competence in writing considerably larger than any of the other strategies for which research was available.

The district staff and its elementary school teachers focused on improving the quality of writing of their students by using the inductive model to help students explore the techniques used by published authors to accomplish tasks such as announcing the main idea clearly, introducing characters, establishing settings, and describing actions. The students, having categorized several devices that authors use for accomplishing similar tasks, then experimented with those devices in their own writing. (The scenarios in Chapters 3, 4, and 5 depict similar approaches.) At intervals throughout the year, the teachers collected samples of the children's writing, and those samples were scored by expert raters who did not know the identity of the children.

By the end of the year, the students' writing had improved dramatically. The example of the fourth grade illustrates how much they improved. (See Table 8.6.) Their end-of-year scores for writing quality were higher than the end-of-year scores for eighth grade students the previous year! They had made greater gains in one year than were normally achieved by comparable students over a period of nearly five years. (The 1.2 gain compares with an average yearly gain of about 0.25 for the students in that district before the inductive process was studied and used by the teachers. Moreover, *all* students had gained substantially—from the ones who started with the poorest writing skills to the ones who began with the most developed skills. A "gender" gap in writing (males often lag behind females in developing writing skills) narrowed significantly (Joyce, Calhoun et al., 1996).

That the same model of teaching reached all the students is surprising to many people, but it is a typical finding in studies of teaching and teaching strategies. Teachers who "reach" the students with poor histories of learning and help them also propel the best students into higher states of growth than they have been accustomed to.

As discussed earlier, the studies of the extensive inductive curriculums appear to indicate that students develop inductive skills by practice with induction and tutoring in the process and that causal reasoning and skills for abstract reasoning can be accelerated through inductive teaching/learning transactions. The inquiry approaches to mathematics demonstrated that the development of mathematical concepts improved computation skills and the ability to solve problems. The Ames study is a field test of the effects of inductive inquiry on writing skill and confirms and extends the thesis put for-

| TABLE 8.6 | Mean Grade Four Scores on Expository Writing for Fall, 1992, and Spring, 1993 |

| | Dimensions | | |
PERIOD	FOCUS/ORG	SUPPORT	GRAMMAR/MECHAN.
Fall			
Mean	1.6	2.2	2.11
SD	0.55	0.65	0.65
Spring			
Mean	2.8	3.2	3.0
SD	0.94	0.96	0.97

ward by Hillocks after his review of the major approaches to the teaching of writing.

How efficient is the model in comparison with customary teaching practices?   A major assumption of the model is that students who build structures for thinking about an area will gain conceptual control of that area, thus increasing their ability to think about it. A corollary is that conceptual control will facilitate the acquisition and retention of information, because the resulting scaffold of ideas provides places to which information is attached, whereas isolated information has to survive on its own in our minds. A number of types of studies have approached this question.

At the Motilal Nehru School of Sports in the state of Haryana, India, two groups of tenth grade students are engaged in the study of a botany unit that focuses on the structure of plant life. The two groups were created after a pretest of knowledge of plant life, so that they were approximately equal in prior knowledge. One group is studying the textbook with the tutorial help of their instructor, who illustrates the structures with plants found on the grounds of the school. We will call this group the presentation-cum-illustration group. The other group, which we will call the inductive group, is taught by Bharati Baveja, an instructor at Delhi University. This group is presented with a large number of plants that are labeled with their names. Working in pairs, Baveja's students build classifications of the plants based on the structural characteristics of their roots, stems, and leaves. Periodically, the pairs share their classifications and generate labels for them. Dr. Baveja also supplies the scientific names for the categories the students invent. Eventually Baveja presents the students with some new specimens and asks them to see if they can predict the structure of one part of the plant from the observation of another part (as predicting the root structure from the observation of the leaves). Finally, she asks them to collect some more specimens and fit them to the categories they have developed so they can determine how comprehensive their categories have become. The students discover that most of the new plants will fit into existing categories but that new categories have to be invented to hold some of them.

After two weeks of study, the two groups take a test over the content of the unit and are asked to analyze some more specimens and name their structural characteristics. The inductive group has gained twice as much on the test of knowledge and can correctly identify the structure of eight times more specimens than the presentation-cum-illustration group.

The experimental treatment (the inductive model of teaching) was apparently effective for the whole population. The lowest score in the experimental group distribution was about where the 30th percentile score was for the control group, and about 30 percent of the students exceeded the highest score obtained in the control.

Another posttest was given ten months later, and the difference in scores was wider. The scores for the inductive group were about the same as in the test given immediately after the unit was taught. The scores of the control group members declined somewhat.

Although substantial in its own right, learning and retention of information was modest when we consider the effect on the students' ability to identify plants and their characteristics, which was measured on a separate test. The scores by members of the experimental group were eight times higher than the scores for the control group. The inference is that the inductive treatment enabled students to apply the information and concepts from the unit much more effectively than the students from the tutorial treatment.

Another study (Worthen, 1968) investigated whether providing students with structures would be as effective in generating long-term retention as would be student development of conceptual structures through induction. This study speaks to a particularly interesting point, because there are quite a few investigations that have shown that presenting students with conceptual structures at the beginning of a course has a considerable effect on the learning and retention of information when compared with procedures where students are presented with information through lectures, readings, films, and other media and conceptual structures are provided directly to them (Lewin and Lewin, 1990; Lawton and Wanska, 1977: see review in Joyce and Weil, 1996). So the question Worthen addressed is not whether learning is enhanced by conceptual structures per se, but whether student construction of structures affects recall of information, including long-term retention. Worthen thus created two conditions, one where students built structures and another where they were presented with structures and tested right after the teaching/learning episodes and at intervals thereafter. He hypothesized that there would be little difference in information-oriented test results immediately after instruction but that considerable differences would emerge as time passed. The results supported his thesis.

At this point we believe the best results will be obtained when students both develop conceptual frameworks and then match those against frameworks developed by teachers or by scholars in the area being studied. We believe that the conceptualizing process itself develops structures that result in more powerful concepts than if those same concepts are simply received from others. When we give students the result of *our* conceptual processes, but they do not engage in the construction of knowledge, the conceptual scaffolds are weaker and less effective in functioning for problem solving and the retention of knowledge. However, if students develop concepts and then check those out against ours or those of scholars, the conceptual structure is both created and recreated, resulting in a firmer and more active scaffold of ideas.

What do you think at this point? You will discover that many people assume that the complex processes of concept formation are less "efficient" than the "chalk and talk," recitation, or direct drill-and-practice procedures so common in schools. ➤

Throughout the book, we have stressed the development of a cooperative learning community. In the next few pages, we'll share a few studies from this line of inquiry.

Inquiries into Cooperative Learning. Most inductive activity is the product of the individual mind. We think about data and form categories. However, our minds do not exist in a social vacuum. The classroom learning environment needs to operate such that students learn to build and test ideas with others, helping one another and testing their minds against the ideas of others. Thus, the classroom becomes a place where individuals learn to share the products of their inquiries and where groups and the whole class plan studies together.

Thus, another assumption related to the inductive model of teaching is that collaborative learning communities can enhance inquiry.

There have been three lines of research on ways of helping students study and learn together, one led by David and Roger Johnson, a second by Robert Slavin, and a third by Shlomo and Yael Sharan and Rachel Hertz-Lazarowitz in Israel.

The Johnsons and their colleagues (1971, 1981, 1990) have studied the effects of cooperative task and reward structures on learning. Their work (1975, 1981) on peers-teaching-peers has provided information about the effects of cooperative behavior on both traditional learning tasks and the effects on values and intergroup behavior and attitudes. Their models of cooperative learning emphasize the development of what they call "positive interdependence," or cooperation where collective action also celebrates individual differences.

Slavin's extensive 1983 review includes the study of a variety of approaches where he manipulates the complexity of the social tasks and experiments with various types of grouping. He reported success with the use of heterogeneous groups with tasks requiring coordination of group members both on academic learning and intergroup relations and has generated a variety of strategies that employ extrinsic and intrinsic reward structures. The Israeli team has concentrated on Group Investigation, the most complex of the social models of teaching.

What is the magnitude of effects that we can expect when we learn to use the cooperative learning strategies effectively? Rolheiser-Bennett's study (1986) compared the effects of the degrees of cooperative structure required by the several approaches (Joyce, Showers, and Rolheiser-Bennett, 1989). On standardized tests in the basic curriculum areas (such as reading and mathematics), the highly structured approaches to teaching students to work together generated effect sizes of an average 0.28 with some studies approaching half a standard deviation. On criterion-referenced tests the average was 0.48, with some of the best implementations reaching an effect of about one standard deviation. The more elaborate cooperative learning models generated an average effect size of somewhat more than one standard deviation, with some exceeding two standard deviations. (The average student was above the 90th percentile student in the control group.) The effects on higher-order thinking were even greater, with an average effect of about 1.25 standard deviations and effects in some studies as high as three standard deviations.

Research that looks at climate of cooperation in schools has gone on for some time. In the early years, these studies were designed on a planned variation model, where schools operating from different stances toward education were compared with one another. For example, fifty years ago the beautifully designed "eight-year study" (Chamberlin and Chamberlin, 1943) submitted the theses of the Progressive Movement (largely cooperative learning–oriented) to a serious (and generally successful) test and defended it against the suggestion that social and personal models of education were dangerous to the academic health of students. Recent research on unusually effective schools have found that one of their most prominent characteristics is a cooperative social climate in which all faculty and students work together to build a supportive, achievement-oriented climate (Levine, 1991).

Taken as a whole, research on cooperative learning is overwhelmingly positive—nearly every study has had from modest to very high effects. Moreover, the cooperative approaches are effective over a range of achievement measures. The more intensely cooperative the environment, the greater the effects; and the more complex the outcomes (higher-order processing of information, problem solving), the greater the effects.

The cooperative environment engendered by these models has substantial effects on the cooperative behavior of the students: increasing feelings of empathy for others, reducing intergroup tensions and aggressive and anti-social behavior, improving moral judgment, and building positive feelings toward others, including those of other ethnic groups.

Hertz-Lazarowitz (1993) recently used one of the models to create integrative interaction between Israeli and Arab students in the West Bank! Margarita Calderon has worked with Lazarowitz and Jusefina Tinajero to adapt a cooperative integrated reading and composition program for bilingual students with some very nice results (Calderon, Hertz-Lazarowitz, and Tinajero, 1991). An adaptation in higher education that organized students into cooperative study groups reduced a dropout rate in engineering from forty percent to about five percent (Bonsangue, 1993). Conflict-resolution strategies have taught students to develop integrative behavior and reduced social tension in some very divided environments in inner-city schools (Johnson and Johnson, 1994).

Group investigation (a cooperative/inductive model) is one of the more cognitively and socially complex of the cooperative learning models. Let's look at its results specifically.

A group of secondary school teachers in Israel, led by Shlomo Sharan and Hana Shachar (1988), demonstrated the rapid acceleration in states of growth when they studied and first began to use the group investigation model. They worked with classes in which the children of the poor (referred to as "Low SES," which is shorthand for "lower socioeconomic status") were mixed with the children of middle class parents (referred to as "High SES," for "higher socioeconomic status"). In a year-long course on the social studies, the teachers gave the students pretests of knowledge as well as final examinations, so that they could measure gains in academic learning and compare them with students taught by the "whole class" format most common in Israeli schools. Table 8.7 shows the results.

You can make several interesting comparisons as you read the table. First, in the pretests, the lower SES students scored significantly lower than their higher SES counterparts. Typically, socioeconomic status is related to the knowledge students bring to the instructional situation, and these students were no exception. Then, the lower SES students taught by group investigation achieved average gains nearly two and a half times those of the lower SES students taught by the whole-class method, and exceeded the scores made by the higher SES students taught with the "whole class" format. In other words, the "socially disadvantaged" students taught with group investigation learned at rates above those of the "socially advantaged" students taught by teachers who did not have the repertoire provided by group investigation. Finally, the "advantaged" students also learned more through group investigation. Their average gain was *twice* that of their whole-class counterparts. Thus, the model was effective by a large margin for students from both low and high SES backgrounds.

TABLE 8.7	Effects of Complex Cooperative Learning in a History Course by SES			
	Cooperative Learning (Treatment)		Whole-Class Learning (Control)	
	HIGH SES	LOW SES	HIGH SES	LOW SES
PRETEST				
M	20.99	14.81	21.73	12.31
SD	9.20	7.20	10.53	7.05
POSTTEST				
M	62.60	50.17	42.78	27.03
SD	10.85	14.44	14.40	13.73
MEAN GAIN	41.61	35.36	21.05	14.92

Summary: Questions Researchers Have Asked

Return to the questions identified earlier as you reflect on the practical value of the inductive model of teaching.

On Competence in Inductive Thinking As a Goal
Does practice with inductive inquiry help students become more effective as inductive thinkers—better able to collect and organize data, build categories, generate and test hypotheses, and convert categories into skill? What do you think? Have these questions been answered affirmatively? Take a few minutes to review what you have been reading. What do you think of the assumption that the inductive model works so well because it capitalizes on a natural disposition to categorize?

On Inquiring Collaboratively
Can we build collaborative classroom communities where collective inquiry is the norm? How long does it take? Does it work out differently with primary, upper grade, and older students? Again, what do you think?

One area that surprises many people is how similar the process is with primary, upper grade, and middle school students, although the content being studied is somewhat different. However, direct experience is important at all age levels. Older students need to conduct experiments, study real writing, and work with real mathematics problems just as much as young children do. Why do you think this is so?

On Students with Varying Learning Abilities and Histories
What are the effects of inductive inquiry on students who come with varying degrees of success in school; those students who initially give the impression of being more or less prepared, by disposition and history, to engage productively in academic study?

If you find yourself being surprised by the research on this subject, you are not alone. Many people believe that students who have had trouble learning will not respond productively to those models of teaching that demand active development of knowledge, but will have to be fed knowledge, bit by bit.

On Synthesizing the Ideas in Learning Resources
Can inductive inquiry increase students' skill in synthesizing information and developing lucid presentations of ideas? Pay particular attention to the Iowa study with respect to this question, where the goal was to have the students develop categories and convert them to skill in writing. Note that the learning rates of the students accelerated to where they were increasing skill in writing several times the rate they were before the curriculum was designed inductively.

On Acquiring and Retaining Information and Skills
How efficient is inductive inquiry for acquiring and retaining information and concepts? Many people tend to think that the inductive process is inherently slow, that if we just tell students what they need to know or how to do things, teaching and learning will be most efficient. What do you think the evidence indicates? Explain why.

How do student characteristics affect the acquisition and retention of information and concepts?

There are many kinds of student characteristics, so let's break the question down and focus on three characteristics: gender, ethnicity, and socioeconomic status.

First, will inductive inquiry work as well with males and females? Traditional schooling generates considerable differences in the cognitive and affective outcomes of education by gender, with females outperforming males in reading and writing and losing self-esteem and confidence in mathematics and science. Looking at the evidence, what do you think at this point? Does inductive work promote gender equity in learning?

Second, how about ethnicity? We have included studies conducted in several countries and in the United States where classrooms and schools serve students with various ethnic backgrounds. Judging from what you have read, what do you think at this point? Again, traditional schooling in the United States generates serious ethnic differences. Will inductive curriculums benefit students of different ethnic backgrounds?

Third, how about socioeconomic backgrounds? Does inductive teaching serve students from different socioeconomic backgrounds equally well?

Coda: Life-Long Inquiry

Clearly, learning about teaching and learning is a lifetime quest filled with formal and informal inquiries.

We hope you will see inquiry in your classroom and in the professional knowledge base as a powerful tool for supporting your continuing development as an educator.

We hope you will find Just Read a productive line of inquiry and will use it to establish the student–parent–teacher connection.

We hope you will address the important questions of gender, socioeconomic status, ethnicity, and linguistic background as long as you teach, searching for productive approaches to learning.

We hope you will simultaneously study your students as inquirers, and what they are learning. As you do so, you will be diagnosing their strengths and weaknesses and planning the next units of study to capitalize on their best skills and strengthen the weaker areas.

We hope that you will improve the inductive teaching model and invent other models as you build or continue your career.

chapter 9

The Teacher/Scholar:
The Professional
Learning Agenda

> *A*t first, when people create or find a new model of teaching
> that works for some purpose, they're so thrilled they try to use
> it for everything. Our job is to provide some order—finding out what
> each model can do and building categories to help folks find the tools
> they need.
>
> —*Bruce Joyce, again and again, in staff*
> *meetings from 1965 to the present*

We have good news for you. There is plenty of support as you add new models of teaching to your repertoire and experiment with them in your teaching. In this final chapter, we'll discuss some of the developed models of teaching you can access and work with. (Consult Joyce and Calhoun, 1997, for an overview of a number of these models, and Joyce and Weil, 1996, for more complex coverage of many of them.) Then we'll discuss how to expend your teaching repertoire—some of the practices that can give you a high probability of success.

An Abundance of Teaching Models

Between us (Bruce and Emily), we have been searching continuously for promising approaches to teaching since the late 1950s. The hunt has many facets. We visit schools (about fifty in the last year alone) and classrooms (about three hundred last year), interview teachers, study research on teaching and learning, and look at people in teaching roles outside of schools, such as therapists and trainers in industrial, military, and athletic settings.

We have found models of teaching in abundance. These models include simple procedures to which students can easily respond and extend to complex strategies that students acquire gradually through patient and skillful instruction. Some aim at specific objectives, while others are broadly useful. Some are quite formal, while others are casual and emergent. Among them, they address a great variety of objectives in the personal, social, and academic domains—our major responsibilities as teachers.

In the United States, from the late 1950s until the mid-1970s, research sponsored by foundations, the Federal government, and school districts refined long-standing models of teaching and developed new ones to a degree not seen before or since. Some of the research was concentrated on specific curriculum areas, especially English, humanities, science, and mathematics.

There was a similar commitment to curriculum development in England during this period. The Schools' Council and Nuffield Foundation, in particular, were highly influential in not only introducing a range of new curricula into the English educational system, but also in establishing a distinctive style of curriculum research and development focused on the teacher (Stenhouse, 1975, 1980). Many of these curriculum projects highlighted the importance of integrating teaching strategies and the learning needs of students into the design of curriculum materials (Hopkins, 1987).

During the same period, research on effective teachers and schools shed light on their practices. During the past twenty years, research on mnemonics and cooperative learning has redeveloped and refined models in those areas, and research on training has clarified how people acquire skills and apply (transfer) them to solve problems. Recent work on how students construct knowledge is enriching those models, as is research on how students develop the "metacognitions" that enable them to consciously improve their strategies for learning.

This rich storehouse of models of teaching can be used by individual teachers and by staff as instructional strategies; as guides when planning lessons, units, courses, and curriculums; and as guides when designing classroom activities and instructional materials.

Studying the Models: An Inductive Activity

Here again the inductive model helped us as learners. To bring order into the study of the growing storehouse of models, we grouped them into four families based on the types of learning they promote and on their orientation toward people and how they learn: the information processing family, the social family, the personal family, and the behavioral systems family.

A criterion of practicability was used to select models from each family that would have considerable utility in instructional settings. Thus, the models we now draw on have long histories of practice behind them: they have been refined through experience so that they can be used comfortably and efficiently in classrooms and other educational settings. Furthermore, they are adaptable: they can be adjusted to the learning styles of students and to the requirements of subject matter. They have lifetime utility: most are useful across the primary and secondary levels, as well as in the university—they are learning tools for life. And finally, there is evidence that they work in enhancing students' ability to learn: all of them are backed by some amount of formal research that tests their theories and their abilities to effect learning. The amount of related research varies from model to model. Some are backed by a few studies, while others have a history of literally hundreds of items of research.

The Information Processing Family

Information processing models emphasize ways of enhancing the human being's innate drive to make sense of the world by acquiring and organizing data, sensing problems and generating solutions to them, and developing concepts and language for conveying them. Some models in this family provide the learner with information and concepts; some emphasize concept formation and hypothesis testing by the learner; and still others generate creative thinking. A few are designed to enhance general intellectual ability. Many information processing models are useful for studying the self and society, and thus for achieving the personal and social goals of education.

Figure 9.1 displays the developers and redevelopers of seven information processing models. The references section of the book includes the primary works of the developers.

The information processing models help students learn how to construct knowledge. They focus directly on intellectual capability. As the term implies, these models help students operate on information obtained either from direct experience or from mediated sources so that they develop conceptual control over the areas they study. The emphases of the various information processing models are somewhat different, however, in the sense that each one has been designed to enhance particular kinds of thinking.

As you know, the **inductive thinking model** induces students to learn to collect and classify information, to build and test hypotheses, and to apply their knowledge and skills. Classification is probably the basic higher-order "thinking skill" and is certainly a necessary skill for mastering large amounts of information.

The **concept attainment model** both helps students learn concepts and also to study how they think. Simultaneously, it leads students to develop

FIGURE 9.1	Information Processing Models: Developers (Redevelopers) and Primary Purposes

MODEL	DEVELOPER (REDEVELOPER)	PURPOSE
Inductive Thinking	Hilda Taba (Bruce Joyce)	Develop classification skills, hypothesis-building and testing, and understanding of how to build conceptual understanding of content areas.
Concept Attainment	Jerome Bruner Fred Lighthall (Bruce Joyce)	Learn concepts, study strategies for attaining and applying them. Build and test hypotheses.
Scientific Inquiry	Joseph Schwab and many others	Learn the research system of the academic disciplines—how knowledge is produced and organized.
Inquiry Training	Richard Suchman (Howard Jones)	Causal reasoning and understanding of how to collect information, build concepts, and build and test hypotheses.
Cognitive Growth	Jean Piaget Irving Sigel Constance Kamii Edmund Sullivan	Increase general intellectual development and adjust instruction to facilitate intellectual growth.
Advance Organizers	David Ausubel (many others)	Increase ability to absorb information and organize it, especially from lectures and readings.
Mnemonics	Michael Pressley Joel Levin (and associated scholars)	Increase ability to acquire information, concepts, and conceptual systems and metacognitive control of information-processing capability.
Synectics	W. W. Gordon	Increase ability to use analogies to reorganize information, solve problems, and write clearly.

concepts and to obtain conceptual control (metacognitive understanding) over their thinking strategies.

Synectics teaches metaphoric thinking—ways of consciously breaking set and generating new ideas.

The recently developed **mnemonics models** have raised the process of memorizing to a surprisingly high conceptual level, by providing tools students can use to learn and analyze information and gain conscious control of their learning processes. They also learn to think about how those processes can be improved.

For maximum effect, these models are used in combinations as students learn to inquire into any given topic. The inductive model can help students collect and analyze information, while concept attainment helps them develop new perspectives on the data. Synectics helps students stretch their ideas and reformulate them. And mnemonics can help students anchor information and ideas in their long-term memory.

The academic curriculum of our schools requires the acquisition and use of massive amounts of information. The information processing family of models provides students with learning strategies to use in gathering, organizing, summarizing, and applying this information, forming and testing hypotheses, making generalizations, and developing concepts that define the content of the disciplines (how language, mathematics, science, and social science work).

The Social Family: Building the Learning Community

When people work together, we generate collective energy called *synergy*. The social models of teaching are constructed to take advantage of this phenomenon by building learning communities. Essentially, classroom management is a matter of developing cooperative relationships in the classroom. The development of positive school cultures is a process of developing integrative and productive ways of interacting and norms that support vigorous learning activity.

Figure 9.2 identifies several social models, the persons who have developed and redeveloped them, and their basic purposes.

The social family of models helps students learn how to sharpen their own cognitions through interactions with others, how to work productively with individuals that represent a range of personalities, and how to work as members of a group. In terms of cognitive and academic growth, the models help students use the perspectives of other persons, both individual and group perspectives, to clarify and expand their own thinking and conceptualization of ideas.

As with the information processing family, the emphases of the various models in the social family are somewhat different, in the sense that each one has been designed to enhance particular kinds of thinking and modes of interaction. Among the developed spectrum of models in the social family, we will look briefly at three models: group investigation (a complex form of cooperative learning), role playing, and jurisprudential inquiry.

Group Investigation.   Group investigation is a direct route to the development of the community of learners. All the simpler forms of cooperative learning are preparation for the rigorous, active, and integrative collective action required in group investigation. John Dewey (1916) developed the idea—extended and refined by a great many teachers and theorists and shaped into powerful definition by Herbert Thelen (1960)—that education in a democratic society should teach democratic process directly. A substantial part of the students' education should be cooperative inquiry into important social and

FIGURE 9.2 Social Models: Developers and Primary Purposes

MODEL	DEVELOPER(S)	PURPOSE
Group Investigation	John Dewey Herbert Thelen Shlomo Sharan Rachel-Hertz-Lazarowitz	Develop skills for participation in democratic process. Simultaneously emphasize social development, academic skills, and person understanding.
Social Inquiry	Byron Massailas Benjamin Cox	Social problem solving through collective academic study and logical reasoning.
Jurisprudential Inquiry	James Shaver Donald Oliver	Analyze policy issues through a jurisprudential framework. Collect data, analyze value questions and positions, study personal beliefs.
Laboratory Method	National Training Laboratory (many contributors)	Understand group dynamics, leadership, personal styles.
Role Playing	Fannie Shaftel	Study values and their role in social interaction. Personal understanding of values and behavior.
Positive Interdependence	David Johnson Roger Johnson Elizabeth Cohen	Develop interdependent strategies of social interaction. Understand self–other relationships and emotions.
Structured Social Inquiry	Robert Slavin and Colleagues	Academic inquiry and social and personal development. Cooperative strategies for approaching academic study.

academic problems. Essentially, the group investigation model provides a social organization within which many other models can be used.

Group investigation has been used in all subject areas, with children of all ages, and even as the core social model for entire schools. The model is designed to lead students to define problems, explore various perspectives on the problems, and study together to master information, ideas, and skills—while simultaneously developing their social competence. The teacher's primary role in this model is to help organize the group process and discipline it, help the students find and organize information, and ensure that there is a vigorous level of activity and discourse.

Role Playing. Role playing leads students to understand social behavior, their roles in social interactions, and ways of solving problems more effectively. Designed by Fannie and George Shaftel (1982) specifically to help students study their social values and reflect on them, role playing also helps students collect and organize information about social issues, develop empathy with others, and attempt to improve their social skills. The model asks students to "act out" conflicts, to learn to take the roles of others, and to observe social behavior. With appropriate adaptation, role playing can be used with students of all ages.

Jurisprudential Inquiry.   As students mature, the study of social issues at community, state, national, and international levels can be made available to them. The jurisprudential inquiry model is designed for this purpose. Created especially for secondary students in the social studies, the model brings the case-study method, reminiscent of legal education, to the process of secondary schooling (Oliver and Shaver, 1966; Shaver, 1995). Students study cases involving social problems in areas where public policy needs to be made (on issues of justice and equality, poverty and power, for example). They are led to identify the public policy issues and the options that are available for dealing with them and the values underlying those options. Although developed for the social studies, this model can be used in any area where there are public policy issues, and most curriculum areas abound with them (ethics in science, business, sports, etc.).

As the term *social* implies, these models help students learn to identify multiple facets of a situation or problem, to understand the reasoning underpinning positions different from their own, and to form disciplined cases and reasoned arguments to support their positions. The interactive mode required by these models also means that students simultaneously practice the complex processes of accessing needed information, using their information-gathering skills and their social skills. These models require intense use of listening comprehension skills, of on-your-feet organization of information, of the ability to formulate and ask questions in such a fashion that the information sought will be forthcoming, and of being able to put it all together to resolve tough issues or negotiate new solutions. **Thus, students are also practicing many of the skills that they will need to participate fully as family members, as citizens, and as successful workers.** To equip our students with these models of learning is a great life-long gift.

The Personal Family

From birth, we are acted on by the world. Our social environment gives us our language, teaches us how to behave, and provides love to us. But our individual selves configure themselves relentlessly and create their own interior environments. Within these interior worlds, each of us creates our identity, and our personalities have remarkable continuity from early in life (White, 1986).

Yet, while much within our interior world remains stable, we also have great capacity to change. We are incomplete without others and can love and receive love, generating perhaps the greatest growth of all. Paradoxically, we also have the capacity to hold tight to behavior that doesn't work—as if to force the world to yield and make our worst features productive. We can adapt to a wide range of environments. We are the greatest! And we can be mulish!

The personal models of learning begin from the perspective of the self-hood of the individual. They can be used to shape education so that we come to understand ourselves better, take responsibility for our education, and learn to reach beyond our current development to become stronger, more sensitive, and more creative in our search for high-quality lives.

The cluster of personal models pays great attention to the individual perspective and seeks to encourage productive independence, so that people become increasingly self-aware and responsible for their own destinies. Figure 9.3 displays the personal models and their developers.

In the personal models of teaching, the emphasis is on the unique character of each human being and the struggle to develop as an integrated, confident, and competent personality. The goal is to help each person "own" his/her development and to achieve a sense of self-worth and personal harmony. The models that comprise this family seek to develop and integrate the emotional and intellectual aspects of personality.

FIGURE 9.3 Personal Models: Developers (Redevelopers) and Purposes

MODEL	DEVELOPER(S)	PURPOSE
Nondirective Teaching	Carl Rogers	Build capacity for personal development, self-understanding, autonomy, and esteem of self.
Awareness Training	Fritz Perls	Increase self-understanding, self-esteem, and capacity for exploration. Develop nterpersonal sensitivity and empathy.
Classroom Meeting	William Glasser	Develop self-understanding and responsibility to self and others.
Self-Actualization	Abraham Maslow	Develop personal understanding and capacity for development.
Conceptual Systems	David Hunt	Increase personal complexity and flexibility in processing information and interacting with others.

The Behavioral Systems Family

A common theoretical base—most commonly called social learning theory, but also known as behavior modification, behavior therapy, and cybernetics—guides the design of the models in this family. The stance taken is that human beings are self-correcting communication systems that modify behavior in response to information about how successfully tasks are navigated. For example, imagine a human being who is climbing (the task) an unfamiliar staircase in the dark. The first few steps are tentative as the foot reaches for the treads. If the stride is too high, feedback is received as the foot encounters air and has to descend to make contact with the surface. If a step is too low, feedback results as the foot hits the riser. Gradually, behavior is adjusted in accordance with the feedback until progress up the stairs is relatively comfortable.

Capitalizing on knowledge about how people respond to tasks and feedback, psychologists (see especially Skinner, 1953) have learned how to organize task and feedback structures to make it easy for human beings' self-correcting capability to function. The result includes programs for reducing phobias, for learning to read and compute, for developing social and athletic skills, for replacing anxiety with relaxation, and for learning the complexes of intellectual, social, and physical skills necessary to pilot an airplane or a space shuttle. Because these models concentrate on observable behavior and clearly defined tasks and on methods for communicating progress to the student, this family of teaching models has a very large foundation of research. Figure 9.4 displays four behavioral models and their developers.

The behavioral systems family, based on the work of B. F. Skinner and the cybernetic training psychologists (K. Smith and M. Smith, 1966), has the largest research literature of the four families. Studies range from programmed instruction to simulations and include training models (Joyce and Showers, 1995) and methods derived directly from therapy (Wolpe and Lazarus, 1966).

There is a great deal of research on the application of social learning theory to instruction (Becker and Gersten, 1982), training (K. Smith and M. Smith, 1966), and simulations (Boocock and Schild, 1968). The behavioral technologists have demonstrated that they can design programs for both specific and general goals (Becker and Gersten, 1982), and, also, that the effective application of those techniques requires extensive cognitive activity and precise interactive skills (Spaulding, 1970).

You may find the results of the research on some of these techniques surprising. A recent analysis by White (1986) examined the results of studies on the application of the DISTAR version of social learning theory to special education. The average effect sizes for mathematics and reading ranged from about one-half to one standard deviation. The effects for moderately- and severely-handicapped students were similar. Perhaps most important, there were a few studies in which the effects on aptitude (measures of intellectual

	Behavioral and Cybernetic Models: Developers (Redevelopers) and
FIGURE 9.4	**Purpose**

MODEL	DEVELOPER(S)	PURPOSE
Social Learning	Albert Bandura Carl Thoresen Wes Becker	The management of behavior. Learning new patterns of behavior, reducing phobic and other disfunctional patterns, learning self-control.
Mastery Learning	Benjamin Bloom James Block	Mastery of academic skills and content of all types.
Programmed Learning	B.F. Skinner	Mastery of skills, concepts, factual information.
Simulation	Many developers; Carl Smith and Mary Foltz Smith provided guidance through the 1960s when design had matured.	Mastery of complex skills and concepts in a wide range of areas of study.
Direct Teaching	Thomas Good Jere Brophy Wes Becker Siegfried Englemann Carl Bereiter	Mastery of academic content and skills in a wide range of areas of study.
Anxiety Reduction	David Rinn Joseph Wolpe John Masters	Control over aversive reactions. Applications in treatment and self-treatment of avoidance and dysfunctional patterns of response.

ability) were included; and where the DISTAR program was implemented for several years, the effect sizes were 1.0 or above, representing an increase of about 10 points in the standard IQ ratio.

Overall, behavioral techniques are amenable to learners of all ages and to an impressive range of educational goals.

Developing a Broad Teaching Repertoire:
A Firm Yet Delicate Hand

As we study the four families of models of teaching, we try to build a mental picture of what each model is designed to accomplish. As we consider when and how to use various combinations of models and, therefore, which learning strategies will get priority for particular units and lessons and groups of students, we take into account the types and pace of learning that are likely to be promoted. We also need to emphasize that each model has both instructional and nurturant effects. For example, a model such as inductive teaching will directly enhance a student's range of concept building strategies; it will also at the same time increase their tolerance of ambiguity and awareness of alternative ways of turning information into knowledge.

We draw on the research to help us determine the sizes and kinds of effects each model has had in its history so that we can estimate its productivity if we use it properly. Sometimes decision making is relatively easy because one model just stands out as though it is crafted for a given purpose. For example, Synectics is immediately useful in helping students learn to write metaphorically—that is, in using a metaphor to organize a written composition.

The decision is more complicated when there are several models of teaching that can achieve the same objective. For example, information can be acquired through inductive inquiry or from readings and lectures developed around advance organizers. Or, the two models can be blended.

The more models of teaching you control, the broader the repertoire you can draw on as you design programs of learning for your students. Consider a program to teach students a new language. One of the early tasks when learning a new language is to develop an initial vocabulary. The link-word method has been dramatically successful in initial vocabulary acquisition, in some cases helping students acquire and retain words as much as twice as fast as normal (Pressley, Levin, and Delaney, 1982), making it a good choice for use early in the program. Students need to acquire skills in reading, writing, and conversation which are enhanced by an expanded vocabulary; then other models that generate practice and synthesis can be used.

To make matters even more complicated, we need to acknowledge, thankfully, that students are not identical. What helps one person learn a given thing more efficiently may not help another as much. Fortunately, there are very few known cases where an educational treatment that helps a given kind of student a great deal has serious damaging effects on another kind, but differences in positive effects can be substantial and need to be taken into account when we design educational environments. Thus, we pay considerable attention to the "learning history" of students, how they have progressed academically, how they feel about themselves, their cognitive and personality development, and their social skills and attitudes.

Also, students will change as their repertoire of learning strategies increases. As they become a more powerful learning community, they will be able to accomplish more and more types of learning more effectively. In a very real sense, increasing aptitude to learn is the fundamental purpose of models of teaching.

Debates about educational method have seemed to imply that schools and teachers should choose one approach over another. However, it is far more likely that for optimum opportunity to learn, students need a range of instructional approaches drawn from the information processing, social, personal, and behavioral families.

Developing Your Teaching Repertoire

We cannot teach you a model of teaching, nor can your professor, staff development coordinator, or favorite teacher. You teach yourself a model by learning its basic moves and their sequence(s) and practicing these moves over and over. A good instructor will design his or her lessons so that you are brought into contact with descriptions and scenarios of what the model looks like in action and its theoretical basis as a learning strategy, will demonstrate the use of the model as part of classroom instruction (or show videotapes), and will provide opportunities for you to develop lessons and units using the model. Then the real learning starts as you design lessons, teach them, and watch how your students respond.

When learning a new model of teaching such as the inductive model, most of us feel much less competent in our actions and interactions with students the first five or six times we try it—sometimes the first fifteen or twenty times. And we often **are** less competent because we are learning/trying on complex new behaviors: simultaneously, we attempt to learn how to do it and to teach our students the routine moves or structures of the model and to watch what happens to the content of the lesson delivered with this new approach. For most of us, it takes numerous practices before we become good at it.

And many of us are harshly judgmental about our performances. It seems particularly illogical for educators who know so much about learning theory to set the unrealistic expectations that most of us place on ourselves as learners: we expect to be comfortable and competent with a complex learning task that requires social and technical changes in our teaching after only a few practices. Without support, most of us will stop after the first, second, or third effort.

Whether you are at the preservice or inservice level of our profession, colleagueship is a big boost to practice. Find a buddy—or two or three buddies—plan lessons together, learn by watching each other practice the model with students (or the children of friends).

See if there are ways to use the model to learn content in other courses you are taking. The inductive model of teaching is a powerful learning strategy; it can help you understand the similarities and differences in geological formations; the table of chemical elements; data presentation modes (e.g., types and uses of graphs); properties of numbers; text structures in expository prose; punctuation; cultural differences. Many, many concepts that form the basis of the structure of the academic disciplines—science, social studies, mathematics, and language arts—can be unlocked for understanding and use through the inductive model. This is true for both the teacher designing the lesson and the student participating in the lesson.

And, you want these practices to cover substantive concepts (for example, in language arts, how letters work in words—all the many ways that *b* works— types of written transitions that move the reader along, ways that authors develop characters, types of organizational structures used in well-written expository pieces), not over trivial content. The information–objects–data the students study must be substantive enough to provide for the formation and testing of generalizations and the use (transfer of useful/truthful generalizations) of these generalizations in their language, science, social studies, and math actions. To ask students to engage in serious inductive reasoning and inquiry on classifying buttons (what can they generalize after they classify them by color and shape?), on words that they cannot pronounce, on shapes, on poorly written sentences, on leaves, and so on, is disrespectful. They can do it, and many will enjoy it, but it trivializes the learning opportunity.

Celebration

Thus, there is much to learn and you have the tools to develop the wide range of models that can serve our students and our society. The great adventure of teaching gives us the gift of being life-long learners in the course of practicing our profession. We have an opportunity to study the process of education, to explore with great depth the content of the curriculum areas we teach, and to have the company of many delightful students.

We wish you the same learning and joy in learning we have experienced in the course of our careers.

appendix A

Peer Coaching Guide: Inductive Model of Teaching

In an ideal teacher education or staff development program, people work in small study groups (two will do) and practice models new to their repertoire in close communication with one another. They share plans and share the experiences they have as they practice with the students. When possible, they observe one another as the phases of a model develop, picking up ideas from watching one another. In a real sense, they take turns demonstrating for one another—in the "peer coaching" relationship, the person who is teaching "coaches" the observer by what he or she does. In the situation where a teacher candidate or intern co-teaches with an experienced teacher or mentor, they can take turns teaching and observing as a unit proceeds.

Peer coaching guides facilitate the use and analysis of the model. They support planning and communication between members of study groups who observe one another and try to profit from the observational experience. The peer coaching guide can be used to support one's individual planning of lessons using the model, and to facilitate sharing of ideas by study group members whether or not observation of one anothers' teaching is included.

Both parties in the peer coaching process use the guides: the teacher who is planning and directing the teaching episode and the partner who is operating as a peer coach. Both parties are involved in a continuing experiment on teaching: to increase their ability to analyze the transactions between teacher and student and their ability to teach students how to learn information and concepts.

The peer coaching guide form assists the teacher being observed in planning the teaching episode (and in using all phases of the model), and in focusing the observation on key features of the model. The teacher prepares the observer by filling out the entries where *Teacher* is indicated, and the observer responds to the questions indicated by *Observer.* Both parties will profit most by making a partnership that studies the student responses and plans how to help the students learn more effectively, for the observer is *not* present to advise the teacher on how to teach better but, rather, to learn by observing and help the teacher by providing information about the students' responses.

The communication of the analysis should proceed matter-of-factly through the phases of the model. The peer coaching guide draws attention to the syntax of the model—the cognitive and social tasks that are presented to the students and how the students respond. The teacher may want to orient the coaching partner (observer) to look closely at a specific phase of the model, such as student response to a particular cognitive or social task, or at her reactions to student responses.

For self-coaching, teachers should use videotapes when possible and, during playback, enter the role of coaching partner, analyzing the transactions as dispassionately as possible.

Using the Peer Coaching Guide for the Inductive Model of Teaching

When you are just learning the model, it's often useful to have a copy of the Syntax Chart (Figure 2.1) as a reference. The teacher or student teacher being observed needs to identify the phases of the model that will be present in this teaching episode; not all lessons will include all phases. More often, the full inductive model will take several days, and with extensive data sets—such as poems, paragraphs on text structures, or statistical/textual data bases on countries or regions—the class may spend several weeks productively moving through, and back and forth among, the six phases of the inductive model. Along with the phases for the lesson to be observed, the teacher may want to identify a particular area of concern, such as how the students study the data set.

Teacher: Do you want to suggest a focus for the analysis? If so, what is it?

The Teaching Process

Most lessons you teach will have both content and process objectives. *Content* objectives identify subject matter (facts, concepts, generalizations, relationships) and content-related skills to be mastered by students, while *process* objectives specify skills and procedures students need in order to achieve content objectives or auxiliary social objectives (e.g., cooperation in a learning task).

The content objectives for inductive thinking reside in the information and concepts embedded in the data set. Students categorize items in the data set by attributes held in common by subsets of items. For example, if the data set consisted of a collection of plants, students might classify plants by types of leaves (size, texture, patterns of veins, shape, connection of leaves to stems, etc.). Content objectives for this data set might include both information about specific plants and the building of a typology. Process objectives might include learning the scientific skill of the discipline (observation and classification) as well as the social skills of cooperative problem solving.

Content Objective(s)

Teacher: What knowledge or skill do you want students to gain from today's tasks?

Process Objective(s)

Teacher: Are the students familiar with the model? Do they need special assistance or training with respect to any aspect of the process? (For example, do students understand how to group items by common attributes? Can they work cooperatively with partners on a classification task?)

Phase One: Domain Identification

Teacher: What domain is being explored? What are the long-term objectives of this exploration?

Phase Two: Collection, Presentation, and Enumeration of Data

The primary activity of phase two of the inductive model involves collection or presentation of a data set. The teacher may provide a data set or instruct students to collect the data that will be categorized. The data that will be scrutinized by the students are extremely important, for they represent much of the information the students will learn from this phase. The choice between data collection or presentation is also important. To continue the above example, if students collect leaves, a different set of data will result than if they had been presented with them.

Data are easier to discuss and to group if enumerated. Continuing with our example of plants, the teacher might place a numbered card under each plant so that students may discuss plants 1, 4, 7, and 14 as sharing a common attribute rather than by plant names (which students may not yet know). However, when young children are dealing with a data set of letter names, numerals, or word cards, enumeration may not be necessary.

Teacher: Please describe the data set to be used in this lesson. Will you provide the data set or have students collect data? If the latter, what will be the sources of information they will use?

Teacher: What, in your opinion, are the critical attributes of the data set? What categories do *you* bring to the set?

Observer: Did the teacher/students enumerate the data before attempting to categorize it?

Yes [   ]   No [   ]

Phase Three: Examination of Data

Once a data set has been presented to students or collected by them, the teacher needs to direct students to review (read, examine, study) all items in the data set.

Teacher: What will you say to students to engage them in a full review of the data set before they begin categorizing the items?

Observer: Did the students examine the items in the data set before they proceeded to classification?

Phase Four: Formation of Concepts by Classifying

Once a data set has been collected by or presented to students, the teacher may want to set parameters for the classification activity by orienting students to relevant attributes. For example, if the data are plants, the teacher may wish to narrow the field of observation by having students classify by "types of leaves." On the other hand, the teacher may wish to leave the parameters open and simply instruct students to classify by common attributes. Generally speaking, the more open-ended the instructions, the better the results and the broader the cognitive engagement of the students.

Items from a data set may be included in only one category, or they may be in multiple categories. You may want to experiment with different instructions regarding the classification of data and observe differences in the categories that result. Generally speaking, leaving open the possibility of multiple category membership for items from the data set provides more energy.

Once students have been instructed on procedures for grouping the data, the teacher will need to attend to the mechanics of the grouping activity. Students may work alone, in pairs, in small groups, or as one large group. Working alone requires the least social skill, and working in small groups, the greatest social skill. If one process objective is to develop students' abilities to work cooperatively, assertively defending their groupings but compromising when appropriate for group consensus, then students will need instruction and practice to develop these skills. If the teacher chooses to work with the entire class as a single group for the categorizing activity, he or she will need to exercise caution so that categories are not inadvertently provided for the students. Structuring students into pairs for the categorizing activity is the simplest way to have all students actively engaged in the task, although the teacher must again use considerable skill in keeping everyone involved while recording and synthesizing reports from the pairs. Teachers will probably want to experiment with different ways of structuring this activity, and pros and cons of each process can be discussed with peer coaches.

Teacher: Please describe how you will instruct the students to classify the data that you have provided or that they have collected.

Observer: In your opinion, did the students understand the criteria and procedures they were to employ during the categorizing activity? Did the teacher inadvertently give clues about what the "right" groups would be?

Teacher: Please describe how you will organize students for the categorizing activity.

Observer: Did the students work productively on the categorizing activity?

Yes [　]   No [　]   Partially [　]

If the teacher had the students work in pairs or small groups, did the students listen as other groups shared their categories?

Yes [　]   No [　]   Partially [　]

Were students able to explain the attributes on which they grouped items within categories?

Yes [　]   No [　]   Partially [　]

Were students able to provide labels or descriptive phrases for their groups which reflected the attributes on which the groups were formed?

Yes [　]   No [　]

Note: The names or labels students attach to groups of items within a data set will often accurately describe the group but not coincide with a technical or scientific name, and this is fine. For example, students may label a group of leaves "jagged edges" while the technical term would be "serrated edges." The teacher may choose to provide technical or scientific terms when appropriate, but not before students have attempted to provide their own labels.

On Phases One through Four

For some lessons, the content objectives will be accomplished at the conclusion of phase four. When the teacher wishes to have students learn information by organizing it into categories and labeling it in order to gain conceptual control of the material, he or she may choose to stop here. Or when the objective is to learn what students see within a data set and what attributes they are unaware of, the grouping activity will accomplish that objective. When, however, the objective is the application of concepts that have been formed through phase four, the remainder of the inductive model is appropriate. Phases five and six result in further processing of the information and ownership of the concepts embedded in the data set and should usually be completed.

Phase Five: Generation and Testing of Hypotheses

The purpose of phase five is to help students develop an understanding of possible relationships between and among categories that they have formed in Phase Four and how (and in what instances) the different categories are useful. The class will need a common set of categories in order to work productively in this kind of discussion. Working off the groups that students developed in Phase Four, the teacher asks questions that focus students' thinking on similarities and differences between the groups. By asking "why" questions, the teacher attempts to develop cause-effect relationships between the groups. The success of this phase depends on a thorough categorizing activity in Phase Four, and the length of Phase Five is relatively short compared with the time required for Phase Four.

Teacher: Although you will not know during your planning what groups the students will form, make a guess about possible categories they might construct, and then write two sample questions that would explore relationships between those groups.

Observer: Were the students able to discuss possible relationships among the groups?

Yes [ ]   No [ ]   Partially [ ]

Did the teacher ask the students to go beyond the data and make inferences about the appropriate use of different groups?

Yes [ ]   No [ ]

If yes, were the students able to do so?

Yes [ ]   No [ ]

If students were unable to make inferences or conclusions, can you think of any ideas to share with your partner that might help them do so?

Teacher: If students were successful in making inferences and conclusions about their data, you may wish to push them a step further and ask them to predict consequences from their data by asking "What would happen if . . ." kinds of questions. Please write one or two examples of hypothetical questions you might ask students about this data set.

Observer: Were students able to make logical predictions based on the foregoing categorization and discussion of relationships?
Yes [   ]   No [   ]

Did the teacher ask the students to explain and support their predictions?
Yes [   ]   No [   ]

If students were unable to make logical predictions based on their previous work with their categories, can you think of questions or examples that might assist students in doing so?

Phase Six: Consolidation and Transfer

The goal of this phase is for students to use the concepts (knowledge and skills) they have been forming. Can they find and create new items that belong to the different groups/categories? Can they write knowledgeably about or use these concepts? Application of the categories and practice in using them through discussion, writing, and/or performance comprise the major portion of this phase.

Teacher: Think about one or two of the categories you believe students will form. Create a writing assignment that would require the application of the content objectives/concepts that have been explored through this data set (or domain, if appropriate).

Observer: Are there other writing assignments or activities that would be appropriate for consolidation and transfer?

For Teacher and Observer Discussion
In order to improve student performance with a model, the first option we explore is whether their performance will improve with practice. That is, will simple repetition of the model give the students a chance to learn to respond more appropriately. Second, we directly teach the students the skills they need to manage the cognitive and social tasks of the model.

Observer: Please comment on the skills with which the students engaged in the activities and suggest any areas where you believe demonstrations by the teacher or further training might be useful. Think especially of the students' ability to group by attributes, to provide labels for groups that accurately described the groups or synthesized attributes characteristic of a given group, to articulate possible relationships among groups, to make inferences regarding use of the different categories, and to use (discuss, write about, demonstrate) the concepts being explored.

appendix B

"Just Read" Forms

My Reading Log for September

My name is _____

My class is _____

WEEK ONE	BOOK #	TITLES OF BOOKS	PAGES READ	BOOK DONE?
	1			
	2			
	3			
	4			
Others		Titles on other side		
WEEK TWO				
	1			
	2			
	3			
	4			
Others		Titles on other side		
September Total			Pages	Books Done
By me				
By my class				
My year to date				
Class year to date				

Class Reading Log for September

Class _____

Student Name	Week 1	Week 2	Week 3	Week 4	Week 5	Total Month	Total Year
NUMBER OF BOOKS							
1.							
2.							
3.							
4.							
5.							
6.							
7.							
8.							
9.							
10.							
11.							
12.							
13.							
Totals							

Class Frequency Distribution for September

Class _____

	ZERO BOOKS (# KIDS)	ONE BOOK (# KIDS)	TWO BOOKS (# KIDS)	THREE BOOKS (# KIDS)	FOUR BOOKS (# KIDS)	MORE (# KIDS) (# READ)	TOTAL BOOKS READ
Week 1							
Week 2							
Week 3							
Week 4							
Week 5							
Total for Month							
Total for Last Month							

School Frequency Distribution for September

School _____

	ZERO BOOKS (# KIDS)	ONE BOOK (# KIDS)	TWO BOOKS (# KIDS)	THREE BOOKS (# KIDS)	FOUR BOOKS (# KIDS)	MORE (# KIDS) (# READ)	TOTAL BOOKS READ
Week 1							
Week 2							
Week 3							
Week 4							
Week 5							
Total for Month							
Total for Last Month							
Total for Year to Date							

District Frequency Distribution for September

District _____

	ZERO BOOKS (# KIDS)	ONE BOOK (# KIDS)	TWO BOOKS (# KIDS)	THREE BOOKS (# KIDS)	FOUR BOOKS (# KIDS)	MORE (# KIDS) (# READ)	TOTAL BOOKS READ
Week 1							
Week 2							
Week 3							
Week 4							
Week 5							
Total for Month							
Total for Last Month							
Total for Year to Date							

References

Adams, A. H., Johnson, M. S., & Connors, J. M. (1980). *Success in kindergarten reading and writing.* Glenview, Ill.: Good Year Books.

Almy, M. (1970). *Logical thinking in the second grade.* New York: Teachers College Press.

Anderson, R. C., & Freebody, P. (1981). Vocabulary knowledge. In J. T. Guthrie (Ed.). *Comprehension and teaching: Research reviews.* Newark: International Reading Association.

Apple, M., & Neane, J. (Eds.). (1995). *Democratic schools.* Alexandria, VA: Association for Curriculum and Supervision Development.

Applebee, A., Langer, J., Jenkins, L., Mullis, I., & Foertsch, M. (1990). *Learning to write in our nation's schools.* Washington, D.C.: U.S. Department of Education.

Aspy, D. N., & Roebuck, F. (1973). An investigation of the relationship between student levels of cognitive functioning and the teacher's classroom behavior. *Journal of Educational Research, 65*(6), 365–368.

Aspy, D. N., Roebuck, F., Willson, M., & Adams, O. (1974). *Interpersonal skills training for teachers.* (Interim report #2 for NIMH Grant #5PO 1MH 1987.) Monroe, La.: Northeast Louisiana University.

Ausubel, D. P. (1960). The use of advance organizers in the learning and retention of meaningful verbal material. *Journal of Educational Psychology, 51,* 267–272.

Ausubel, D. P. (1963). *The psychology of meaningful verbal learning.* New York: Grune and Stratton.

Ausubel, D. P. (1968). *Educational psychology: A cognitive view.* New York: Holt, Rinehart & Winston.

Ausubel, D. P. (1977). *Behavior modification for the classroom teacher.* New York: McGraw-Hill.

Ausubel, D. P. (1980). Schemata, cognitive structure, and advance organizers: A reply to Anderson, Spiro, and Anderson. *American Educational Research Journal, 17*(3), 400–404.

Ausubel, D. P., & Fitzgerald, J. (1962). Organizer, general background and antecedent learning variables in sequential verbal learning. *Journal of Educational Psychology, 53,* 243–249.

Ausubel, D. P., Stager, M., & Gaite, A. J. H. (1968). Retroactive facilitation of meaningful verbal learning. *Journal of Educational Psychology, 59,* 250–255.

Ball, S., & Bogatz, G. A. (1970). *The first year of Sesame Street.* Princeton, N.J.: Educational Testing Service.

Baveja, B. (1988). An exploratory study of the use of information-processing models of teaching in secondary school biology science classes. Delhi, India: Delhi University. Ph.D. thesis.

Becker, W., & Gersten, R. (1982). A followup of Follow Through: The later effects of the direct instruction model on children in the fifth and sixth grades. *American Educational Research Journal, 19*(1), 75–92.

Bellack, A. (1962). *The language of the classroom.* New York: Teachers College Press.

Bloom, B. S. (1984). The 2 sigma problem: The search for group instruction as effective as one-to-one tutoring. *Educational Researcher, 13,* 4–16.

Bonsangue, M. (1993). Long term effects of the Calculus Workshop Model. *Cooperative Learning, 13*(3), 19–20.

Bonstingl, J. J. (1992). *Schools of quality: An introduction to total quality management in education.* Alexandria, VA: Association for Supervision and Curriculum Development.

Boocock, S. S., & Schild, E. (1968). Simulation games in learning. Beverly Hills: Sage Publications.

Bredderman, T. (1983). Effects of activity-based elementary science on student outcomes: A quantitative synthesis. *Review of Educational Research, 53*(4), 499–518.

Brophy, J. E., & Good, T. (1986). Teacher behavior and student achievement. In Merlin Wittrock (Ed.). *Handbook of research on teaching* (3rd ed.), 328–375. New York: Macmillan.

Bruner, J. (1961). *The process of education.* Cambridge: Harvard University Press.

Bruner, J., Goodnow, J. J., & Austin, G. A. (1967). *A study of thinking.* New York: Science Editions.

Calderon, M., Hertz-Lazarowitz, R., & Tinajero, J. (1991). Adapting CIRC to multi-ethnic and bilingual classrooms. *Cooperative Learning, 12,* 17–20.

Carroll, J. (1977). A revisionist model of school learning. *Review of Educational Research, 3,* 155–167.

Ceram, C. W. (1951). *Gods, graves, and scholars: The story of archeology.* New York: Random House.

Chall, J. S. (1983). *Stages of reading development.* New York: McGraw-Hill.

Chamberlin, C., & Chamberlin, E. (1943). *Did they succeed in college?* New York: Harper and Row.

Chesler, M., & Fox, R. (1966). *Role-playing methods in the classroom.* Chicago: Science Research Associates.

Clark, C., & Peterson, P. (1986). Teachers' thought processes. In M. Wittrock (Ed.). *Handbook of Research on Teaching.* New York: Macmillan.

Clark, C., & Yinger, R. (1979). *Three studies of teacher planning.* (Research Series No. 55) East Lansing: Michigan State University.

Clark, H. H., & Clark, E. V. (1977). *Psychology and language: An introduction to psycholinguistics.* New York: Harcourt, Brace, Jovanovich.

Dewey, J. (1916). *Democracy in education.* New York: Macmillan.

Dewey, J. (1937). *Experience and education.* New York: Macmillan.

Duncan, D. (1996). *The West: An illustrated history for children.* Boston: Little, Brown.

El-Nemr, M. A. (1979). Meta-analysis of the outcomes of teaching biology as inquiry. Unpublished doctoral dissertation, University of Colorado, Boulder.

Encyclopaedia Britannica (Vol. 13). (1993). Chicago: Encyclopaedia Britannica.

Force, R. W., & Force, M. T. (1991). *The American Indians.* Chelsea House Publishers.

Freedman, R. (1992). *Buffalo hunt.* New York: Scholastic.

Gardner, H., (1983). *Frames of mind:* The *Theory of multiple intelligences.* N.Y.: Basic Books.

Glass, G. V. (1982). Meta-analysis: An approach to the synthesis of research results. *Journal of Research in Science Teaching, 19*(2), 93–112.

Glasser, W. (1969). *Schools without failure.* New York: Harper and Row.

Glickman, C. D. (1993). *Renewing America's schools: A guide for school-based action.* San Francisco: Jossey-Bass.

Goodlad, J., & Klein, F. (1970). *Looking behind the classroom door.* Worthington, Ohio: Charles Jones.

Grouws, D., & Ebmeier, H. (1983). *Active mathematics teaching.* White Plains, N.Y.: Longman.

Hendrickson, R. (1987). *The Henry Holt encyclopedia of word and phrase origins.* New York: Henry Holt.

Hertz-Lazarowitz, R. (1993). Using group investigation to enhance Arab-Jewish relationships. *Cooperative Learning, 11*(2), 13–14.

Hillocks, G. (1987). Synthesis of research on teaching writing. *Educational Leadership, 44*(8), 71–82.

Hirsch, E. (1987). *Cultural literacy: What every American needs to know.* Boston: Houghton Mifflin.

Hoetker, J., & Ahlbrand, W. (1969). The persistence of the recitation. *American Educational Research Journal, 6,* 145–167.

Hopkins, D. (1987). *Improving the quality of schooling.* Lewes: Falmer.

Houghton Mifflin. (1991). *A message of ancient days.* Boston: Houghton Mifflin.

Hunt, D. E. (1983). The MOTAC studies. In Joyce, Brown, and Peck (Eds.). *Flexibility and teaching.* White Plains, N.Y.: Longman.

Hunt, D. E., & Hardt, R. H. (1967). The role of conceptual level and program structure in summer Upward Bound programs. Paper presented to the Eastern Psychological Association, Boston.

Hunt, D. E., & Joyce, B. (1967). Teacher trainee personality and initial teaching style. *American Educational Research Journal, 4,* 253–259.

Hunt, D. E., & Sullivan, E. V. (1974). *Between psychology and education.* Hinsdale, Ill.: Dryden.

Hunt, D. E., Butler, L. F., Noy, J. E., & Rosser, M. E. (1978). *Assessing conceptual level by the paragraph completion method.* Toronto: Ontario Institute for Studies in Education.

Hunt, D. E., Greenwood, J., Brill, R., & Deineka, M. (1972). From psychological theory to educational practice: Implementation of a matching model. Symposium presented at the annual meeting of the American Educational Research Association, Chicago.

Hunt, D. E., Joyce, B., & Del Popolo, J. (1964). An exploratory study of the modification of student teachers' behavior patterns. Syracuse University, unpublished paper.

Hunt, D. E., Joyce, B., Greenwood, J., Noy, J., Reid, R., & Weil, M. (1981). Student conceptual level and models of teaching. In Joyce, Bruce, Peck, Lucy, Brown, & Clark. *Flexibility in teaching.* White Plains, N.Y.: Longman.

Johnson, D. W., & Johnson, R. T. (1974). Instructional goal structure: Cooperative, competitive, or individualistic. *Review of Educational Research, 44,* 213–240.

Johnson, D. W., & Johnson, R. T. (1975). Learning together and alone. Englewood Cliffs, N.J.: Prentice Hall.

Johnson, D. W., & Johnson, R. T. (1979). Conflict in the classroom: Controversy in learning. *Review of Educational Research, 49*(1), 51–70.

Johnson, D. W., & Johnson, R. T. (1981). Effects of cooperative and individualistic learning experiences on inter-ethnic interaction. *Journal of Educational Psychology, 73*(3), 444–449.

Johnson, D. W., & Johnson, R. T. (1990). *Cooperation and competition: Theory and research.* Edina, Minn.: Interaction Book Company.

Johnson, D. W., & Johnson, R. T. (1993). *Circles of learning.* Edina, Minn.: Interaction Book Company.

Johnson, D. W., & Johnson, R. T. (1994). *Leading the cooperative school.* Edina, Minn.: Interaction Book Company.

Johnson, D. W., & Johnson, R. T. (1996). Conflict resolution and peer mediated programs in elementary and secondary schools: A review of the research. *Review of Educational Research, 66*(4), 459–506.

Johnson, D. W., Maruyama, G., Johnson, R., Nelson, D., & Skon, L. (1981). Effects of cooperative, competitive, and individualistic goal structures on achievement: A meta-analysis. *Psychological Bulletin, 89*(1), 47–62.

Joyce, B., & Calhoun, E. (1997). *Creating learning experiences.* Alexandria, VA: The Association for Supervision and Curriculum Development.

Joyce, B., & Calhoun, E. (Eds.). (1996). *Learning experiences in school renewal.* Eugene, Oregon: The ERIC Clearinghouse on Educational Management.

Joyce, B., & Joyce, E. (1968). *Data Banks for Children.* New York: Teachers College, Columbia University.

Joyce, B., & Weil, M. (1996). *Models of teaching.* Boston: Allyn and Bacon.

Joyce, B., & Wolf, J. (1996). Readersville: Building a culture of readers and writers. In Joyce and Calhoun (Eds.). *Learning experiences in school renewal.* Eugene, Oregon: ERIC Clearinghouse.

Joyce, B., Calhoun, E., Halliburton, C., Simser, J., Rust, D., & Carran, N. (1994). The Ames Community Schools staff development program. Paper presented at the annual meeting of the Association for Supervision and Curriculum Development, Chicago.

Joyce, B., Calhoun, E., Halliburton, C., Simser, J., Rust, D., & Carran, N. (1996). University town. In Joyce and Calhoun (Eds.). *Learning experiences in school renewal.* Eugene, Oregon: ERIC Clearinghouse.

Joyce, B., & Calhoun, E. (Eds.). *Learning experiences in school renewal.* Eugene, Oregon: ERIC Clearinghouse.

Joyce, B., & Showers, B. (1983). *Power in staff development through research on training.* Washington: Association for Supervision and Curriculum Development.

Joyce, B., & Showers, B. (1995). *Student achievement through staff development.* White Plains, N.Y.: Longman.

Joyce, B., Showers, B., & Bennett, B. (1987). Synthesis of research on staff development: A framework for future study and a state-of-the-art analysis. *Educational Leadership, 45*(3), 77–87.

Kagan, S. (1990). *Cooperative learning resources for teachers.* San Juan Capistrano, Calif.: Resources for Teachers.

Kidron, M., & Segal, R. (1991). *The new state of the world atlas.* New York: Simon & Schuster.

Kitchen, B. (1992). *Somewhere today.* Cambridge, Mass.: Candlewick Press.

Lawton, J., & Wanska, S. (1977). The effects of different types of advance organizers on classification learning. *The American Educational Research Journal, 16*(3), 223–239.

Levin, M., & Levin, J. (1990). Scientific mnemonics. *American Educational Research Journal, 27*, 301–321.

Levine, D. (1991). Creating effective schools. *Phi delta kappan, 72*(5), 389–393.

Maslow, A. (1962). *Toward a psychology of being.* New York: Van Nostrand.

Massialas, B., & Cox, B. (1966). *Inquiry in social studies.* New York: McGraw-Hill.

Menyuk, P. (1971). *The acquisition and development of language.* Englewood Cliffs, N.J.: Prentice Hall.

National Assessment of Educational Progress (NAEP). (1992). *The Reading Report Card.* Washington, D.C.: National Center for Educational Statistics, U.S. Department of Education.

Neill, A. S. (1960). *Summerhill.* New York: Holt, Rinehart, and Winston.

Nelson, J. (1971). Collegial supervision in multi-unit schools. Ph.D. Thesis, University of Oregon.

Oakes, J. (1986). *Keeping track: How schools structure inequality.* New Haven: Yale University Press.

Oliver, D., & Shaver, J. P. (1966). *Teaching public issues in the high school.* Boston: Houghton Mifflin.

Perls, F. (1968). *Gestalt therapy verbatim.* Lafayette, Calif.: Real People Press.

Pinnell, G. S. (1989). Helping at-risk children learn to read. *Elementary School Journal, 90*(2), 161–184.

Pressley, M., Levin, J. R., & Delaney, H. D. (1982). The mnemonic keyword method. *Review of Educational Research, 52*(1), 61–91.

Quellmatz, E. S., & Burry, J. (1983). *Analytic scales for assessing students' expository and narrative writing skills.* Los Angeles: Center for the Study of Evaluation, UCLA Graduate School of Education. (CSE Resource Paper No. 5).

Roebuck, F., Buhler, J., & Aspy, D. (1976). A comparison of high and low levels of humane teaching/learning conditions on the subsequent achievement of students identified as having learning difficulties. Final Report: Order No. PLD 6816–76. The National Institute of Mental Health. Denton, Texas: Texas Woman's University Press.

Rogers, C. (1961). *On becoming a person.* Boston: Houghton Mifflin.

Rogers, C. (1969). *Freedom to learn.* Columbus: Charles E. Merrill.

Rogers, C. (1971). *Client centered therapy.* Boston: Houghton Mifflin.

Rogers, C. (1981). *A way of being.* Boston: Houghton Mifflin.

Rogers, C. (1982). *Freedom to learn for the eighties.* Columbus: Charles E. Merrill.

Rolheiser-Bennett, C. (1986). Four models of teaching: A meta-analysis of student outcomes. Ph.D. thesis, University of Oregon.

Sagan, C. (1995). *The demon-haunted world: Science as a candle in the dark.* New York: Random House.

Schwab, J. (1965). *Biological sciences curriculum study: Biology teachers' handbook.* New York: John Wiley and Sons.

Schwab, J. (1982). *Science, curriculum, and liberal education: Selected essays.* Chicago: University of Chicago Press.

Schwab, J., & Brandwein, P. (1962). *The teaching of science.* Cambridge, Mass.: Harvard University Press.

Shaftel, F., & Shaftel, G. (1982). *Role playing in the curriculum.* Englewood Cliffs, N.J.: Prentice-Hall.

Sharan, S., & Shachar, H. (1988). *Language and learning in the cooperative classroom.* New York: Springer-Verlag.

Shaver, J. P. (1995). Social studies. In G. Caweelti (Ed.). *Handbook of Research on Improving Instruction.* Arlington, VA: Alliance for Curriculum Reform.

Sigel, I. E. (1984). *Advances in applied developmental psychology.* New York: Ablex.

Sirotnik, K. (1983). What you see is what you get. *Harvard Educational Review, 53*(1), 16–31.

Skinner, B. F. (1953). *Science and human behavior.* New York: Macmillan.

Skinner, B. F. (1968). *The technology of teaching.* Englewood Cliffs, N.J.: Prentice-Hall.

Skinner, B. F. (1971). *Beyond freedom and dignity.* New York: Knopf.

Slavin, R. E., & Madden (1995). Success for all: Creating schools and classrooms where all children can read. In J. Oakes and K. Quartz (Eds.). *Creating New Educational Communities. The ninety-fourth yearbook of the National Society for the Study of Education.* Chicago: The University of Chicago Press, pp. 70–86.

Slavin, R. E. (1983). *Cooperative learning.* New York: Longman.

Smith, K., & Smith, M. (1966). *Cybernetic principles of learning and educational design.* New York: Holt, Rinehart, and Winston.

Smith, M. L. (1980). Effects of aesthetics education on basic skills learning. Boulder, Colo.: Laboratory of Educational Research, University of Colorado.

Spaulding, R. (1970). *E.I.P.* Durham, N.C.: Duke University Press.

Stille, A. (February 10, 1997). Perils of the Sphinx. *The New Yorker.* New York: New Yorker Magazine.

Stenhouse, L. (1975). *An introduction to curriculum research and development*. London: Heinemann.

Stenhouse, L. (1980). *Curriculum research and development in action*. London: Heinemann.

Suchman, R. J. (1981). *Idea book for geological inquiry*. Trillium Press.

Taba, H. (1966). *Teaching strategies and cognitive functioning in elementary school children*. (Cooperative Research Project 2404.) San Francisco: San Francisco State College.

Thelen, H. (1960). *Education and the human quest*. New York: Harper and Row.

Time-Life Books. (1993). *The wild west*. New York: Warner Books.

White, W. A. T. (1986). The effects of direct instruction in special education: A meta-analysis. Ph.D. Thesis. University of Oregon.

Whitehead, A. (1929). *The aims of education*. New York: Macmillan.

Wolpe, J., & Lazarus, A. (1966). *Behavior therapy techniques: A guide to the treatment of neuroses*. Oxford: Pergamon Press.

Worthen, B. (1968). A study of discovery and expository presentation: Implications for teaching. *Journal of Teacher Education, 19*, 223–242.

Yue, C., & Yue, D. (1986). *The Pueblo*. Boston: Houghton Mifflin.

*I*ndex